Accounting with Pegasus

D1826998

Accounting with Pegasus Single-User Version 2

David Royall BSc (Econ) PGCE

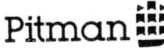
Pitman

Pitman Publishing
128 Long Acre, London WC2E 9AN

A Division of Longman Group UK Limited

First published in 1990

© Longman Group UK Ltd 1990

British Library Cataloguing in Publication Data

Royall, David
   Accounting with Pegasus Single-User Version 2.
   1.   Accounting. Applications of computer systems. Software packages
   I.   Title
   657' .028'553

ISBN 0 273 03159 7

All rights reserved; no part of this publication may be
reproduced, stored in a retrieval system, or transmitted in any
form or by any other means, electronic, mechanical, photocopying,
recording, or otherwise without either the prior written
permission of the Publishers or a licence permitting restricted
copying in the United Kingdom issued by the Copyright Licensing
Agency, 33 – 34 Alfred Place, London WC1E 7DP. This book may not be
lent, resold, hired out or otherwise disposed of by way of trade
in any form of binding or cover other than that in which it is
published, without the prior consent of the Publishers.

Typeset, printed and bound in Great Britain

Contents

Preface

The main aim of this book is to give either students or practitioners a sound knowledge of the Pegasus Single-User Version 2 software package as well as to significantly improve both book-keeping and financial analysis skills. Although some previously gained computing skills would be an advantage to becoming expert in computerised accounts it is by no means essential. This book assumes that the reader has little or no computing knowledge. When embarking on computerised accounts, readers will soon appreciate that accounting skills are more important than computing ones. This book, however, can be used by students who are studying accounts and should prove a useful vehicle for improving their knowledge and skills in this area.

The book offers practical guidance to any potential Pegasus user, giving them an opportunity to reflect on the use and application of the package away from the computer as well as structured guidance of the package while using the computer. The book uses a semi-tutorial approach that can be best used by reading the book in the chapter sequence presented with access to the Pegasus package.

The book begins with an introduction to the concepts of computing, the basic requirements for computerised accounts, and methods a business might adopt when deciding on a computerisation project. The book then works through the Pegasus modules in a way that develops skills and understanding of both the package and the basic functions that the modules attempt to computerise. A good deal of effort on the part of the reader is encouraged to understand exactly what the computer is trying to do, rather than simply operating the system mechanically.

The book ends by introducing users to some of the more advanced features of the package and examines three case studies of the way different firms went about implementing Pegasus into their businesses.

The book may be of particular interest to those students of accounting working for a qualification with one of the professional accounting bodies such as the AAT, ACCA or ICMA. The book not only deals with fundamental book-keeping and accounting principles, but also with computing and data-processing concepts in an integrated manner, a requirement of almost all the professional accounting qualifications.

The book will also serve as a useful text to students and tutors involved with BTEC National and Higher Awards in Business & Finance and those students studying Small Business Systems and Concepts on BTEC courses in business and computer studies areas. With the growing emphasis on the need to integrate many business and information technology skills in a practical way, this book, along with the appropriate computing resources, offers a way of meeting such requirements.

By the time readers have worked through the entire book, they should have gained an insight into the way a business information system operates as well as useful skills in computerised accounts – an essential skill even if the reader never uses Pegasus Business Software again.

A glossary of computerised accounting terms is provided in Appendix 1 should readers have any difficulty with the vocabulary used in this book.

1 Introduction

Using a computer to help a business with its accounts can, if implemented incorrectly, cause more problems than it solves. When a computer system and associated software is purchased there are a number of points that should be examined.

1 Identifying the need to use computers

One of the first starting points for a business is to decide whether or not a computer would benefit it. This can be a difficult need to identify if the person(s) is not aware of what a computer can do and also its limitations.

It is always wise to investigate how a computer can perform tasks and gain a little experience by attending exhibitions, short courses at the local technical college or even contacting a business associate who uses a computer, in order to benefit from the experience of others. For most businesses a computer, if properly used and administered, can be a great benefit to the accounting function and prove to be an enjoyable experience.

Important in the early stages is to assess exactly what work the business wants the computer to do. Also, establishing the amount of work that has to be done will help any supplier to ensure that an adequate system is provided. When a business decides to purchase a motor vehicle, it must have some idea on the amount of work such a vehicle has to do and the amount of freight it has to carry in order to purchase a vehicle that is capable of handling the work. Exactly the same must apply to a computer system.

Having established this, it is a good idea to put such details in writing and send them to a number of potential suppliers to see what they can offer. Such a document might include the following:

- The nature of the business.
- What a computer would be expected to do.
- The amount of information processing expected from a system.
- The number of staff currently doing the work and approximately how much time is spent on such processing activities.

1

There is no reason, of course, why a more experienced person could not purchase a complete system through a magazine, catalogue or high street shop and make a success of using it. But, however 'ideal' a resulting system might be, the success of such a system will still be dependent upon the way it is implemented and maintained.

The essence of a computerised accounting system is no different to that of a manual system. The introduction of calculators has not altered the basic rules of arithmetic and mathematics and, likewise, the introduction of computers has not altered the basic rules of book-keeping and accounts, just the way we might approach them.

One of the most difficult aspects of using a computerised system will be the process of setting it up. In most businesses, transactions are being generated on a very regular basis and details about such things as stock quantities, customer account details and so on would be difficult to assess accurately at any given point. When setting up a computer system, we will need to enter all the details about the state of a company's accounts before we can start. The problem here is that by the time all the required information has been compiled and entered to the system, it has become out of date – it is the classic problem of trying to computerise a moving target.

Many of the above issues will be raised in this book, along with some ideas about how to overcome some of the problems and dilemmas facing a firm wishing to computerise its accounting system.

2 Some expected benefits of using computers for accounts

The saving of time with respect to transactions processing and the production of a whole series of reports is an obvious benefit we would want from computerising accounts. The basic principle of any accounting system is depicted in Figure 1.1:

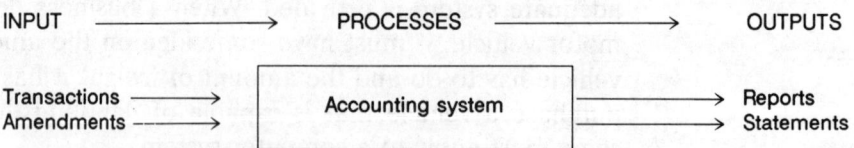

Figure 1.1

The aim of a computerised accounting system is to perform the processing stage electronically, which should be much quicker than if it were done manually. However, transactions and amendment details have to get into the process in the correct form, in the correct order and in a timely manner. Although there is scope to use electronic methods, it will require a good deal of human initiative and an organised way of doing things. Further time saving can be achieved by automatic output of reports such as trading and profit and loss accounts, customer statements, sales analyses and trial balances. Such reports and statements can be produced by the computer searching through information generated and saved by the accounting system.

Effective reporting would often be required as a way of improving the decision-making process. For example, a computer system should be capable of detecting when a customer appears to be running up excessive debts with the company, offering us the chance to take action before the whole thing gets out of hand. Another area is the need to remain within budgets. Many business expenses can get out of hand if they are not checked at regular intervals. What a computerised accounts system should be capable of is an activity called exception reporting – a process of issuing early warning messages to operators when something appears to be out of order. In a manual system, the situation often occurs when many errors or unwanted transactions go unnoticed until too late or until they have already incurred unnecessary costs to the firm.

For many businesses, the need to produce monthly and annual returns such as VAT and payroll stoppages can be lengthy, tedious and unrewarding. The use of a computer system to assist in this process can be effective in speeding up the process and reducing the monotony of producing lengthy and uninteresting reports with large amounts of figure work. In many cases, firms find that they can use computer printouts or even data on computer disks instead of having to complete official forms.

Improved accuracy may be one of the more obvious benefits of any kind of computer system, which is especially the case with accounting, where numerous calculations have to be carried out.

More job satisfaction and more effective use of operator time can be an added bonus to computerisation. For example, if a firm computerises its stock records, an operator's job of keeping records properly maintained will be much the same as was the case in the manual system. However, with instant reporting facilities available, such as a list of all stock items that may be in short supply, the operator can produce details almost instantly. This will allow an operator the facility of keeping a much closer check on stock levels. Also, if time can be saved in producing stock reports, the operator may have more time to 'chase up' suppliers who are not delivering on time or 'shop around' the market for better suppliers and products.

Many more benefits of computerisation will become apparent as you work your way through this book. It is worth noting that the extent and type of the benefits will vary from firm to firm. It may even be the case that a firm can derive no benefit at all from computerisation.

Once a computer system is working properly, managers will often find themselves extracting reports that under a manual system could not be achieved within a time scale that would serve a useful purpose. The improved reporting and analysis that can be achieved by computerisation should improve the whole decision-making process within a firm.

3 Differing computer systems

A basic requirement will, of course, be the need for a computer system consisting of hardware and software. In most instances, a decision about the software will be made first. Software is that part of a system that instructs it about the processing of the data in order to produce the information requirements of a computer system. Such software will come at two levels.

The first level is the computer's operating system. This software, as its name suggests, will operate all parts of the computer system, such as keyboard input, screen output, printing and internal processing of data inside the computer itself. All computer systems will have one, but not necessarily the same operating system. Such operating systems come in many forms such as Microsoft Disk Operating System (MSDOS), Operating System/2 (OS/2) and Xenix. Such operating systems are designed differently and have changed in nature over the years. As computers have become more advanced and their operating environment has changed, the operating system has also changed. The second level of software is that of an applications package. This adds to the software by offering the added features required to perform specific tasks, such as accounting. When purchasing an applications package, such as Pegasus, it is important that the correct version is purchased to match the operating system. In turn, the operating system must match the computer system. In others words, compatibility must exist between operating system and applications package.

Deciding on the hardware will become easier once the software decision has been made and it is clear what work a system has to do.

The type of system that would normally meet the needs of most small- to medium-sized businesses will fall into one of three categories: stand alone, network and multi-user/tasking systems.

Stand alone Such a system will consist of one screen, one keyboard, one disk drive and enough memory in order to run the software. For a firm with relatively small data-processing needs and no need for more than one operator to be at a keyboard at any time such a system could prove quite adequate. Even so, it would probably be advisable to have a system with a **hard disk** as opposed to floppy disks, for ease of operation.

A network of micros This allows the linking up of micro-computers in such a way that they are able to share information and permit the centralisation of the data-processing system. In other words, someone working on a computer on a network system can update information on a customer which allows another person on a different machine to be aware of the update on inspecting that customer account. Such a set-up is of particular use in a larger firm that requires the accounting and related data-processing function to be divided between a number of staff. It also allows management to extract reports without having to disturb the accounts staff.

Such networks are not fixed in size. They can vary according to the requirements of the firm from two micro-computers on a network to dozens of micro-computers. Firms should always take advice when deciding on the number of micro-computers to network together. Too many on a network can, at times, lead to congestion.

Multi-user/tasking Such a set-up offers much the same as that of a network. The difference lies in the fact that the system is one computer with a number of terminals attached to it. In other words, each keyboard is not a computer in its own right. Such a system means that the familiar MS-DOS or OS/2 operating system associated with a micro-computer will be replaced with a different operating system such as Xenix.

Choosing which type of system is appropriate for which kind of business is not an easy task. It is important to bear in mind that all packages of software will not work on all machines. Compatibility across a system is a key issue in the decision-making process.

4 Printing

All users of computerised accounts will need to print information such as customer statements, invoices, order forms, audit trails and reports. It is worth noting at this point that it is unlikely that computerising the accounting functions will significantly reduce the amount of physical paper. In fact many new users have found that the computer results in more paper not less.

Different types of printers are available for computer systems. Any firm using computers will need to assess how many printers are required and the quality of printing that needs to be achieved.

The most commonly used printer is the matrix printer. Such a printer produces character images on to paper by dot patterns one character at a time. Most matrix printers are capable of printing a full page (A4 size) of text in under a minute and at a very reasonable quality. For most accounting function printing output, this kind of printing is both economic and adequate. Stationery for such printers includes continuous paper (fanfold) which is a cheap way of acquiring printed output.

For improved output quality, a laser printer is another option. The quality of print is better, the machines are not as noisy and they normally accept only standard size single sheets of paper. For most accounts reports this is probably a little extravagant. For graphics output and good quality letter production, a laser printer may be a viable option.

Other types of printers are available for serving differing types of needs, some of which are:

1 Daisy wheel printers, which are designed as letter-quality impact printers. The characters to be printed are superimposed on the spokes of a wheel, which is used to create the impact on paper. They will produce high-quality letters but are restricted to one set of character fonts at a time (changeable by changing wheels) and will not produce any graphics.
2 Ink jet printers. These can be a cheap non-impact printer, although they can be slow. There are a number of cheap colour printers available on the market.
3 Plotters. These are really used for graphics printing and work by drawing on paper with pen-like actions.

The term hard copy is often used to refer to printed output as opposed to soft copy which refers to screen output.

5 Staff training

Another major issue in implementing computerised accounts will be the need to ensure that staff are adequately prepared and trained, which can be done in a number of ways.

(a) Purchase a system and the required software from a firm who also offers staff training.
(b) Send a member of staff on a course. Such courses are available at differing times of the year from both private institutions and local technical colleges.
(c) Employ someone who is already trained.
(d) Hope that an employee can learn the package and computer system as they implement it, giving them time to research and experiment. (Although this option is extremely risky, it is an option often used.)

Staff training is an expense of implementing a computer often overlooked by firms. Poorly trained staff can lead to the downfall of **any** system, not just a computerised one.

In conclusion to this section on implementing computerised accounts, anyone responsible for its computerisation should be aware that a degree of time and patience is required. Computerising a manual book-keeping system cannot be done overnight; it may well take weeks or months. In Chapter 14 of this book there are three case studies which will put a lot of this into some kind of perspective.

THE DATA PROTECTION ACT

Most firms who make extensive use of computers for accounts, Payroll and any other applications that involve details of personal individuals would be well advised to register with the **Data Protection Board.**

The Act defines a **data user** as someone who makes use of **personal data** that is on a computer. Basically, personal data is data held about individuals. A **data subject** as defined by the Act is any person who has data about them on a computer. Such data on a computer has to be processed by the computer's software before it becomes information. It is this information that the Data Protection Registrar wants to know about.

Essentially, the data user must declare what information he has access to on a data subject and the uses he will put that information to. The main objective of the Act is to ensure that individuals are aware of what is being held about them on business computers and allow them access to this information. There are, however, many exemptions such as medical records, criminal records and information deemed necessary to be kept secret in the national interest.

If a firm is using the Sales Ledger or Purchase Ledger only for preparing and sending invoices and statements and does not use the 'comment' functions for a contact name, then registration may not be necessary. Also, if customers and suppliers are companies and individuals cannot be identified in the data, registration is not necessary. In the same way with wages, if all a firm does with the data is to pay wages and prepare statutory returns, registration is not necessary. If customer and supplier lists are used for sending out sales promotions, the firm must register, likewise, if a firm uses data on the Payroll for management information about staff sickness or any form of staff monitoring.

Forms for registration are available at any main post office. These forms require the firm to reveal the kind of data it holds on individuals and the purpose for which it wants to use it. The firm must also give details on how data subjects can find out what data is held on computer about them.

In addition to the possible need to register, firms must comply with certain practices with regard to holding personalised data on computer. They are:

1   Data must be obtained fairly and lawfully.
2   Data can only be used for the specified purpose set out in original submission to the Registrar. If the firm wishes to change the way it uses such data, then it must re-apply.
3   Data must not be disclosed to unauthorised parties. Again, authorised parties must be stated within the original application.
4   Data held must be adequate, relevant and not excessive for the purposes for which it is being held.
5   Data must be kept accurate and up to date. This principle should really apply to **all** data in an accounting system if the system is being managed and run properly.
6   Data must not be kept longer than is necessary.
7   Any 'data subject' must be allowed to see the data held on them in readable and legible form. This means firms must have the mechanism for extracting a complete profile kept on an individual if requested. If a data subject does approach a firm requesting such information, the data user can demand a fee to cover any administration costs.
8   A data user must have appropriate security against unauthorised access.

If a firm is in doubt, then it should always register as the cost of registration is small.

The information sent to the Registrar is available to any member of the public for inspection.

2 The Sales Ledger

INTRODUCTION

This chapter starts us off with the Pegasus package by looking at the way it handles sales. Once you have loaded Pegasus into the computer you will see a **menu** listing the modules available in the Pegasus package as follows:

PEGASUS	Business System		{ Date }
	1	Sales Ledger	
	2	Purchase Ledger	
	3	Nominal Ledger	
	4	Sales Invoicing	
	5	Stock Control	
	6	Payroll	
	7	Job Costing	
	8	Bill of Materials	
	9	Utilities	
	R	Retail Accounting	
	0	Finish	

A menu is a list of the options available to a user if the software is available on the system. Not all the modules listed above will be available to the user unless they have purchased the complete set. The first option in this menu is the Sales Ledger. To select this option, you would simply press the number **1** key. On pressing the 1 key, you will then be confronted with another menu:

PEGASUS	Sales Ledger		{ Date }
	1	Ledger Processing	
	2	Period End	
	3	Analysis	
	4	Parameter Update	
	5	Reports	
	6	VAT Report (Cash Accounting)	
	R	Report Generator	

To go back to the original menu, you need to press the **ESC** key.

The Pegasus system is a hierarchy of menus which allows an operator the facility of 'homing in' on the activity required by pressing appropriate number keys and then using the ESC key to 'back track'. A little practice may now be in order, as little more will be said about this point. Figure 2.1 illustrates the structure of activities available in the Sales Ledger function.

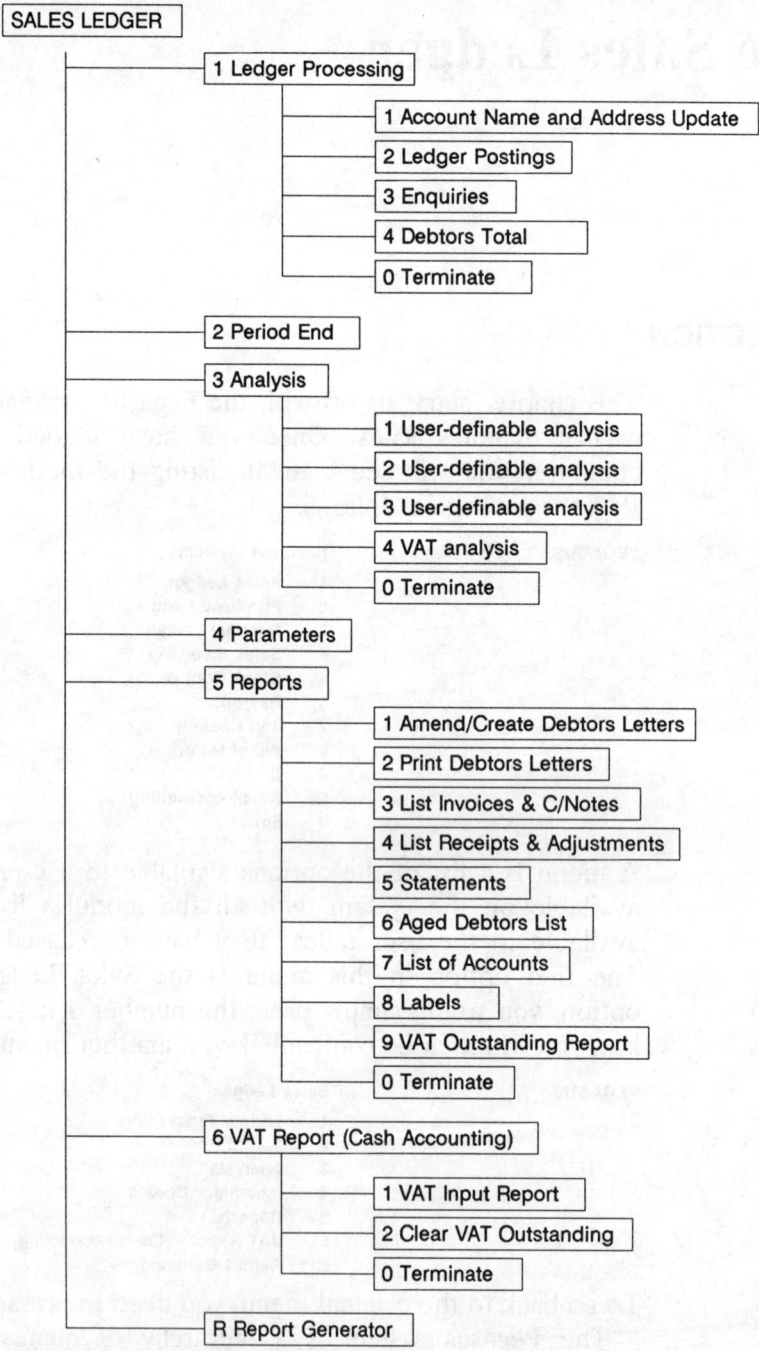

Figure 2.1

The purpose of a Sales Ledger is to record and help manage sales to customers or clients. The Sales Ledger can be used just as effectively for services rendered as it can for goods sold (or a combination of both). Such facilities offered by a Sales Ledger must allow a user the ability to create, delete and amend customer details on the ledger as well as record all transactions between firm and customer. Additional requirements would be good reporting on the Sales Ledger to ensure the firm is aware of how much is owed to it and by whom. Another important part of the Sales Ledger to many firms is to assist in offering information on VAT collected from sales.

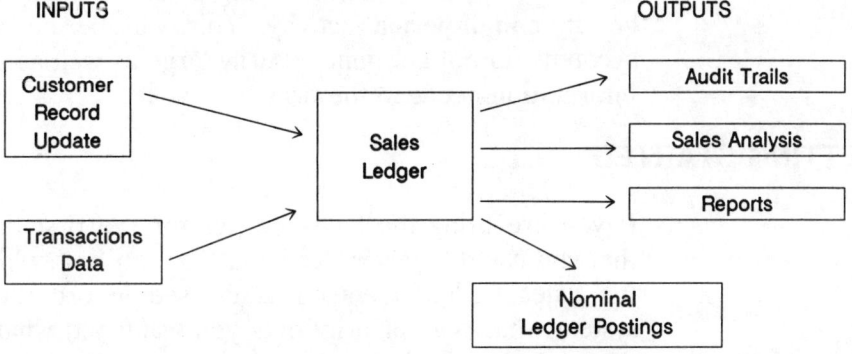

Figure 2.2 Sales Ledger Processing

Figure 2.2 gives an overview of the function of a sales ledger with input activities showing the maintenance of customer records and entry of transactions data. The output activities will consist of the customer statements, audit trails and reports

The audit trail will be a series of lists indicating all the data that have been entered into the Sales Ledger during a current period. This will be required for checking for omissions and errors and is required for subsequent auditing purposes.

An important requirement of a Sales Ledger is to provide details of sales, receipts and debtors to the Nominal Ledger. This will be dealt with at some length in Chapters 4 and 5.

In addition to supplying the firm's needs, there is also a requirement to supply information to those customers and clients that the firm is selling to. Such information requirements may include details on invoices sent to them in the past and regular statements of account. This part of the package will meet most requirements quite easily, along with some others. There are other reporting facilities available for, in particular, management information that will be dealt with in Chapter 14.

The Sales Ledger can be used in isolation to all other facilities offered by Pegasus. This chapter will assume that you are setting up the Sales Ledger system in isolation to any other accounting function. An integrated approach with other functions will be tackled in Chapter 5.

When operating a Sales Ledger, it is often a good idea to **batch process** much of the work. For example, when adding transactions to the Sales Ledger, it is often best to do a few at the same time (say weekly) rather than enter them to the ledger on an *ad-hoc* basis. This will save both time and possible confusion caused by making a large number of visits to the computer to enter small amounts of transactions data.

At the end of each accounting period (usually monthly) there will be an **end-of-period** activity. This will be necessary for ensuring accounts do not get unnecessarily large as well as supplying important information needs to the firm.

GETTING STARTED

If you are using the Sales Ledger for the first time, it is important that you use the **parameter update** option first, which is option **4** from the Sales Ledger menu. This is used in order to tell the Pegasus system what type of print-outs you want and what should appear on them, plus other characteristics.

When using the parameter settings for the first time, you will be required to enter a password. The password builds in some security to the system in a way that prevents any unauthorised persons from interfering with the processes. When entering your password, try not to forget it!

Having specified the password you will be confronted with a form to be completed that makes up the required parameters file. On most machines, drive locations A and B normally refer to floppy disks, while drive C is a hard disk. If you are storing your company data on a file server (as could be the case on a network), then you should check either with the manual or the network manager about the drive location. The following offers a suggested response with an explanation:

Sales Parameters - { Date }

Company	Name	Pegasus Users Enterprises
	Address Line 1	100 High Street
	Address Line 2	Biddlesdon
	Address Line 3	Wessex
	Address Line 4	England WSX 999
	1st Tel No.	0002 82991
	2nd Tel No.	0001 19928
	Telex No.	72781
	VAT Reg No.	

This information will ensure that any documentation sent to outside organisations or customers will have your company details on it. The exact use of this information will depend on the way some other parameters are set.

Printer	Type	0	(For use on a draft printer)
	TOF Code	12	(ASCII Code to start new page)
	Columns	132	(No. of characters on printer)
	Lines/Page	66	(No. of lines per page)

When a package is first installed, it will not know what kind of printer you have opted to use on your system. These printer settings are used to ensure a degree of **compatibility** with the package and printer. The following options allow you to **tailor** the package more closely to the needs of the firm.

Option No. 1 Y

This will ensure that an invoice and receipt list will show the customer name. There is no need to do this, but clearly it makes analysis of lists more effective. Such lists will be needed to ensure that transactions entered are complete as well as correct. It is, therefore, up to the user to decide if such lists with customer names on them will assist or hamper work.

Option No. 2 Y

Invoice and credit note analysis codes will have exactly **four** characters. The implication of this will become apparent when we examine sales analysis and post transactions to the Nominal Ledger.

VAT Code for Analysis SVAT

This will be needed later when integrating the Sales Ledger with the Nominal Ledger. It affects the way the VAT data is posted to the Nominal Ledger.

Option No. 3 Y

A new page is generated after printing each customer statement.

Option No. 4 Y

Allows analysis of invoices and credit notes under different rates of VAT. If there is only **one** rate of VAT (such as 15%), setting this to 'Y' has little effect.

Option No. 5 N

All customers with zero balances at end-of-period run will **not** be deleted from the Sales Ledger. Setting this to 'N' does not mean you are obliged to keep customer details on file after you have finished trading with them. When a firm deals with many customers on a 'one-off' sale arrangement, setting this option to 'Y' can save a good deal of time.

Option No. 6 Y

This allows the ageing of debt to be made other than by month, but by some user-defined period. The package determines the length of debt in months.

Option No. 7   Y

This allows the use of alternative stationery such as pre-printed forms for customer statements. This will be fairly normal practice for a firm needing to print a large number of such documents. Pre-printed stationery can be purchased from many computer system suppliers, Pegasus or stationers.

Option No. 8   Y

This allows calculation of interest on debt not paid after a user-specified time. For example, you may decide to add 1.5% to a debt owing by a customer if it is not paid within the first accounting period.

Option No. 9   Y

This gives you the opportunity to establish a password for operators to gain access to other areas of the Sales Ledger. If the answer to this section is 'Y', then when items are selected from the menu of the Sales Ledger, the user will be prompted for the entry of the password before being allowed to proceed.

Option No. 10   Y

This allows you to instruct the system to allow sub-totalling on the aged debtors list, based on a change in the first character of the customer account number.

Option No. 11   Y

This option allows you to integrate the Sales Ledger to the bank reconciliation facilities within the Nominal Ledger. This will enable receipt postings to be given a cheque and batch reference for the purpose of bank reconciliation.

Option No. 12   Y

This option is pertinent to those companies who account for VAT on a cash basis – that is, when you pay VAT on money received rather than invoiced amounts.

Sales Analysis 1   – Sequence
                       – Narrative
Sales Analysis 2   – Sequence
                       – Narrative
Sales Analysis 3   – Sequence
                       – Narrative

These sales analysis parameters will be discussed fully in Chapter 6. For now you can leave them blank.

Please note: while you are writing the parameters, at no point should you press the ESC key unless you want to completely give up what you are doing and start again. This principle will apply whenever you are in the middle of entering a set of data.

The parameters can be re-set at any time in the future without doing any harm to your accounting information. On each subsequent amendment you will be given the opportunity to change the password. Also, if at a later stage you change the parameters, you will be asked if you want the old files erased. If you answer 'Y' to this question, **all** sales information will be erased. Only the parameters will remain.

At the end of entering the parameters data, the highlighted bar at the bottom of the screen will instruct you what to do. One of the instructions is to request what kind of output you require: Printer, Screen or Spooler. If you keep pressing the RETURN or ENTER key you will see the output name 'nudged' between the output options. Stop at the one required and use the 'SPACE' bar to start the output. The outputs are:

(a) Printer. A list of the parameters is sent to the printer. Ensure the printer is on and prepared for printing.

(b) Screen. A list of the parameters is scrolled on to the screen for inspection.

(c) Spooler. A list of the parameters is sent to a file on your specified data disk for printing at a later stage or used for possible word processing.

Controlling where data is output to is a regular feature of the Pegasus package and you should try and become acquainted with it as soon as possible.

MAINTAINING CUSTOMER RECORDS

This section will form the main set of activities that will be typically performed on a Sales Ledger function. It requires details to be entered regarding customers, invoices, credit notes, receipts, account adjustments, statements, listings and some basic reports.

The activities are contained in option 1 of the Sales Ledger menu, Ledger Processing. This produces the following menu:

```
1   Account Name and Address Update
2   Ledger Postings
3   Enquiries
4   Debtors Total
0   Terminate
```

The main purpose of this activity is to:

(a) Enter new customer details.
(b) Delete customer accounts that are no longer needed.
(c) Amend details of existing customer, such as a change in address or credit limit.

Figure 2.3 illustrates the structure of customer records.

A/C No.	Name & Address	Interest Terms		Comments	Credit Limit	Analysis Code	A/C type O/B	Turnover
0001	J Hunt	1.5	1	Local	12000	L9	0	12344

Figure 2.3 Customer records held in the Sales Ledger

It is important that each customer has a **unique** account number. Each record will, as indicated, hold details of one customer with details being broken down into **fields**. The field that holds the customer account number is a **key field** in that it identifies the customer record. In order to achieve this, no two customers can have the same account number, hence the concept of a unique field. It is quite acceptable for one customer to have more than one account with a firm, often the case when the customer is a large corporation with many different departments.

To add a customer record to the file, you simply enter a new customer account number and then complete the remaining fields. The name and address box should contain a full postal address. Many of a firm's customers could be overseas, so it is important to enter the postal address applicable to the country where the firm is based. This will be the only reference in the system that contains the customer address.

The boxes containing interest terms will only be displayed if option 8 of the parameters is set to 'Y'. If the first entries in two boxes are 1.5% and 2, then 1.5% of the outstanding debt is added to a debt that has been owing for more than 2 periods. If the second row reads 2% and 3, then the amount added rises to 2% if the debt has still not been settled after 3 periods. In most cases, the period being referred to is one calendar month.

The comment field serves no accounting purpose and is left for the firm's own use. Such a comment box could, for example, hold a contact name for the customer or a telephone number or a code to indicate how good a customer is at paying bills.

The field containing credit limit is used to enter the amount of debt you are willing to allow a customer. When an invoice is entered to the Sales Ledger and will result in the customer exceeding his credit limit, the package will warn you of this fact and give you the option of cancelling the transaction.

The analysis code field is for use by the firm and will allow future analysis of sales, a topic to be discussed in Chapter 6.

The account type field is used to indicate whether the account is open item or balanced. If the account is open item it means the customer will always pay against invoices and that at the end of a period the unpaid invoice will be carried across to the next period. If the account is balanced it means the customer will always pay against a balance and that at the end of a period, the balance only will be carried across to the next period.

The turnover field records the amount of sales made with the customer in either the current period or since the start of trading. It is useful in order to inspect the value of a customer to the firm.

When an account is no longer needed, it can be deleted by entering the characters DELETE in the name and address box in the top left-hand corner. This record will remain on the file until an end-of-period has been run.

To amend a customer record, simply enter the customer account number in the appropriate box. The record details will appear, leaving the operator with the job of simply altering any fields that appear.

TRANSACTION PROCESSING

Entering a transaction is available as option 2 (Ledger Postings) of the Ledger Posting menu in the Sales Ledger. This option allows the entry of a number of different types of transactions. All transactions will be kept in a transactions file, of which the record structure is as shown in Figure 2.4.

A/C No.	Trans Date	Trans Type	Ref.	Trans Value	Goods Value	VAT or Disk
0001	130789	Invoice	783478	234.89	200.00	34.89
0981	120789	Receipt	r 386	120.00		

Figure 2.4 Transaction records held in the Sales Ledger

The account number refers to the key field in the customer file. When entering this in the transactions screen, customer details will be displayed to assist the operator. In this instance, the customer code can appear more than once in the transactions file, once for each transaction.

The date that appears will normally be the system date. Most computers have a facility for keeping note of the date in much the same way an electronic watch keeps the time. A battery in the computer keeps the date correct; some batteries are rechargeable while the computer is on. This date can be altered if you wish to post-date or pre-date the transaction.

There are six transaction types which can be entered. Each transaction type has to be indicated by a code (I, C, R, F, A and X).

1 I = Invoice

The effect on the customer account is to **increase** the amount of debt owing by the customer. The reference box can be used in this instance for anything the company wishes, but will normally hold the invoice number. The transaction value box holds the **total invoice** price, including VAT.

The box headed **VAT** or **Disk** will contain (for this transaction type) the VAT total on the invoice. On your screen a period box may appear, which is for balanced accounts only, and indicates against which period the invoice is to be matched.

The analysis boxes will need to be filled. They are designed to show a breakdown of the value of goods that appear on the invoice. If your screen displays a code column, then this should contain either a stock code or a nominal code, depending on how the package is to be used. The value box contains the selling price of the product(s), exclusive of VAT.

The VAT column is for reference purposes and will not affect the amount of VAT collected. It is used to indicate the type of VAT that a particular item is subject to, and can be one of:

1   To indicate standard rate.
Z   To indicate zero rate.
E   To indicate exempt of VAT.

Although Exempt and Zero rate VAT have the same actual effect on the amount of VAT charged, Exempt refers to those items that are exempt from VAT under Common Market regulations while Zero rated is a zero rate chosen by the member country's government.

When all values in the analysis column plus the VAT equal the total amount held in the value box, the system will automatically post the details to the transactions file and proceed with the next transaction.

A special note is worth making at this stage with regard to the collection and payment of VAT. When a company collects VAT it will have to pass it on to H.M. Customs and Excise at the end of each month. The amount passed on will be the amount actually invoiced, not collected. This is an assumption made by the Pegasus package which is applicable to the majority of firms.

2 C = Credit note

The effect on the customer account is to **reduce** the amount of debt owing by the customer. Entry details are exactly the same as that for invoice. Such documents are often issued when the customer returns goods delivered to them or may come about because they were inadvertently overcharged on a previous invoice.

Not only will the amount owing to the firm fall, but also the amount of VAT collected will also fall – a fact that has to be reflected in VAT monthly returns.

In Chapter 7 covering Sales Invoicing, the entry of many of these details will be automated, further reducing the amount of data entry required by the operator.

3 R = Receipts

A receipt is a transaction that comes about when a customer makes a payment and consequently **reduces** the balance outstanding.

The value box must contain the total payment made by the customer. The reference box can be used in this instance for anything the company wishes, such as the customer cheque number or method of payment.

The box headed VAT or Disk will contain (for this transaction type) the discount total offered to the customer. This amount will further reduce the amount of debt owing by the customer. The period box is for balanced accounts only, and indicates against which period the payment is to be matched.

When a payment is made on an open item account, you will be given the option of deciding whether the amount is to be paid on account. If you answer 'Y' to this, the system will start clearing the longest outstanding invoice (a usual practice when payments are made). If 'N' is answered, the operator will have to decide which invoices are to be paid and by how much.

4 F = Refunds

This refers to money refunded by the firm to a customer account and has the opposite effect to a credit note and **increases** the amount of debt owing by the customer to the firm. If this appears confusing to readers, then think of it as a debit note.

5 A = Adjustments

This simply allows an adjustment to be made on an individual account and can either **increase** or **reduce** the amount of debt owing. The important difference in this entry is that a negative (−) sign is placed in front of the value amount if it is to reduce the balance. The reference plays an important part in the documenting of this transaction.

The references that may be used to indicate the type of adjustment must appear in UPPER CASE (Capitals) and are:

(a) **CONTRA** indicates that a part or all of a customer's account has been adjusted because of another transaction counteracting it. For example, a particular customer who owes us £500, has also acted as a supplier and supplied £300 worth of goods. Rather than go through the process of demanding £500 and then subsequently paying £300, it seems more logical to make a CONTRA adjustment of −£300 on the account in the Sales Ledger to indicate that only £200 is now owing followed by a CONTRA adjustment of +£300 in the appropriate Purchase Ledger account. This method of accounting is perfectly legitimate but should, naturally, be handled with care.

(b) **BAD DEBT** will normally be a negative value and indicates that a customer has defaulted on payment and the account is to be written off.

(c) **WRITE OFF** is used in much the same way as a bad debt, but may be done as a gesture of goodwill or because all goods have been returned from a one-off sale.

(d) **MISPOST** simply indicates the correction of an error.

(e) **DISCOUNT** is usually negative and allows you to offer a subsequent discount to a customer.

(f) **INTEREST** is usually positive and allows you to add interest on a customer account for late payment.

Any other adjustment entry not known by the system will be documented as **sundry**.

The important point to consider is that **all** adjustments will be treated in exactly the same way with regard to the effect that they have on accounts. The purpose of entering a reference that matched the kind of adjustment required is to allow proper and meaningful documentation.

6 X = Allocations

This type of transaction will only be allowed on open item accounts. In a customer account, there may appear both positive and negative amounts. An allocation allows one figure to offset another. For example, a credit note may appear on an account which can then be used to offset a particular invoice. This may have an affect on discounts and interest charges on accounts as well as influencing the unpaid invoices that have to be carried forward to the next period.

REPORTS

This section contains some standard reports which can be run. These reports can be complemented by using the Report Generator facility explained further in this book.

The reports in this section are found from option 5 of the Sales Ledger menu, **Reports**. This produces the following menu:

```
1  Amend/Create Debtors Letters
2  Print Debtors Letters
3  List Invoices and Credit Notes
4  List Receipts and Adjustments
5  Statements
6  Aged Debtors List
7  List of Accounts
8  Labels
9  VAT Outstanding Report
0  Terminate
```

Options 1 and 2, **Amend/Create Debtors Letters** and **Print Debtors Letters**, concentrate on the letters sent to debtors. This facility allows letters to be set up and printed for (say) all customers with a debt outstanding for three months.

By setting up a number of letters for differing circumstances, an operator has the facility for automating the distribution of letters that are personalised (some computer operators call this 'mail merge').

Option 3, **List Invoices and Credit Notes**, will produce part of an audit trail giving details along with a summary of all such transactions. The negative or positive sign is used to indicate the effect each transaction has had on the account.

Option 4, **List Receipts and Adjustments**, does exactly the same. Between the two listings, all Sales Ledger transactions will be listed and form an important part of an audit trail.

Option 5, **Statements**, produces customer statements of accounts. The option will reveal two boxes indicating from which account you wish to start producing statements and to which account you wish to print to. If you simply press ENTER in response, leaving both boxes empty, all customer accounts will have statements. This principle is used elsewhere in the package.

Option 6, **Aged Debtors List**, produces a statement of which customers owe debt to the firm, how much each customer owes and how long the debt has been owing.

Option 7, **List of Accounts**, does exactly this. It is worth noting that the order in which accounts records are stored, listed and processed will, for the first time, be in the same sequence as they were entered. The end-of-period run will re-arrange the accounts records in customer account order: the accounts starting with numbers coming before alphabetic ones.

Option 8, **Labels**, enables the operator to print self-adhesive labels for all or a range of customers.

Option 9, **VAT Outstanding Report**, provides a listing of the outstanding VAT on the Sales Ledger for cash accounting purposes.

VAT REPORT (CASH ACCOUNTING)

Pegasus Single-User provides for the accounts of companies whose VAT is paid on invoice value, or those smaller companies that pay VAT only on the amount received during the tax period.
This function has a small sub-menu attached to it:

```
1   VAT Input Report
2   Clear VAT Outstanding
0   Terminate
```

The VAT input report gives details of invoices, credit notes, receipts and payments, with the VAT received and paid. On the report, invoices, receipts and the VAT received are shown as positive quantities, whereas credit notes, payments and the VAT refunded are shown as negatives. It would be usual to produce this report every quarter in order to calculate VAT due, after which the file is cleared for the next period.
The 'clear VAT outstanding' option is used only once when you first utilise 'cash accounting' methods on changing over from standard accounting.

STAGES FOR END-OF-PERIOD (MONTH) RUN

At the end of any accounting period, normally monthly, all accounts are closed and re-opened with new balances from the previous month, unless the accounts are open items, where only unpaid invoices are passed over to the new month. The end of month also deletes accounts which have DELETE typed in their name and address field, re-arranges the accounts records in customer account order and sets turnovers to zero (if you require this). Option 2, **Period End**, performs this activity. In using this option, the operator should be carefully prepared and should go through a number of procedures before commencing.

Because of the importance of this process, a password will be asked for.

You are not advised, at this stage, to perform this activity, until you have thoroughly investigated the other activities associated with the Sales Ledger.

The following are the stages that should be gone through:

1 Finish posting all transactions for month. A good deal of an operator's time can be spent trying to chase up invoices and receipts that have not yet been entered to the system.

2 Back-up on to a floppy disk ALL data files for the month, being careful to label your disk as data files as at END OF MONTH. The need for backing up cannot be over-emphasised. Once a computer system has been running for some time, it is often the case that the data generated is worth more in value than the entire computer system. Once data is properly backed up, there can be no such thing as a disaster in terms of data processing.

3 From **Nominal Ledger** select **Analysis as Sales and Purchases** in order to post any remaining transactions to the Nominal Ledger. A transaction list will then be required. This will be explained in some detail in a later chapter.

4 Print an **Aged Debtors Report** and check the **Outstanding Debtors total** against the Nominal Ledger **Sales Ledger Control Account**.

5 Print statements of account so that customers can be notified of the state of their accounts.

6 Produce any other relevant lists that will make up the required audit trail.

7 Print any analysis report and the **VAT analysis.**

8 Run **end-of-period** program.

9 Back-up data files again, being careful to label your disk as data files as at BEGINNING OF MONTH.

If backing up has been done properly **at both stages** and it is found that a mistake or omission has been made, then you will always be able to restore the back-up and start the end-of-month process.

Many of the processes stated here require integration with the Nominal Ledger. If the Sales Ledger is being operated as a stand-alone module, then the printed reports will serve the purpose of supplying sufficient information for postings to be made to a manual or separate computerised Nominal Ledger.

SALES ANALYSIS

This appears in the Sales Ledger menu as option 3. Much of the analyses in this section are dependent upon how the Sales Ledger has been organised. It is important to note that the organisation of a Sales Ledger is dependent upon the type of business it is being used for. For example, customer accounts can be grouped by department, geographical location, importance of customer or client, type of customer. The analysis uses reports that have already been set up by an operator using the option 'update parameters'.

VAT analysis is an exception to this, in that it comes as part of the package and shows a breakdown of VAT collected by the firm. This information has to be passed on to H.M. Customs and Excise along with settlement. If the firm has also paid VAT, then a further statement is needed, so that the firm can deduct this from the amount collected to arrive at a net figure which becomes the settlement figure. We shall return to this problem in a later chapter.

REPORT GENERATOR

Many firms' managers require the kind of reports that the package does not readily cater for. This routine goes a long way to setting up reports. Such reports may well involve a more detailed analysis of the type of customers on the Sales Ledger or the nature of debt owed to the firm. They are essential for effective management information.

CONCLUSION AND EXERCISES

Some important issues raised in this chapter have been covered lightly because they require a knowledge of other modules. Some further issues regarding the Sales Ledger will be raised in later chapters, in particular Chapter 6 which looks in some depth at reporting procedures and debtors' letters.

As a way of gaining practice, you should have a go at performing the following tasks:

1   Create a parameters file based on the information given in this Chapter.
2   Create at least 15 customer accounts using a variety of account types.
3   Generate for each customer at least 2 invoices.
4   Generate for 4 of your customers 2 credit notes.
5   Receive a payment from 5 of your customers.
6   Produce a full list of transactions showing:
    (a) List Invoices and Credit Notes.
    (b) List Receipts and Adjustments.

7 Generate an enquiry on 2 accounts.
8 Produce a statement of account for 2 customers.
9 Produce an aged debtors list.
10 Produce a list of accounts.
11 Determine the outstanding debtors total

Please note: It is not essential to produce printer listings of all of these, but to simply be able to access such information – in other words, a listing to the screen will suffice.

3 The Purchase Ledger

THE PURPOSE AND STRUCTURE OF THE PURCHASE LEDGER FUNCTION

The Purchase Ledger can be used in isolation to all other facilities offered by Pegasus. This chapter will assume that you are setting up the Purchase Ledger system in isolation, although reference will have to be made with regard to the Nominal Ledger. An integrated approach with other functions will be tackled in Chapter 5.

The purpose of a Purchase Ledger is to record and help manage **all** Purchases from suppliers. The Purchase Ledger can be used just as effectively for services acquired as it can for goods bought (or a combination of both). As depicted in Figure 3.1, such facilities offered by a Purchase Ledger must allow a user the ability to create, delete and amend suppliers' details on the ledger as well as record all transactions between firm and supplier. Additional requirements would be good reporting on the Purchase Ledger to ensure the firm is keeping within defined budgets and is not building too much expensive debt. Controlling expenditure will always be an important part of business management, and although an efficient Purchase Ledger will not, by itself, control expenditure, it should be capable of reporting any problems quickly so they can be rectified. Another important part of the Purchase Ledger to many firms is to assist it in offering information on VAT collected from its sales.

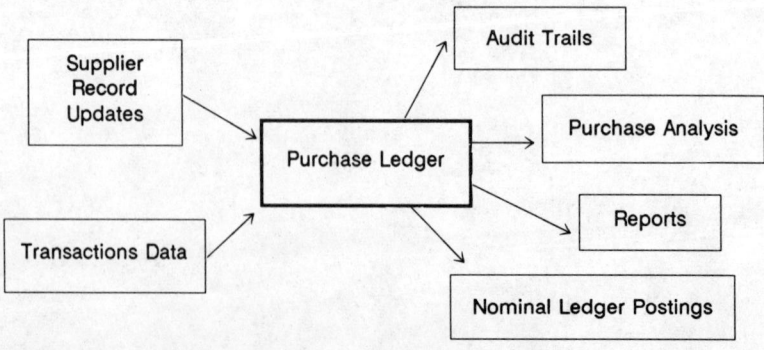

Figure 3.1 Purchase Ledger Processing

In general, purchases can fall into one of three categories:

(a)   Purchases for trading such as the purchase of raw materials that will go into stock for future manufacturing purposes, or purchases of stock for later re-sale.

(b)   Purchases related to business expenses, such as wages, stationery, electricity, rates and general office supplies. Such purchases can be regarded as trading expenses.

(c)   Capital purchases such as new buildings, warehouses or the purchase of fixtures and fittings.

In many businesses, other categories may be identified. Regardless of the type and nature of a purchase, the Purchase Ledger will treat them all in exactly the same way. The need to be aware of the category of goods or services purchased will have to be considered when the invoice details are entered to the Ledger and when the purchase details need to be posted to the Nominal Ledger.

The Purchase Ledger, in many ways, is the inverted function of the Sales Ledger. In other words, it does almost the same as the Sales Ledger, but goods and services enter the business and payments result in money leaving the business bank accounts.

The activities within the Purchase Ledger are similar to that of the Sales Ledger. The structure of activities, however, do vary and it is a good idea at this stage to compare the differences illustrated in Figure 3.2.

This part of the package will meet most requirements stated quite easily, along with some others. There are other reporting facilities available for, in particular, management information that will be a topic in Chapter 6.

As a useful tip in operating the Purchase Ledger, it is often a good idea to **batch process** much of the work. For example, when adding transactions to the Purchase Ledger, it is often best to do a few at the same time (say weekly) rather than enter them to the ledger on an *ad-hoc* basis. This will save both time and possible confusion.

At the end of each accounting period (usually monthly) there will be an **end-of-period** activity. This will be necessary for ensuring accounts do not get unnecessarily large as well as supplying important information needs to the firm.

Using a computer for a Purchase Ledger works in much the same way as that for a manual system. Also, the operation is very similar to the Sales Ledger. A typical set of procedures may look something like this:

When invoices arrive, check them for completeness and batch them until there is a sufficient number of invoices to warrant entering to the computer.

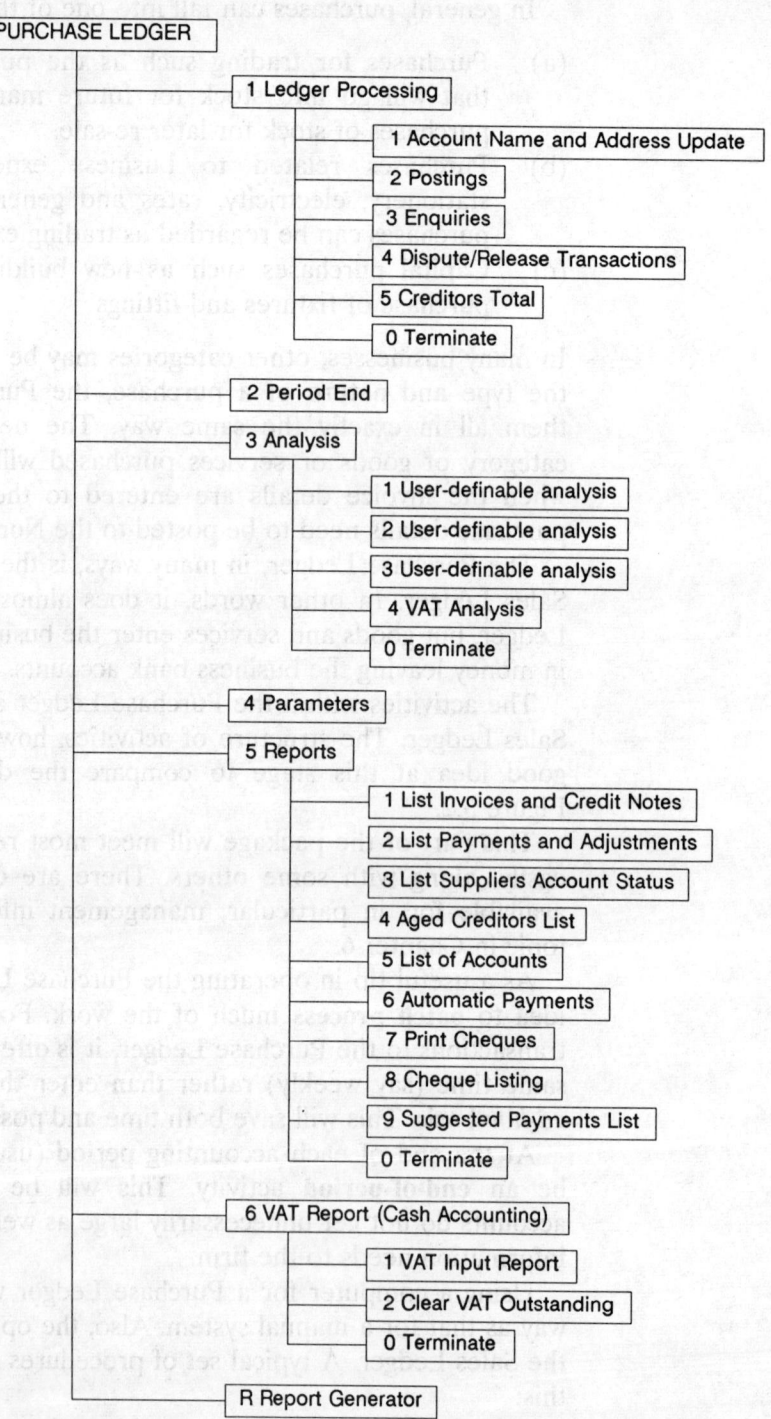

```
                    ┌─────────────────────┐
                    │  PURCHASE LEDGER    │
                    └─────────────────────┘
                              │
              ┌───────────────────────────────────┐
              │         1 Ledger Processing        │
              └───────────────────────────────────┘
                      │     ┌──────────────────────────────────────┐
                      ├─────│ 1 Account Name and Address Update     │
                      │     └──────────────────────────────────────┘
                      │     ┌──────────────────────────────────────┐
                      ├─────│ 2 Postings                            │
                      │     └──────────────────────────────────────┘
                      │     ┌──────────────────────────────────────┐
                      ├─────│ 3 Enquiries                           │
                      │     └──────────────────────────────────────┘
                      │     ┌──────────────────────────────────────┐
                      ├─────│ 4 Dispute/Release Transactions        │
                      │     └──────────────────────────────────────┘
                      │     ┌──────────────────────────────────────┐
                      ├─────│ 5 Creditors Total                     │
                      │     └──────────────────────────────────────┘
                      │     ┌──────────────────────────────────────┐
                      └─────│ 0 Terminate                           │
                            └──────────────────────────────────────┘
              ┌───────────────────────────────────┐
              │         2 Period End               │
              └───────────────────────────────────┘
              ┌───────────────────────────────────┐
              │         3 Analysis                 │
              └───────────────────────────────────┘
                      │     ┌──────────────────────────────────────┐
                      ├─────│ 1 User-definable analysis             │
                      │     └──────────────────────────────────────┘
                      │     ┌──────────────────────────────────────┐
                      ├─────│ 2 User-definable analysis             │
                      │     └──────────────────────────────────────┘
                      │     ┌──────────────────────────────────────┐
                      ├─────│ 3 User-definable analysis             │
                      │     └──────────────────────────────────────┘
                      │     ┌──────────────────────────────────────┐
                      ├─────│ 4 VAT Analysis                        │
                      │     └──────────────────────────────────────┘
                      │     ┌──────────────────────────────────────┐
                      └─────│ 0 Terminate                           │
                            └──────────────────────────────────────┘
              ┌───────────────────────────────────┐
              │         4 Parameters               │
              └───────────────────────────────────┘
              ┌───────────────────────────────────┐
              │         5 Reports                  │
              └───────────────────────────────────┘
                      │     ┌──────────────────────────────────────┐
                      ├─────│ 1 List Invoices and Credit Notes      │
                      │     └──────────────────────────────────────┘
                      │     ┌──────────────────────────────────────┐
                      ├─────│ 2 List Payments and Adjustments       │
                      │     └──────────────────────────────────────┘
                      │     ┌──────────────────────────────────────┐
                      ├─────│ 3 List Suppliers Account Status       │
                      │     └──────────────────────────────────────┘
                      │     ┌──────────────────────────────────────┐
                      ├─────│ 4 Aged Creditors List                 │
                      │     └──────────────────────────────────────┘
                      │     ┌──────────────────────────────────────┐
                      ├─────│ 5 List of Accounts                    │
                      │     └──────────────────────────────────────┘
                      │     ┌──────────────────────────────────────┐
                      ├─────│ 6 Automatic Payments                  │
                      │     └──────────────────────────────────────┘
                      │     ┌──────────────────────────────────────┐
                      ├─────│ 7 Print Cheques                       │
                      │     └──────────────────────────────────────┘
                      │     ┌──────────────────────────────────────┐
                      ├─────│ 8 Cheque Listing                      │
                      │     └──────────────────────────────────────┘
                      │     ┌──────────────────────────────────────┐
                      ├─────│ 9 Suggested Payments List             │
                      │     └──────────────────────────────────────┘
                      │     ┌──────────────────────────────────────┐
                      └─────│ 0 Terminate                           │
                            └──────────────────────────────────────┘
              ┌───────────────────────────────────┐
              │         6 VAT Report (Cash Accounting) │
              └───────────────────────────────────┘
                      │     ┌──────────────────────────────────────┐
                      ├─────│ 1 VAT Input Report                    │
                      │     └──────────────────────────────────────┘
                      │     ┌──────────────────────────────────────┐
                      ├─────│ 2 Clear VAT Outstanding               │
                      │     └──────────────────────────────────────┘
                      │     ┌──────────────────────────────────────┐
                      └─────│ 0 Terminate                           │
                            └──────────────────────────────────────┘
              ┌───────────────────────────────────┐
              │         R Report Generator         │
              └───────────────────────────────────┘
```

Figure 3.2

Record them on the computer, ensuring that any invoices received are checked for completeness. Any invoices that are to be questioned should be placed **in dispute**. Pegasus has the facility of doing this by making an invoice reference have a **D** in the last position in the reference box. The effect of this is that invoices are treated in the normal way but do not get paid until they are brought out of dispute. It also has the effect of bringing the disputed invoices to the attention of those concerned. If in doubt, placing invoices in dispute may be the safest option.

For the invoices in dispute, check the invoice(s) against the purchase order or with the person who authorised the order; check that goods or services have been received and are in as ordered; check that prices and extensions are correct and any available discounts have been deducted.

Release the invoice(s) using the **dispute/release transaction** activity.

Pay the invoice at an appropriate time, keeping the invoice with all its accumulated signatures on file to settle queries and for the auditors. Never throw away any of these **source documents** as they are the real proof of a transaction taking place.

Produce summary reports of the transactions data entered at the end of each batch-process run, and check that the data entries are complete and accurate.

The Sales Ledger function will have the Invoicing part of the package to assist it in much of the transactions entry – a topic to be covered in a later chapter. Such a facility is now available to assist us with the Purchase Ledger. Consequently, an operator should use as many checks as possible to ensure good data entry. In many instances, firms will use someone else to check for completeness and accuracy of data input to the person(s) who entered it.

As an important point, do not destroy or dispose of any invoices. Once their details have been entered to the computer, such documents should be filed in a safe place in case they are required for future reference; and a good number of them always will.

The principle, therefore, of effective Purchase Ledger management has to be to establish a routine and stick to it, a principle that applies to manual book-keeping systems as well.

GETTING STARTED

If you are using the Purchase Ledger for the first time, it is important that you use the **Parameter Update** option first, which is option **4** from the Purchase Ledger menu. This is used in order to tell the

Pegasus system what type of print-outs you want and what should appear on them.

When using the parameter settings for the first time, you will be required to enter a password. A password is needed to build in some security to the system in a way that prevents any unauthorised persons from interfering with the processes. When entering your password, try not to forget it. This was also required with respect to the Sales Ledger. The situation may arise where different personnel operate the two accounting functions, in which case they can have different passwords.

Having specified the password, you will be confronted with a form to be completed that makes up the required parameters file. The following offers a suggested response with explanation:

Purchase Parameters - { Date }

Company Name		Pegasus Users Enterprises
	Address Line 1	100 High Street
	Address Line 2	Biddlesdon
	Address Line 3	Wessex
	Address Line 4	England WSX 999
	1st Tel No.	0002 82991
	2nd Tel No.	0001 19928
	Telex No.	72781

Company details stated above will appear on any remittance notes produced by the system. A remittance advice note is a statement of payment to a supplier. Such documents are of particular use as a hard-copy record of payment.

The same document can then be sent to the supplier to assist them in keeping their records and ensure clarity of transaction.

VAT Reg No.	000 1990 00

Nearly all businesses require a VAT Registration Number which is obtainable from H.M. Customs and Excise Department (VAT) on application.

Printer Type	0
TOF Code	12
Columns	132
Lines/Page	66

As with the Sales Ledger, these printer settings are used to ensure a degree of **compatibility** with the package and printer.

The following options allow you to **tailor** the package more closely to the needs of the firm.

Option No. 1	Y

This ensures lists of transactions will also contain suppliers' names – useful when dealing with a large number of suppliers or when you are unfamiliar with the supplier codes.

Option No. 2	Y

This ensures that when invoice details are entered to the Purchase Ledger, invoice analysis codes are inserted with a four-digit code in the same format as the Nominal Ledger. This allows integration with the Nominal Ledger and is discussed in Chapter 5 in some detail.

VAT Code for Analysis   **PVAT**

Again, this is to allow future integration with the Nominal Ledger. With respect to purchases, if the firm has to pay VAT to its suppliers, it will have the right to claim it back from H.M. Customs and Excise. In practice, most firms collect more VAT from Sales than they pay through Purchases, which requires a settlement of the difference with H.M. Customs and Excise. Such settlement is normally done quarterly (every 3 months).

Option No. 3   **Y**

By setting this to 'Y', the system will print a remittance note each time a payment is posted to the Nominal Ledger. Payments can be made in two ways using the Purchase Ledger function:

(a) From the main Purchase Ledger option 1, Ledger Processing, and from there option 2, Ledger Postings. This allows the entry of a payment.

(b) From the main Purchase Ledger option 5, Special Reports has an option in it of **Automatic Payments** which allows the automatic payment of accounts. Paying an account by this method will settle all invoices that are not in dispute.

Option No. 4   **N**

An entry of 'Y' here will allow for an analysis of invoices and credit notes over different rates of VAT. At the time of writing there were only two rates of VAT applicable in the United Kingdom (0% and 15%). Setting this to 'N' will, of course, reduce the size and complexity of such a report.

Option No. 5   **N**

If this is set to 'Y' then all zero balance accounts at the end of the period run will be deleted. This can be a nuisance if you use certain suppliers on a regular basis because you will have to create another supplier record every time you wish to restart trading with a supplier. On the other hand, the type of business that purchases from many suppliers on a 'one-off' basis, will find this facility useful as it will reduce the size of the supplier file and make it easier to locate supplier information.

Maintaining a list of suppliers, even if not used in the current period, offers useful information in its own right. For example, if a manufacturer requires a supply of goods or raw materials quickly, then it has at hand details of a number of suppliers to draw on.

Option No. 6   **N**

This is used to integrate the Purchase Ledger with the Job Costing function of the Pegasus package and will be discussed in a later chapter.

Option No. 7   **N**

This allows the operator to affect what is placed into a supplier record. If the option is set at 'N', a comment field is used, permitting the entry of a comment about the account to be stored.

If the option is set at 'Y', the details on settlement and discount terms can be entered. This informs the firm of any discounts that may be allowed for prompt payment and will, in some cases, affect the decision about the timing of payments.

Option No. 8

This option allows the operator to establish a password that he would enter for access to the parameters in other areas of the Purchase Ledger. When items are selected from the menu of the Purchase Ledger, the user will be prompted for entry of the password before being allowed to proceed.

Option No. 9

This will allow smaller companies to account for VAT on a cash basis as opposed to an invoiced basis.

Purchase Analysis 1	– Sequence	12/3456
	– Narrative	Supplier/Stock Type
Purchase Analysis 2	– Sequence	3456/12
	– Narrative	Stock Type/Supplier
Purchase Analysis 3	– Sequence	
	– Narrative	

These Purchase Analysis details are used to determine the type of report required as a way of analysing what has been purchased. They require the use of a special supplier code along with a code on what has been purchased. These codes and the reports they generate will be discussed Chapter 6.

Cheque Format	Details – Lines/Chqe
Date	Position – Line/Col
Payee	Position – Line/Col
Amnt	Position – Line/Col
10000	Position – Line/Col
1000	Position – Line/Col
100	Position – Line/Col
10	Position – Line/Col
1	Position – Line/Col
Upper Cheque Limit	

The Purchase Ledger function permits the production of cheques on special stationery that can be provided by arrangement with the firm's bank. When a firm has a lot of suppliers to pay, it can be time-saving to produce all the cheques automatically at (say) the end of each month. However well the cheques are printed, they will still have to be signed by authorised signatories.

As with the Sales Ledger, the parameters can be re-set at any time. When parameters are re-set, answer the questions, as prompted, accurately. When the system asks if you want to erase old data files, and you answer 'Y' to this, then **all** Purchase Ledger data will be destroyed from the disk. This could be fatal if you get it wrong.

MAINTAINING SUPPLIER RECORDS

The activity is contained in option 1 of the Purchase Ledger menu, Ledger Posting. This produces the following menu:

1 Account Names and Address Update
2 Ledger Postings
3 Enquiries
4 Dispute/Release Transactions
5 Creditors Total

Option 1 from here is used to maintain supplier record details. Figure 3.3 illustrates the structure of supplier records.

Supplier a/c number	Name & address	Disc. rate terms	Days to pay	Credit limit	Analysis code	a/c type O/B
0200	KJ Right 1 Low Rd	2% 1 1% 2	99	3,000	P1	B
0210	PB Left 21 King St	1.3% 1	99	4,000	P1	O

Figure 3.3 Supplier records held in Purchase Ledger

The purpose of the Account Names and Address Update activity is to:

(a)   Enter new supplier details.
(b)   Delete supplier records that are no longer needed.
(c)   Amend details of existing suppliers, such as a change in address or credit limit.

It is important that each supplier has a **unique** account number. Each record will, as indicated, hold details of one supplier with supplier details being broken down into **fields**. The field that holds the supplier account number is a **key field** in that it identifies the supplier record. The account number is derived from the firm, not the supplier. Circumstances may arise when a supplier supplies different categories of goods and services to the firm, such as raw materials and office materials. In this case, it may be wise to create more than one account on this supplier to cater for this. Differentiating the types of purchases can also be made within the posting of invoices to the Ledger, thereby avoiding the need for more than one account. Whatever method is used, it must be tailored to suit the firm's accounting needs.

To add a supplier record to the file, you simply enter a new supplier account number and then complete the remaining fields. The name and address box should contain a full postal address. Many of a firm's suppliers could be overseas, so it is important to enter the postal address applicable to the country where the supplier is based. This will be the only reference in the system that contains the supplier address. A telephone number in this field may also be useful, especially if you need to get in touch with suppliers quickly.

The boxes containing settlement discount will only be displayed if option 7 of the parameters is set to 'Y'. If the first entries in two boxes are 2.0% and 30 days, then a discount of 2% is allowed off the invoice if it is settled within 30 days of the invoice date. If a second row reads 1% and 60, then the discount allowed falls to 1% if the invoice is paid after 30 days but within 60 days.

The days to pay indicates the number of days allowed before payment is due. This is particularly useful if you are using the automatic payments activity, as payment can be delayed until the stipulated number of days. For example, if the number of settlement days was set at 20, then no settlement of the invoice would be considered until 20 days had lapsed.

If option 7 is set to 'N', a comment field appears instead of discount details. The comment box serves no accounting purpose and is left for the firm's own use. Such a comment box could, for example, hold a contact name for the supplier or a telephone number or a code to indicate how reliable a supplier is at meeting orders.

The field containing credit limit is used to enter the amount of credit a supplier has allowed the firm. Such credit limits are common in trading and work in much the same way as credit cards. When an invoice is entered to the Purchase Ledger and will result in the account exceeding the credit limit, the package will warn you of this fact. Payments to suppliers may then have to be made prior to an order being placed.

The account type field is used to indicate whether the account is open item or balanced. If the account is open item it means the firm will always pay against invoices and that at the end of a period, the unpaid invoice(s) will be carried across to the next period. If the account is balanced it means the firm will always pay against a balance and that at the end of a period, the balance will be carried across to the next period.

The analysis code field is for use by the firm and will allow future analysis of purchases, a topic to be discussed in Chapter 6.

When an account is no longer needed, then it can be deleted by entering the characters **DELETE** in the name and address box in the top left-hand corner. This record will remain on the file until an end-of-period has been run.

To amend a supplier record, simply enter the customer account number in the appropriate box. The record details will appear, leaving the operator with the job of simply altering any fields that appear.

TRANSACTION PROCESSING

Entering a transaction is available as option 2, Ledger Postings, of the Ledger Posting menu in the Purchase Ledger. This option allows the entry of a number of different types of transactions. In practice not all transaction types have to be entered through this activity. As mentioned earlier in this chapter, it is always wise, where possible, to batch the work in such a way that a number of transactions are entered in one go rather than being entered as they occur.

All transactions will be kept in a transactions file, of which the record structure is illustrated in Figure 3.4.

Supplier a/c Number	Trans Date	Trans Type	Ref	Trans Value	Goods Value	VAT or Disc.
0200	130789	Paymt	Chq 2132	543.00	500.00	43.00
0210	140789	Invce	19801	229.99	210.00	19.99

Figure 3.4 Transaction records held in the Purchase Ledger

The account number refers to the key field in the supplier file. When entering this through the transactions screen, supplier record details will be displayed to assist the operator. In this instance, the supplier code can appear more than once in the transactions file, once for each transaction.

The date that appears will normally be the system date. This date can be altered if you wish to post-date or pre-date the transaction.

There are six transaction types which can be entered. Each transaction type has to be indicated by a code (I, C, P, F, A and X).

1 I = Invoice

The effect on the customer account is to **increase** the amount of debt owed to the supplier. The reference box can be used in this instance for anything the company wishes, but will normally hold the invoice number. The value box holds the total invoice price, including VAT.

The box headed **VAT or Disc** will contain (for this transaction type) the VAT total on the invoice. The period box is for balanced accounts only, and indicates against which period the invoice is to be matched.

The analysis boxes will need to be filled. They are designed to show a breakdown of the value of goods that appear on the invoice. The code column will contain either a stock code or a nominal code, depending on how the package is to be used. The value box contains the selling price of the product(s) exclusive of VAT. It is in this analysis box that the type of purchase will be indicated. For example, a nominal code indicating the acquisition of office furniture may be E421; in which case this is the code that should appear if the purchase amount is to be posted to this account later on when the functions are integrated.

The VAT column is for reference purposes and will not affect the amount of VAT collected. It is used to indicate the type of VAT that a particular item is subject to, and can be one of:

1   To indicate Standard Rate.
Z   To indicate Zero Rate.
E   To indicate Exempt of VAT.

Although Exempt and Zero rate VAT has the same actual effect on the amount of VAT charged, Exempt refers to those items that are exempt from VAT under Common Market regulations while Zero Rated is a zero rate chosen by the member country's government. In Chapter 8, we shall store this information in the stock record relating to each item of stock, avoiding the need to keep entering it in ourselves.

It is also possible to set the system up so that information on where the details of a purchased item should be posted to in the Nominal Ledger is also contained within the stock files.

When all values in the analysis column plus the VAT equal the total amount held in the value box, the system will automatically post the details to the transactions file and proceed with the next transactions.

Placing a **D** in the last space in the reference box will place an invoice **in dispute**. At some point in the future, we must take the invoice out of dispute using the special reports facility within the Purchase Ledger function.

2 C = Credit Note

The effect on the supplier account is to **reduce** the amount of debt owing to the supplier. Entry details are exactly the same as for Invoice. Such documents are often issued when the goods are returned to the supplier, or the firm has been inadvertently overcharged on a previous invoice.

Not only will the amount owed by the firm fall, but also the amount of VAT paid will fall – a fact that has to be reflected in VAT returns.

3 P = Payments

A payment is a transaction that comes about when a supplier is paid and consequently **reduces** the balance outstanding. Automatic payments can be used instead of this option.

The value box must contain the total payment made to the supplier. The reference box can be used in this instance for anything the company wishes, such as cheque number or method of payment.

The box headed **VAT or Disc** will contain (for this transaction type) the discount allowed by the supplier. This amount will further reduce the amount of debt owing to the supplier. The period box is for balanced accounts only, and indicates against which period the payment is to be matched.

The amount owed is reduced by both the value of the payment and the discount allowed.

When a payment is made on an open item account, you will be given the option of deciding whether the amount is to be paid on account. If you answer 'Y' to this, the system will start clearing the longest outstanding invoice (a usual practice when payments are made). If 'N' is answered, the operator will have to decide which invoices are to be paid and by how much.

4 F = Refunds

This refers to money refunded by the firm to its supplier and has the opposite effect to a credit note and **increases** the amount of debt owing to the supplier by the firm. If this appears confusing to readers, then think of it as a debit note.

5 A = Adjustments

This simply allows an adjustment to be made on an individual account and can either **increase** or **reduce** the amount of debt owing. The important difference in this entry is to place a negative (−) sign in front of the value amount if it is to reduce the balance. Also the reference plays an important part in the documenting of this transaction.

The references that may be used to indicate the type of adjustment must appear in UPPER CASE (Capitals) and are exactly the same as that for the Sales Ledger and work in the same way. Namely:

CONTRA
WRITE OFF
MISPOST
DISCOUNT

Any other adjustment entry not known by the system will be documented as **sundry**.

The important point to consider is that all adjustments will be treated in exactly the same way with regard to the effect that they have on accounts. The purpose of entering a reference that matches the kind of adjustment required is to allow proper and meaningful documentation.

6 X = Allocations

This type of transaction will only be allowed on open item accounts. In a customer account, there may appear both positive and negative amounts. An allocation allows one figure to offset another. For example, a credit note may appear on an account which can then be used to offset a particular invoice.

As a way of summarising this section on transaction, Table 3.1 shows the effect on the supplier account of each transaction type:

Table 3.1

Transaction Type	Code	Effect on Balance
Invoice	I	+
Credit Note	C	−
Payments	P	−
Refunds	F	+
Adjustments	A	+ or −
Allocation	X	nothing

Other options

Option 3, **Enquiries**, allows an investigation to be made on an individual account and lists all transactions made during the current accounting period.

Option 4, **Dispute/Release Transactions**, allows the alteration of the status of a previously stored invoice. You will be required to enter the supplier account number. A list of invoices not yet paid will appear, indicating whether any are in dispute or not. This status can be altered.

Option 5, **Creditors Total**, simply gives a single figure showing the net total amount owing by the firm to its suppliers.

TRANSACTION REPORTS

The remainder of the Ledger Posting options are, to some extent, self-explanatory.

Option 1, **List Invoices and Credit Notes**, will produce part of an audit trail, giving details along with a summary of all such transactions. The NEGATIVE and POSITIVE sign is used to indicate the effect each transaction has had on the account. In most transaction entries, the system knows when to decrease or increase an account balance; the only exception to this is when using adjustments which require a negative sign to reduce an account.

Option 2, **List Payments and Adjustments**, does exactly the same. Between the two listings, all Purchase Ledger transactions will be listed and form an important part of an audit trail.

Option 3, **List Suppliers Account Status**, produces a detailed statement of a supplier's account and serves as a record of all transactions undergone between the firm and the supplier.

Option 4, **Aged Creditors List**, produces a statement of which suppliers are owed money by the firm, how much each supplier is owed and how long the debt has been owing.

Option 5, **List of Accounts**, does exactly this. It is worth noting that the order in which accounts records are stored, listed and processed will, for the first time, be in the same sequence as they were entered. The end-of-period run will re-arrange the accounts records in supplier account order.

END-OF-PERIOD RUN

At the end of any accounting period, normally monthly, all accounts are closed and re-opened with new balances from the previous month (unless the accounts are open items, where only unpaid invoices are passed over to the new month). In using this option, the operator should be carefully prepared and should go through a number of procedures before commencing with this option. Because of its importance, a password will be asked for. The following is a suggestion of how an end-of-month activity might be performed:

1 Finish posting all transactions for the month. This means collecting all those invoices and payment details that have not been accounted for. In practice, this can be an irritating job for an operator.

2 Any payments that still have to be made should now be done and entered to the computer. A suggested payment list can be extracted from this function and automatic payments made.

3 Back-up on to a floppy disk ALL data files for the month, being careful to label your disk as data files as at END OF MONTH. If for some reason the end-of-month operation fails, the process can always be repeated by restoring the back-up and starting again.

4 From the **Nominal Ledger** an activity **Analysis as Sales and Purchases** will be used in order to post any remaining transactions to the Nominal Ledger. A transaction list will then be required.

5 From the Job Costing program (if in use) run the **Purchase Ledger Analysis** program.

6 Print an audit trail which may include, among others, aged creditors report, outstanding creditors total, lists of transactions.

7 Produce any listings that may be required by user departments.

8 Print any analysis report and the **VAT Analysis**.

9 Run **end-of-period** program.

10 Back-up data files again, being careful to label your disk as data files as at BEGINNING OF MONTH. If during the month an accident led to the loss of data, then at the worst, the transactions can be re-entered starting at the beginning of the month. Hopefully, regular backing up of files will be more frequent than just monthly, reducing the effect of any computing disasters.

The end-of-period run also has the effect of deleting those accounts with DELETE in their names and address field. In addition to this, accounts are re-organised into account number order. Any accounts records added to the supplier file will be placed at the end of it until re-organised at this stage.

Analysis

Much of the analysis in this activity is dependent upon how the Purchase Ledger has been organised. It is important to note that the organisation of a Purchase Ledger is dependent upon the type of business it is being used for. For example, supplier accounts can be grouped by department, geographical location, raw materials, office supplies, etc. The analysis uses reports that have already been set up by an operator using the option 'update parameters'. This will be discussed fully in Chapter 6.

VAT analysis is an exception to this, in that it comes as part of the package and shows a breakdown of VAT paid by the firm. As we are dealing with a business, it should be remembered that the firm can claim the VAT back from Customs and Excise.

SPECIAL REPORTS

These activities are grouped together as they differ quite substantially from anything available in the Sales Ledger function. The menu reveals the following activities:

6 **Automatic Payments**
7 **Print Cheques**
8 **Cheque Listing**
9 **Suggested Payments List**

Automatic Payments from account to account will record that supplier accounts are to be settled. It will NOT settle those accounts still in dispute, nor will it settle accounts whose settlement days are not yet due.

Print Cheques. The conditions for using this option are:

1 The first cheque number needs to be entered with numbers incremented by one for each cheque printed.
2 The word CHQ must appear in the reference box for the invoice.
3 Cheques will only be printed ONCE. Any mistakes or your printer not functioning correctly will cause a loss of cheques. It may be wise to back-up before running this activity in case something goes wrong.
4 Special stationery will be required in the printer.

Cheque Listing simply lists all cheques automatically printed in the previous activity.

Suggested Payments List gives suggestions on paying suppliers. A list of who to pay and how much is to be paid is given, based on settlement days' criteria and discounts being offered.

REPORT GENERATOR

Many firms' managers require the kind of reports that the package does not readily cater for. This routine goes a long way to allowing setting up reports. Such reports may well involve a more detailed analysis of the type of suppliers on the Purchase Ledger or the nature of debt owing to suppliers or efficiency of suppliers to meet orders in time. They are essential for effective management information.

This topic will be covered in some detail in Chapter 14.

CONCLUSION AND EXERCISES

Some important issues raised in this chapter have been covered lightly because they require a knowledge of other modules. Some further issues regarding the Purchase Ledger will be raised in later chapters.

As a way of gaining practice, you should have a go at performing the following tasks:

1 Create a parameters file based on the information given in this chapter.
2 Create 15 supplier accounts using a variety of account types.
3 Generate for each supplier at least two invoices with some of them left in dispute. Also use the CHQ reference in some of them in order to make use of automatic payments later.
4 Generate for four of your suppliers two credit notes.
5 Produce a suggested payments list.
6 Use automatic payments to pay some of your suppliers AND pay some of them through the ledger postings activity.
7 Amend the parameters file in order to allow for the production of cheques and produce a cheque listing report.
8 Produce a full list of transactions showing:
(a) List Invoices and Credit Notes.
(b) List Receipts and Adjustments.
9 Generate an enquiry on two accounts.
10 Produce a List Suppliers Account Status for at least two suppliers.
11 Produce an Aged Creditors List.
12 Produce a List of Accounts.
13 Determine the Outstanding Creditors Total.

Please note: It is not essential to produce printer listings of all of these, but to simply be able to access such information – in other words, a listing to the screen will suffice.

4 The Nominal Ledger

PURPOSE AND ROLE

The Nominal Ledger is used to record all dealings involving, on one side, ASSETS of the firm such as buildings, stock, work in progress, and, on the other side, LIABILITIES of the firm such as amounts owing to suppliers, loan capital and share capital. In addition to this, the Nominal Ledger is used to produce trial balances, balance sheets and other reports required by the firm.

The Nominal Ledger can be used in conjunction with the Sales and Purchase Ledgers. The next chapter will concentrate on integrating the three ledgers with the use of an extensive worked example.

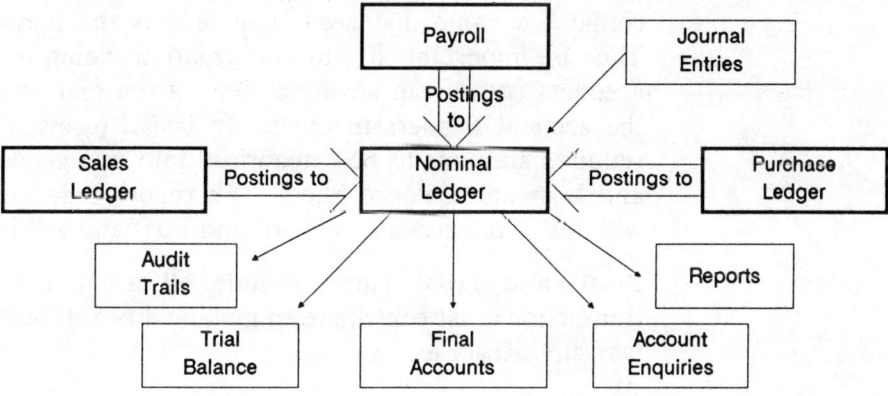

Figure 4.1

The Nominal Ledger, by its very nature, is very much the 'pillar stone' of an accounting system where, in varying forms, ALL business transactions will pass. It is worth noting that all business transactions do not necessarily involve money, as we have already seen. The Nominal Ledger uses the principle of **double-entry**, a process whereby any transaction entered to the nominal accounts must have a source and destination (credit and debit). As you work through this chapter and the remaining ones it is hoped you will gain an understanding of this principle. However, a knowledge of double-entry book-keeping beforehand will assist understanding.

ORGANISING NOMINAL ACCOUNTS

A nominal account is a record containing details about the type of transactions that have features in common. For example, a nominal account called 'Electricity' will be used to relate all transactions regarding electricity, such as a statement of how much electricity has been consumed and any payments to made. Also, a nominal account called 'purchase of stock' will relate to all transactions regarding acquisition of such stock. The nominal account, therefore, contains a number of nominal header records with the structure shown below.

Number	Name	Budget	Report Code
E101	Electric		P10
E103	Stationery	1,200	P76

Figure 4.2 Nominal header records

In practice the Nominal Ledger will hold many headers, possibly running into hundreds. It is important that the header **name** field contains a name that accurately reflects the purpose of the header. This is important if any information being extracted from the accounts is to mean anything. One of the first stages is to decide on the account headers to create. In broad terms, the Pegasus system requires accounts to be categorised into two general headings: Profit and Loss and Balance Sheet. The **report code** field will be prefixed with a **P** if the account is Profit and Loss and a **B** if Balance Sheet.

Profit and Loss: These include all account headers relating to transactions that contribute to making a profit. Such accounts fall into two sub-categories:

1   Trading: accounts relating to buying stock and selling goods and services. Such accounts will also include any goods returned to us by customers or returned by us to suppliers.

2   Expenses: as the name suggests, accounts incurring expenses or running costs to the business come into this category. Many expense accounts will have a BUDGET attached to them, which is an indicator as to how much such an expense should reach.

Balance Sheet: Such accounts fall into four groupings:

1   Long-term liabilities (or financed by). Such accounts are used to hold transactions regarding the long-term financing of a

company such as, share capital, long-term loans and accumulated retained profits.

2   Current liabilities. Such accounts refer to those debts owed by the company that will need repaying in the near future. An obvious example of this will be the sums owing to trade creditors as recorded in the Purchase Ledger. Another example would be any loans or overdrafts arranged over a short period of time (ranging from months to a few years).

3   Fixed assets. These record transactions relating to the permanent assets of the firm such as land, buildings, machinery, furniture, fixtures, fittings and motor vehicles.

4   Current assets. This holds transaction details regarding those assets of the company that will be required to operate the company, and so will be temporary in nature, examples of which are, stocks, trade debtors, and money held in the bank.

Figure 4.3 is designed to clarify this and shows a possible structure.

Most account headers will fall into their categories quite easily. Some accounts, however, will require some experience before they become obvious. In practice, an accountant will be involved in the process of setting up the structure of the nominal account system. If you are in any doubt about where account headers should fall, then ASK; do not attempt to guess.

Figure 4.3 shows 4-digit codes indicating the **account number** associated with each header. Each group heading within the diagram has a code ending with '00'. The Pegasus system allows us to reserve such account names to these kind of group headings. This facility is particularly useful when designing the Trading and Profit/Loss statements and the Balance Sheet, discussed in the next chapter. Each actual nominal account has a code closely related to its group heading, essential if the accounts are to be grouped together at a later stage. Such a design of structure will vary considerably from firm to firm and there is no reason why different coding techniques could not be developed. The Pegasus system will also need to know if an account header belongs to a Balance Sheet account or a Profit and Loss account.

In the account header records, a field is reserved for a **budget** figure. Such a figure, if it appears, sets a budget on an account which would be used as an attempt to control or monitor expenditure. It is important to note that only expense accounts and fixed assets should realistically be given a budget figure. Even here, there may be little point setting a budget on certain accounts, such as local authority taxes which are out of the control of the firm. The whole issue of budgeting will be discussed in a later chapter.

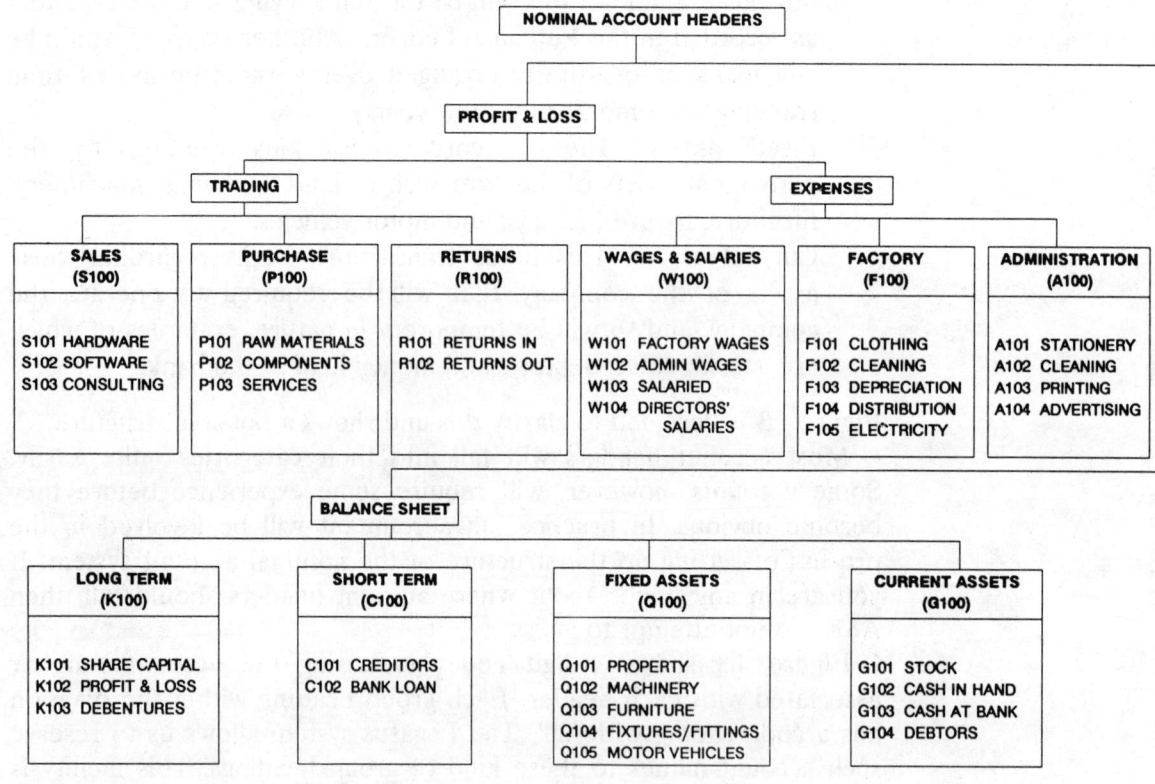

Figure 4.3

GETTING STARTED

When first loading the Nominal Ledger program (option 3 from the main Pegasus menu), the following options appear:

Nominal Ledger

1   Ledger Processing
2   Period End
3   Transfer of Sales and Purchase
4   Parameters
5   Reports
6   Bank Reconciliation
7   Report Generator

From this the structure of the Nominal Ledger function looks something like Figure 4.4.

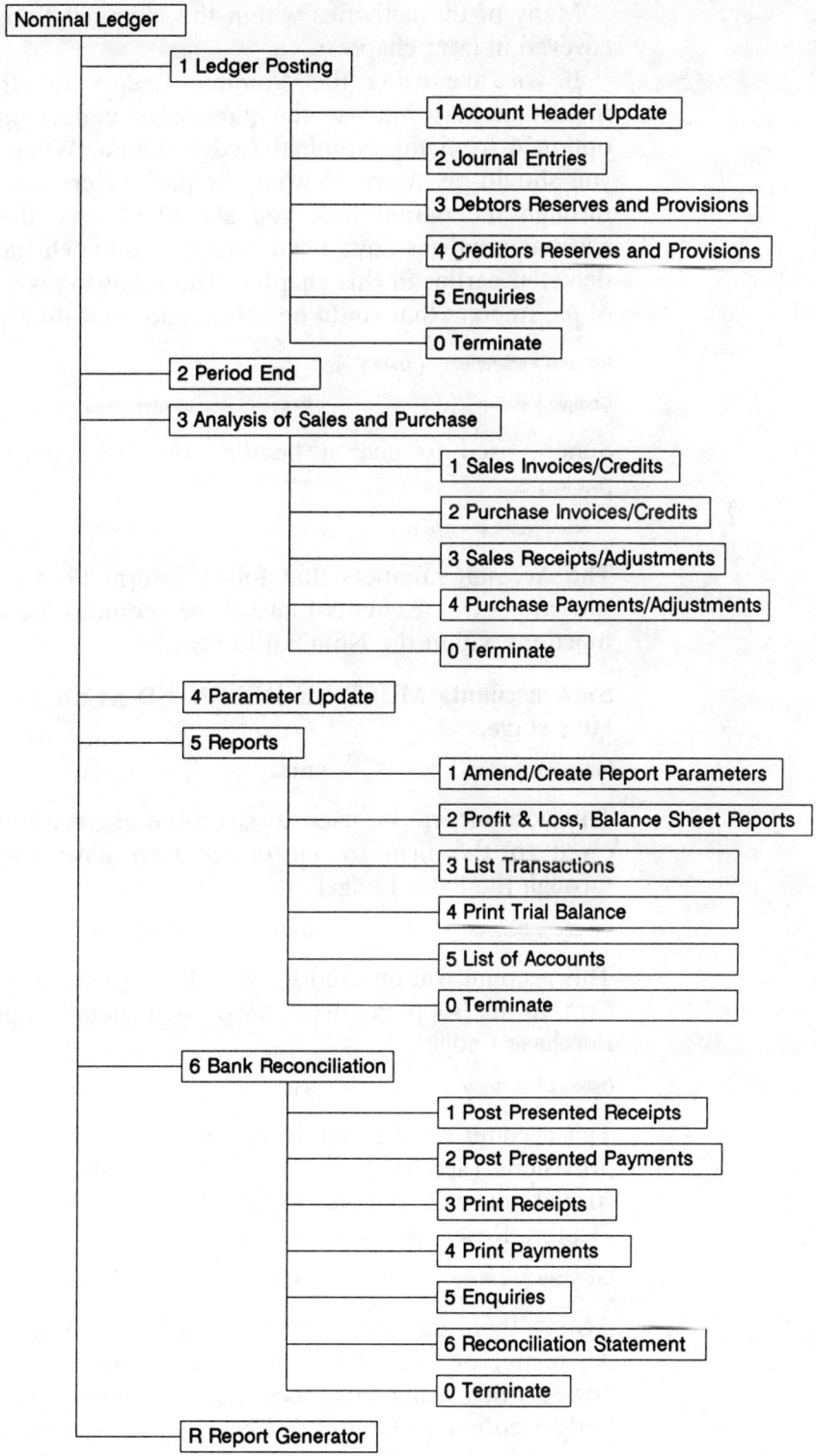

Figure 4.4

Many of the activities within the Nominal Ledger function will be covered in later chapters.

If you are using the Nominal Ledger for the first time, it is important that you use the **parameter update** option first, which is option **4** from the Nominal Ledger menu. When calling this option, you should be aware of what the parameters are for. When working through the parameters, you should observe the way some of the account numbers have been selected to match the nominal structure depicted earlier in this chapter. The following is a sample of the kind of parameters that **could be set up** and what their purpose is:

Nominal Parameters - { Date }

Company Name   **Pegasus Users Enterprises**

Simply used to give a heading on the reports produced by the package.

Account Number - A/c No.

The Account numbers that follow inform Pegasus where it will find special control accounts that will be required for many of the special functions within the Nominal Ledger.

Such accounts MUST BE REPEATED as an accounts heading at a later stage.

Debtors Control   **G104**

This account will be used to store the aggregate outstanding amount owed to the firm by customers who have their details updated through the Sales Ledger.

Creditors Control   **C101**

This account will be used to store the aggregate amount owing by the firm to its suppliers who have their details updated through the Purchase Ledger.

Debtors Res/Prov   **G105**

This account records details on sales reserves (pre-payments) or sales provisions (accruals) that are automatically posted when using the special journals entries facility from Nominal Ledger option 1 - Debtors Reserves and Provisions.

Creditors Res/Prov   **C103**

Again, this account records details on purchase reserves (pre-payments) or purchase provisions (accruals) that are automatically posted when using the special journals entries facility from Nominal Ledger option 1 - Creditors Reserves and Provisions.

Opening Stock   **G111**

Used to **bring forward** (normally from previous year) the value of the firm's opening stock. In other words, a current year's opening stock is normally the previous year's closing stock.

Closing Stock   **G101**

This will be required at the end of the year as a figure to help determine:

(a) Gross profit made by the firm.
(b) Total value of the firm's current assets.
(c) The amount that will form the next year's opening stock.

Discount Given   **A111**

This must match the account number to which all discounts given in the Sales Ledger match. It is used to store the aggregate of discounts given to customers on the settlement of their accounts. This account is updated during the nominal analysis of Sales Ledger.

Discount Taken   **A112**

This must match the account number to which all discounts taken in the Purchase Ledger match. It is used to store the aggregate of discounts taken from suppliers on the settlement of their accounts. This account is updated during the nominal analysis of Purchase Ledger.

Profit and Loss   **K102**

Used to **bring forward** (normally from previous year) the value of the profit or loss. This figure must appear on the firm's balance sheet at the end of year.

Bank Account   **G103**

This must match the account number to which all Sales Ledger receipts **and** Purchase Ledger payments are made. This account is updated during the nominal analysis of Purchase Ledger and Sales Ledger.

Debtors Suspense   **G199**

The situation will often arise where a sales invoice posted through the Sales Ledger does not possess a nominal code that exists in the Nominal Ledger (i.e. the Nominal Ledger does not know what category of stock/service is being sold). In this event, postings will be made to this account during the nominal analysis of the Sales Ledger. It will then be up to the operator to make the necessary re-postings and adjustments through journal entries after the analysis has been made. In other words, this balance must end up as a zero figure. It is often good practice to generate a **bogus code** for a sales posting as a way of getting the process of issuing an invoice under way and then posting it from the suspense account to the relevant nominal account at a later date (usually at the end of an accounting period). In many cases, the absence of a nominal code is a simple entry error.

Creditors Suspense   **C199**

The situation will often arise where a purchase invoice posted through the Purchase Ledger does not possess a nominal code that exists in the Nominal Ledger (i.e. the Nominal Ledger does not know what category of purchase is being made). In this event, postings will be made to this account during the nominal analysis of the Purchase Ledger. It will then be up to the operator to make the necessary re-postings and adjustments through journal entries after the analysis has been made. In other words, this balance must end up as a zero figure. It is often good practice to generate a **bogus code** for a purchase posting as a way of getting the process of receiving an invoice under way and then posting it from the suspense account to the relevant nominal account at a later date (usually at the end of an accounting period). In many cases, the absence of a nominal code is a simple entry error.

Some of these codes do not appear on the structure given earlier and would need to be included in the structure, along with many other accounts. Although there will have to be a header record with each of these control accounts, the names held in the header account do not have to match.

Printer	**Type**	**0**
	TOF Code	**12**
	Columns	**132**
	Lines/Page	**66**

The printer settings here are the same as for the Purchase and Sales Ledgers in that they determine the settings required to achieve hard-copy output.

Start of Year   **01**

This indicates the month number (01 being January) in the year where a company starts its financial year. This facility comes into use when producing budget reports.

Option No. 1   **Y**

Ensures customer and supplier names appear on audit trails.

Option No. 2   **Y**

Group totals will appear on the trial balance. In the example above, the account numbers prefixed with (say) **C** will be grouped together, with the sub-total display for these accounts. This was assumed in the diagram depicting the Nominal Ledger structure.

Option No. 3   Y

This ensures that the Nominal Ledger will produce a Profit and Loss report and a Balance Sheet. As a result of this, the operator is forced to enter a special report code within each nominal header. As will be seen later, the special report code will have to be prefixed with **B** (for a Balance Sheet account) or **P** (for a Profit and Loss account)

Option No. 4   Y

This will suppress zero values on nominal accounts appearing on the trial balance.

Option No. 5   N

Prevents the generation number check for the nominal analysis from being overridden.

Option No. 6   N

This option is not in use and therefore should be set to N.

Option No. 7

This option allows you to enter the password you enter for access to the parameters in other areas of the Nominal Ledger. When items are selected from the menu of the Nominal Ledger, the user will be prompted for entry of the password before being allowed to proceed.

Option No. 8

This option allows for group totals to be printed on the trial balance report based on a change in the second character of the account code. This only applies if you have selected the option for group totals (option 2 above).

Option No. 9

You can choose to omit the page headings on all but the first page of the profit and loss or balance sheet by entering a 'Y'.

Option No. 10

To use the bank reconciliation facility of the Nominal Ledger enter a 'Y'.

Sales and Purchase masks

The sales and purchase masks are used to assist in integrating the Sales and Purchase Ledgers with the Nominal Ledger, in that entries made to these ledgers can have their data posted to the nominal accounts in a way that avoids an operator having to enter such sales and purchase details as journal entries. Chapter 5 will demonstrate the use of this facility by example.

PREPARING ACCOUNTS

When starting the Nominal Ledger for the first time, no account headers will have been installed. As a starting point, it is a good idea to repeat all those control accounts set up in the parameters with account headers. To do this, the numbers must be the same, but the operator may alter the account names to suit the business requirements.

Following this, all other required accounts should be entered. Additional headers **may be added at any time in the future**, as and when they are required.

The special report code is used to segregate accounts into either Balance Sheet or Profit and Loss accounts, The special report code, therefore, will have to be prefixed with **B** (for a Balance Sheet account) or **P** (for a Profit and Loss account). This will only be required if option 3 was set to 'Y' in the parameters.

Deleting of unwanted accounts can be done by entering **DELETE** in upper case at the beginning of the account name. Only a period end will permanently remove an account. To remove any account, it must have a zero balance.

PROCESSING ACCOUNTS

Having performed the first two routines, it is now possible to proceed with entering transactions. A transaction record takes the form illustrated in Figure 4.5.

Entry Number	Trans Date	Account Number	Debit Amt	Credit Amt	Comment
1	120789	E101	234.12		Electric Bill
2	120789	E103	761.12		Rates Bill

Figure 4.5 Nominal Ledger transactions records

The transaction file will hold records for each transaction, numbering the entries automatically. Ledger postings can be made in one of three ways:

1   Direct Journal Entries.
2   Special Journal Entries for pre-payments and accruals.
3   Automatic transfer from Sales and Purchase Ledgers.

Whichever method is used at any time, all credit entries must be accounted for by similar debit entries; and, all debit entries must be accounted for by similar credit entries. This basic principle of double-entry will be imposed on an operator, through the program, although it does not mean that an operator can get away without a knowledge of double-entry.

For each transaction, there will be at least two records entered to the transaction file, one for a credit item and another for a debit item. In many cases, a single entry can result in many transaction records being generated. Each record must hold the transaction date and the nominal account number to which a value is either credit or debit.

Journal Entries

This is used to make direct entries into the nominal accounts. It is wise at this stage to have a listing of the nominal accounts with you in order to enter the correct nominal a/c no.

When entering the debit and credit values, the totals at the bottom of the columns will be accumulated and displayed as an operator makes the entries. These figures will have to balance before you can leave this option and post the values to the accounts. When the figures have been entered and the balances are equal, an entry of END in the **a/c no.** column will terminate the entry and post the figures to their respective accounts.

This option will be used frequently for direct entries, but on starting up a computerised nominal system, this would be used to enter the opening balances for the nominal accounts.

Special Journal Entries

This routine handles reserves and provisions for both debtors and creditors. At this point, some definitions may be helpful:

(a) **Reserve** A reserve represents profit withheld from distribution for the purpose of strengthening the financial base of the company or for covering any unforeseen losses that may occur.

(b) **Provision** Provision is part of the profit held back for a specific purpose, such as depreciation of assets or bad debts.

(c) **Pre-payment** Pre-payments are payments made in advance of the current accounting period. An example of this is on some rents and rates where payments are made in advance.

With a knowledge of the above definitions, this option works in a similar way to the journal entries. The difference between this and journal entries is that ALL debtors' provisions and reserves will be assumed as credit, with the accumulated sum being entered as a debit item to the **'Debtors Res/Prov'** account set up in the parameters and given a heading 'account headings options'. In turn, ALL creditors' provisions and reserves will be assumed as debit, with the accumulated sum being entered as a credit item to the **'Creditors Res/Prov'** account set up in the parameters and given a heading in account headings options.

The importance of this section becomes apparent when producing a Profit and Loss account and Balance Sheet, a topic to be discussed in Chapter 6.

INFORMATION RETRIEVAL

The remainder of this part on the Nominal Ledger concerns itself with simple, but essential, information retrieval. A **List of Transactions** can be made at any time and will list all nominal transactions made during the current period (i.e. since the last end-of-period run).

Account Enquiries will give a detailed list of transactions made on an account or group of accounts during the current period (i.e. since the last end-of-period run).

Printing the **Trial Balance** will show how credit and debit net figures are distributed amongst the nominal accounts. This option will allow you a detailed list or brief summary. If group totals were requested on option 2 of the parameters, then groups will be based on the first character(s) of the nominal account code.

Printing a **List of Accounts** will serve as useful reference when making journal entries. It will also be useful for showing budget summaries (if used). Listings will always be in account number order, an important point to consider when deciding on account numbers.

Period-end procedures do the following:

(a) Removes deleted accounts from the ledger.
(b) Re-organises accounts into account number order.
(c) Removes all transactions from accounts and carries forward net balance to the next period.
(d) Removes all reserves and provisions.
(e) If the period-end is the year-end, then all balances are set to zero.

Exercise

As an exercise and preparation for the next chapter, perform the following tasks.

1 Prepare a parameters file based on the settings in this chapter.
2 Create all the header records that match the control accounts set out in the parameters. Table 4.1 will help you identify the type of account each is:

Table 4.1

Control Account	Account Type
Debtors Control	Balance Sheet
Creditors Control	Balance Sheet
Debtors Res/Prov	Balance Sheet
Creditors Res/Prov	Balance Sheet
Opening Stock	Profit & Loss
Closing Stock	Balance Sheet
Discount Given	Profit & Loss
Discount Taken	Profit & Loss
Profit and Loss	Balance Sheet
Bank Account	Balance Sheet
Debtors Suspense	Balance Sheet
Creditors Suspense	Balance Sheet

3 Now create the remaining headers required to complete the set-up indicated in the nominal structure in this chapter.
4 Using the journal entry, enter opening balance in a way that uses ALL accounts.
5 In order to prepare ourselves for automatic postings from the Sales and Purchase Ledgers to the nominal accounts, create two nominal account headers for Value Added Tax with the codes and details shown in Table 4.2.

Table 4.2

Account Number	Header Name	Report Code
SVAT	VAT Collected from Sales	B13
PVAT	VAT Paid on Purchases	B13

6 Extract the following reports:

(a) A list of nominal accounts.
(b) A list of transactions showing the opening balances that were entered.
(c) A summary trial balance.

The exercise above is designed to give you a good start to using the Nominal Ledger and prepare for the next two chapters. Before commencing with the next chapter, check your reports with the ones that follow.

The Nominal Ledger is designed to reflect the way the nominal accounts are structured (*see* Table 4.3). The account numbers ending with '00' are used as group headings. Also the report codes reflect the way accounts should be grouped. This will be required in order to extract a Trading, Profit and Loss statement and a Balance Sheet. The budget figures have been left blank intentionally as this is a topic to be covered in a later chapter.

Table 4.3

	Pegasus Users Enterprises		
{ Date }	Nominal Accounts		
A/c	Account Name	Budget	Report Code
S100	SALES	0	
S101	SALES – HARDWARE	0	P01
S102	SALES – SOFTWARE	0	P01
S103	SALES – CONSULTANCY	0	P01
P100	PURCHASES	0	
P101	PURCHASES – RAW MATERIALS	0	P02
P102	PURCHASES – COMPONENTS	0	P02
P103	PURCHASES – SERVICES	0	P02
R100	RETURNS	0	
R101	GOODS RETURNED – INWARDS	0	P03
R102	GOODS RETURNED – OUTWARDS	0	P03
W100	WAGES & SALARIES	0	
W101	FACTORY WAGES	0	P04
W102	ADMINISTRATION WAGES	0	P04
W103	SALARIED STAFF	0	P04
W104	DIRECTORS SALARIES	0	P04
F100	FACTORY EXPENSES	0	
F101	CLOTHING – FACTORY STAFF	0	P05
F102	CLEANING – FACTORY	0	P05
F103	DEPRECIATION OF MACHINERY	0	P05
F104	DISTRIBUTION	0	P05
F105	ELECTRICITY – FACTORY	0	P05
A100	ADMINISTRATION EXPENSES	0	
A101	STATIONERY	0	P06
A102	OFFICE CLEANING	0	P06
A103	PRINTING & PUBLISHING	0	P06
A104	ADVERTISING	0	P06
A111	DISCOUNTS GIVEN	0	P07
A112	DISCOUNTS TAKEN	0	P08
K100	LONG TERM LIABILITIES	0	
K101	SHARE CAPITAL	0	B01
K102	PROFIT & LOSS	0	B01
K103	DEBENTURES	0	B01
C100	SHORT TERM LIABILITIES	0	
C101	CREDITORS	0	B02
C102	SHORT TERM BANK LOAN	0	B02
C103	CREDITORS RESERVES/PROVISIONS	0	B02
C199	CREDITORS SUSPENSE	0	B06
Q100	FIXED ASSETS	0	
Q101	PROPERTY	0	B03
Q102	PLANT & MACHINERY	0	B03
Q103	FURNITURE	0	B03
Q104	FIXTURES and FITTINGS	0	B03
Q105	MOTOR VEHICLES	0	B03

Table 4.3 Continued

A/c	Account Name	Budget	Report Code
G100	CURRENT ASSETS	0	
G101	CLOSING STOCK	0	P02
G102	BANK ACCOUNT	0	B04
G103	CASH IN HAND	0	B04
G104	DEBTORS	0	B04
G105	DEBTORS RESERVES/PROVISIONS	0	B04
G111	OPENING STOCK	0	P02
G199	DEBTORS SUSPENSE	0	B05
PVAT	VAT PAID THROUGH PURCHASES	0	B11
SVAT	VAT COLLECTED THROUGH SALES	0	B11

Transaction list

The opening balances – as illustrated in Table 4.4 – were entered in one single entry. In order to get out of the option you must:

(a) Ensure the debit and credit columns balance.
(b) Enter END in the account number column.

At no time should you press the ESC key as this will terminate the entry and will not add anything to the records.

Table 4.4

	Pegasus Users Enterprises		
{ Date }	Transaction List		

Entry 1 08.02.90 Type = Journal

A/c	Account Name	Dr	Cr	
S101	SALES – HARDWARE		112,000.00	O/BAL
S102	SALES – SOFTWARE		115,000.00	O/BAL
S103	SALES – CONSULTANCY		78,000.00	O/BAL
P101	PURCHASES – RAW MATERIALS	43,000.00		O/BAL
P102	PURCHASES – COMPONENTS	34,500.00		O/BAL
P103	PURCHASES – SERVICES	1,500.00		O/BAL
R101	GOODS RETURNED – INWARDS	3,350.00		O/BAL
R102	GOODS RETURNED - OUTWARDS		4,400.00	O/BAL
W101	FACTORY WAGES	20,000.00		O/BAL
W102	ADMINISTRATION WAGES	6,000.00		O/BAL
W103	SALARIED STAFF	12,000.00		O/BAL
F101	CLOTHING – FACTORY STAFF	900.00		O/BAL
F102	CLEANING – FACTORY	400.00		O/BAL
F103	DEPRECIATION OF MACHINERY	2,000.00		O/BAL
F104	DISTRIBUTION	1,200.00		O/BAL
F105	ELECTRICITY – FACTORY	780.00		O/BAL
K101	SHARE CAPITAL		500,000.00	O/BAL
K102	PROFIT & LOSS		12,000.00	O/BAL
K103	DEBENTURES		200,000.00	O/BAL
C101	CREDITORS		9,000.00	O/BAL
C102	SHORT TERM BANK LOAN		10,000.00	O/BAL
Q101	PROPERTY	253,000.00		O/BAL
Q102	PLANT & MACHINERY	120,000.00		O/BAL

Table 4.4 Continued

Q103	FURNITURE	121,000.00	O/BAL
Q104	FIXTURES & FITTINGS	166,000.00	O/BAL
Q105	MOTOR VEHICLES	90,000.00	O/BAL
G101	CLOSING STOCK	21,000.00	O/BAL
G102	BANK ACCOUNT	20,770.00	O/BAL
G103	CASH IN HAND	3,000.00	O/BAL
G104	DEBTORS	120,000.00	O/BAL

Input By DR	1,040,400.00	1,040,400.00
Grand Total		
	1,040,400.00	1,040,400.00

Trial balance

The trial balance illustrated in Table 4.5 shows the NET figures in every nominal account. If each DEBIT transaction entry has to be matched with a CREDIT transactions entry, then the two columns (Dr and Cr) must add up to the same figure.

Observe the effect of the groupings with respect to the trial balance.

Table 4.5

	Pegasus Users Enterprises	
{ Date }	Summary Trial Balance	
	Dr	**Cr**
G104 DEBTORS	120,000.00	
Total Group G	120,000.00	.00
C101 CREDITORS		9,000.00
Total Group C	.00	9,000.00
Total Group G	.00	.00
Total Group C	.00	.00
G101 CLOSING STOCK	21,000.00	
Total Group G	21,000.00	.00
Total Group A	.00	.00

Table 4.5 Continued

{Date}	Pegasus Users Enterprises Summary Trial Balance	Dr	Cr
K102	PROFIT & LOSS		12,000.00
	Total Group K	.00	12,000.00
G102	BANK ACCOUNT	20,770.00	
	Total Group G	20,770.00	.00
	Total Group C	.00	.00
S101	SALES – HARDWARE		112,000.00
S102	SALES – SOFTWARE		115,000.00
S103	SALES – CONSULTANCY		78,000.00
	Total Group S	.00	305,000.00
P101	PURCHASES – RAW MATERIALS	43,000.00	
P102	PURCHASES – COMPONENTS	34,500.00	
P103	PURCHASES – SERVICES	1,500.00	
	Total Group P	79,000.00	.00
R101	GOODS RETURNED – INWARDS	3,350.00	
R102	GOODS RETURNED – OUTWARDS		4,400.00
	Total Group R	3,350.00	4,400.00
	Total Group S	.00	.00
	Total Group P	.00	.00
	Total Group R	.00	.00
W101	FACTORY WAGES	20,000.00	
W102	ADMINISTRATION WAGES	6,000.00	
W103	SALARIED STAFF	12,000.00	
	Total Group W	38,000.00	.00
F101	CLOTHING – FACTORY STAFF	900.00	
F102	CLEANING – FACTORY	400.00	
F103	DEPRECIATION OF MACHINERY	2,000.00	
F104	DISTRIBUTION	1,200.00	
F105	ELECTRICITY – FACTORY	780.00	
	Total Group F	5,280.00	.00
	Total Group A	.00	.00

Table 4.5 Continued

{Date}	Pegasus Users Enterprises Summary Trial Balance		
		Dr	Cr
K101	SHARE CAPITAL		500,000.00
K103	DEBENTURES		200,000.00
Total Group K		.00	700,000.00
C102	SHORT TERM BANK LOAN		10,000.00
Total Group C		.00	10,000.00
Q101	PROPERTY	253,000.00	
Q102	PLANT & MACHINERY	120,000.00	
Q103	FURNITURE	121,000.00	
Q104	FIXTURES and FITTINGS	166,000.00	
Q105	MOTOR VEHICLES	90,000.00	
Total Group Q		750,000.00	.00
G103	CASH IN HAND	3,000.00	
Total Group G		3,000.00	.00
Total Group P		.00	.00
Total Group S		.00	.00
Grand Totals		1,040,400.00	1,040,400.00

5 Integrating the Ledgers

AIMS OF THIS CHAPTER

Until now, you will have learnt how to work with the three ledgers independently of each other. The purpose of this chapter is to:

(a) Consolidate your knowledge of the ledgers.
(b) Learn how to integrate the three ledgers.
(c) Perform end-of-period routines.

The chapter will take you through a worked example as a way of developing understanding. In the previous chapter you have already set up a nominal parameter file, entered opening balances and extracted a trial balance. This chapter will work from that point. While you are working through the material you should try to expand on the suggested data entry if you feel confident.

MAKING JOURNAL ENTRIES

Making journal entries will require a double entry so that each credit entry has to be accounted for by equal debit entry amounts. However, some basic rules are worth observing:

1   Make a separate entry for each posting. Do not attempt to make several entries on one entry number. It is important at a later date to see *who* made an entry and exactly what the nature of the entry is. Consequently, entries will often be small but informative.

2   Give a general narrative *that makes easy sense*. This is required as one of the fields in the transaction record that makes up a journal entry and is used to explain the nature of the transaction.

3   The journal entry allows you to place a comment for each item on the entry. Use it to explain where the entry is being posted. In other words, if the transaction is a debit item, it is a good idea to state where the corresponding credit item is. If the debit is to be split across more than one account for credits, then some generic explanation should be given.

In order to gain some experience on entering data through the journal, attempt the following transactions:

1   Create a new account for depreciation on fixtures and fittings with the account number F106 in order to make it fit in with our structure.

2   Now depreciate the fixtures and fittings account (Q104) by £12,000 by debiting the depreciation account and crediting the fixtures and fittings account. Please note: in most instances a special fixed asset account will normally be created specifically to credit depreciation on fixtures and fittings in order to help produce a more informative Balance Sheet later.

3   Transfer £760 from the bank account (G102) to the cash account (G103).

4   Pay an electricity bill of £156.99 from the bank.

5   Record cash sales (S102 SOFTWARE SALES) of £981.89.

6   Create a petty cash account under G106. Transfer £5,000 cash to this account.

7   Create a bad debts account as an expense account with number F107 and debit £2,345 from the debtors account (G104)

8   Use the special journals entry to provide for £4,000 bad debts and £12,000 depreciation of machinery.

9   Now transfer all of the petty cash to the following accounts:

Table 5.1

Account	Account Number	Amount £
CLOTHING – FACTORY STAFF	F101	1,300
* SUNDRY EXPENSES	F108	580
* ENTERTAINMENT ALLOWANCES	F109	850
CLEANING – FACTORY	F102	1,120
PURCHASES – SERVICES	P103	1,150
		5,000

(* Indicates the need to create a new account header)

10   Produce

(a)   A detailed trial balance.
(b)   A list of all nominal accounts.
(c)   A list of transactions.

Having performed these tasks, compare your results with the ones that follow. If you feel you need more practice, then attempt to make your own journal entries and see what happens to the trial balance and transactions.

The entries resulting from the exercises may look like this:

Entry 1 was the opening balance entered in the previous chapter.

Table 5.2

Entry 2 09.02.90 Type = Journal	Dr	Cr	
Q104 FIXTURES AND FITTINGS		12,000.00	DEPRECIATION
F106 DEPRECIATION OF FIXTURES	12,000.00		FIXT/FITTINGS
Input by DR	12,000.00	12,000.00	

In Entry 2, shown in Table 5.2, fixtures and fittings are credited by £12,000 which will have the result of lowering the value of these assets. Alternatively, the depreciation account is debited which will increase the amount in an expense account.

Table 5.3

Entry 3 09.02.90 Type = Journal	Dr	Cr	
G102 BANK ACCOUNT		760.00	CASH
G103 CASH IN HAND	760.00		BANK
Input by DR	760.00	760.00	

Table 5.3 shows that £760 has been withdrawn from the bank (Cr) and placed into cash in hand.

Table 5.4

Entry 4 09.02.90 Type = Journal	Dr	Cr	
F105 ELECTRICITY – FACTORY	156.99		BANK
G102 BANK ACCOUNT		156.99	ELECTRICITY
Input by DR	156.99	156.99	

Table 5.4 shows that the electricity account has been debited by £156.99 which has the effect of increasing an expense account while decreasing the amount in the bank by the same figure. When payments are made, the effect is to credit the bank or cash, so reducing the balance.

Table 5.5

Entry 5 09.02.90 Type = Journal	Dr	Cr	
S102 SALES – SOFTWARE		981.89	CASH
G103 CASH IN HAND	981.89		SALES SOFTWARE
Input by DR	981.89	981.89	

When a sale is made, whether cash or not, a sales account will be credited, while, in Table 5.5, the cash account is debited.

Table 5.6

Entry 6 09.02.90 Type = Journal

	Dr	Cr	
G106 PETTY CASH	5,000.00		CASH
G103 CASH IN HAND		5,000.00	PETTY CASH
Input by DR	5,000.00	5,000.00	

In Table 5.6 £5,000 has been transferred from cash (credit) to the petty cash (debit). Again, when cash leaves an account it will be entered as a credit item.

Table 5.7

Entry 7 09.02.90 Type = Journal

	Dr	Cr	
F107 BAD DEBTS	2,345.00		DEBTORS
G104 DEBTORS		2,345.00	BAD DEBT
Input by DR	2,345.00	2,345.00	

In Table 5.7 the bad debts account has been debited by £2,345.00 which has the effect of increasing an expense account while decreasing the amount that is owed to the business in the debtors account.

Table 5.8

Entry 8 09.02.90 Type = Journal

	Dr	Cr	
G106 PETTY CASH		5,000.00	ALLOCATION
F101 CLOTHING – FACTORY STAFF	1,300.00		PETTY CASH
F108 SUNDRY EXPENSES	580.00		PETTY CASH
F109 ENTERTAINMENT ALLOWANCES	850.00		PETTY CASH
F102 CLEANING – FACTORY	1,120.00		PETTY CASH
P103 PURCHASES – SERVICES	1,150.00		PETTY CASH
Input by DR	5,000.00	5,000.00	

On Entry 8, shown in Table 5.8, the petty cash value of £5,000 has been transferred (credited) to a number of accounts (debited) which has the effect of reversing an earlier process where cash was put in. Figure 5.1 diagram depicts what has happened.

	Journal Entry	Function		Journal Entry

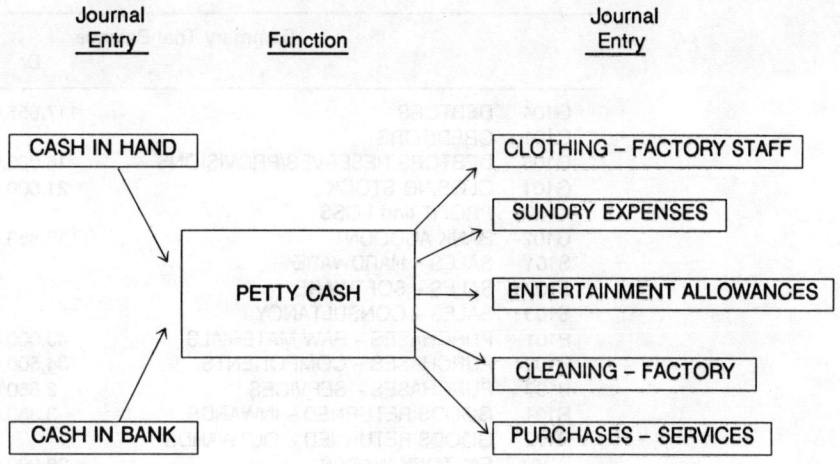

Figure 5.1

This process is quite normal, as the petty cash function is used to prevent a whole series of small cash purchase transactions being entered to the nominal accounts. The petty cash function, therefore, receives a lump sum into it and outputs aggregate totals to a whole series of nominal accounts, leaving the petty cash with a zero balance.

Table 5.9

Entry 9 09.02.90 Type = Journal	Dr	Cr	
G105 DEBTORS RESERVES/PROVISIONS	16,000.00		
F107 BAD DEBTS		4,000.00	PROVISION
F103 DEPRECIATION OF MACHINERY		12,000.00	PROVISION
Input by DR	16,000.00	16,000.00	

The entry in Table 5.9 was made as a special journal entry and shows what exactly has happened.

The resulting trial balance illustrated in Table 5.10 will show the effect of the journal entries. The trial balance will also show the new accounts added during the exercise. When observing the trial balance, you will probably see that the *order* in which accounts appear are the same as entered. This will cause a problem in the report, which will be rectified at period-end. Table 5.10 is a brief summary to avoid lengthy reports. You should have examined a detailed trial balance in order to get a much better picture.

Table 5.10

| | | Summary Trial Balance | | |
			Dr	Cr
G104	DEBTORS		117,655.00	
C101	CREDITORS			9,000.00
G105	DEBTORS RESERVES/PROVISIONS		16,000.00	
G101	CLOSING STOCK		21,000.00	
K102	PROFIT and LOSS			12,000.00
G102	BANK ACCOUNT		19,853.01	
S101	SALES – HARDWARE			112,000.00
S102	SALES – SOFTWARE			115,981.89
S103	SALES – CONSULTANCY			78,000.00
P101	PURCHASES – RAW MATERIALS		43,000.00	
P102	PURCHASES – COMPONENTS		34,500.00	
P103	PURCHASES – SERVICES		2,650.00	
R101	GOODS RETURNED – INWARDS		3,350.00	
R102	GOODS RETURNED – OUTWARDS			4,400.00
W101	FACTORY WAGES		20,000.00	
W102	ADMINISTRATION WAGES		6,000.00	
W103	SALARIED STAFF		12,000.00	
F101	CLOTHING – FACTORY STAFF		2,200.00	
F102	CLEANING – FACTORY		1,520.00	
F103	DEPRECIATION OF MACHINERY			10,000.00
F104	DISTRIBUTION		1,200.00	
F105	ELECTRICITY – FACTORY		936.99	
K101	SHARE CAPITAL			500,000.00
K103	DEBENTURES			200,000.00
C102	SHORT TERM BANK LOAN			10,000.00
Q101	PROPERTY		253,000.00	
Q102	PLANT and MACHINERY		120,000.00	
Q103	FURNITURE		121,000.00	
Q104	FIXTURES and FITTINGS		154,000.00	
Q105	MOTOR VEHICLES		90,000.00	
G103	CASH IN HAND			258.11
F106	DEPRECIATION OF FIXTURES		12,000.00	
G106	PETTY CASH		.00	
F107	BAD DEBTS			1,655.00
F108	SUNDRY EXPENSES		580.00	
F109	ENTERTAINMENT ALLOWANCES		850.00	
	Grand Totals		1,053,295.00	1,053,295.00

SALES LEDGER FUNCTION

By now you should be getting a good idea about using the Nominal Ledger. The next stage is to move to the Sales Ledger and generate some transactions with a view to automating the posting of sales to the Nominal Ledger.

The first stage is to set up the parameters correctly from the Sales Ledger menu (option 4). The following is an example:

Sales Parameters

Company Name		**Pegasus User Enterprises**
	Address Line 1	**100 High Street**
	Address Line 2	**Newtown**
	Address Line 3	**Wessex**
	Address Line 4	
	1st Tel No.	**01 001 0001**
	2nd Tel No.	
	Telex No.	
	VAT Reg No.	
Printer Type		**0**
	TOF Code	**12**
	Columns	**80**
	Lines/Page	**66**
Option No. 1		**Y**
Option No. 2		**Y**
VAT Code for Analysis		**SVAT**
Option No. 3		**1**
Option No. 4		**Y**
Option No. 5		**N**
Option No. 6		**N**
Option No. 7		**Y**
Option No. 8		**N**
Sales Analysis 1	**– Sequence**	**12/3456**
	– Narrative	**Customer/Transaction**
Sales Analysis 2	**– Sequence**	**3456/12**
	– Narrative	**Transaction/Customer**
Sales Analysis 3	**– Sequence**	
	– Narrative	

The use of the Sales Analysis 1 and 2 will become apparent in the next chapter.

Having done this, a set of accounts will be required in order to process. The listing below is an example set of accounts to help you:

0001	A J Amber	Personal Account
	33 Littleston Road	Code P1
	Wilmington Green	Type O
	Hiltshire	Cr. Limit 900
		T/Over
0002	P M Bluesdale	Personal Account
	120 High Street	Code P1
	Forresdon	Type O
	Panktonshire	Cr.Limit 1,500
	F1 5RR	T/Over
0100	K K Schwarz	Personal Foreign
	12 Haupstrasse	Code P3
	Dusseldorf	Type O
	West Germany	Cr.Limit 1,500
		T/Over
0101	A P Klingen	Personal Foreign
	123 Schmidt Strasse	Code P3
	Vienna	Type O
	Austria	Cr.Limit 1,000
		T/Over

0200	Wessex County Council	Local Authority
	Town Square	Code L1
	Newtown	Type B
	Wessex	Cr.Limit
		T/Over
0300	Blackman Software Ltd	Business Account
	High Street	Code B1
	Wincarton	Type O
	Wessex	Cr.Limit 5,000
		T/Over
0303	Microchip Hardware	Business Account
	Supplies	Code B1
	Silicon Road	Type O
	Processor Valley	Cr.Limit 10,000
	Diskshire	T/Over
0400	Connells Enterprises Inc.	Foreign Business
	1232 Street	Code B5
	New York	Type B
	U.S.A.	Cr.Limit 6,500
		T/Over

In setting up these accounts, a code has been given to each account which is used at a later stage in conjunction with the Sales Analysis in the next section.

The type of account is set at **O** for an open account where invoices are settled, whereas type **B** is used for a balance account where settlements are simply made on outstanding balances rather than on particular invoices. The type of account will have an influence on the end-of-period run.

The next stage is to perform some transactions on the accounts by issuing:

I Invoices to customers
R Receipts from customers
A Adjustments of invoices
C Credit notes to customers
F Refunds to customers
X Allocation of receipts

Table 5.11, giving transaction records, is an attempt at using most of the ledger posting types. It is important to bear in mind that this activity **will not** update the Nominal Ledger, only the Sales Ledger. Making postings to the Nominal Ledger is an activity that will be done at a later stage.

Table 5.11

A/C	Date	Type	Reference	Value	Goods	Vat disc	Period
0001	11.02.90	I	0000000001	320.00	290.00	30.00	
0002	11.02.90	I	0000000002	990.00	850.00	140.00	
0100	11.02.90	I	0000000003	100.00	100.00	.00	
0101	11.02.90	I	0000000004	800.00	650.00	150.00	
0200	11.02.90	I	0000000005	115.00	100.00	15.00	
0300	11.02.90	I	0000000006	12,000.00	10,500.00	1,500.00	
0303	11.02.90	I	0000000007	8,500.00	7,300.00	1,200.00	
0400	11.02.90	I	0000000008	120.00	100.00	20.00	
0001	12.02.90	I	0000000009	98.00	80.00	18.00	
0200	12.02.90	I	0000000010	56,900.00	50,000.00	6,900.00	
0303	13.02.90	I	0000000011	450.00	400.00	50.00	
0400	13.02.90	I	0000000011	5,000.00	5,000.00	.00	
0002	14.02.90	C	C1	−90.00	−80.00	−10.00	
0303	14.02.90	C	C2	−100.00	−100.00	.00	
0100	14.02.90	R	CHQ 123991	−96.00		−4.00	
0200	14.02.90	R	CHQ 222111	−43,000.00		−2,300.00	2
0303	15.02.90	R	CHQ 232112	−8,500.00		−300.00	
0400	15.02.90	R	CASH	−4,000.00			2
0002	16.02.90	R	DEBIT 1001	120.00			
0001	16.02.90	A	DISCOUNT	−18.00			
0100	16.02.90	A	MISPOST	110.00			
0101	16.02.90	A	WRITE OFF	−200.00			
0300	16.02.90	A	DISCOUNT	−1,000.00			
0300	21.02.90	R	CHQ 1231	−10,500.00			
0300	21.02.90	D	CHQ 1231	−500.00			

Listing invoices and credit notes and receipts and adjustments from the above transactions will reveal the following totals:

Total Invoices	85,393.00	75,370.00	10,023.00
Total Cr.Notes	−190.00	−180.00	−10.00
Total Discounts	−3,104.00		
Total Receipts	−66,096.00		
Total Refunds	120.00		
Total Adj – Contras	.00		
Total Adj – Bad Debts	.00		
Total Adj – Write Offs	−200.00		
Total Adj – Misposts	110.00		
Total Adj – Discounts	−1,018.00		
Total Adj – Sundry	.00		

When entering invoice and credit note details, you will be required to enter analysis codes. In order to allow automatic postings later, it may be a good idea to enter nominal codes for one of the sales accounts. The sales nominal codes set up in our example are:

S101 SALES – HARDWARE
S102 SALES – SOFTWARE
S103 SALES – CONSULTANCY

With this information, enter each of the transactions to match the table of transaction records given. At the end produce from the ledger processing the following reports:

1 List of Invoices and Credit Notes   (option 3)
2 List of Receipts and Adjustments   (option 4)
3 Account Enquiries on some accounts   (option 5)
4 A set of customer Statements of account   (option 6)
5 An Aged Debtors List   (option 7)

Figures 5.2 and 5.3 are example accounts belonging to two of the customers on the Sales Ledger that will reflect the transactions carried out.

K K Schwarz 12 Haupstrasse Dusseldorf West Germany		Account 0100 T/Over	100/Feb	11 Feb 1990 Cr.Lim 1,500		
Date	Type	Reference	Status	Debit	Credit	Balance
11.02.90	Invoice	0000000003		100.00		
14.02.90	Receipt	CHQ 123991			96.00	
14.02.90	Discnt	CHQ 123991			4.00	
16.02.90	Adjust	MISPOST		110.00		
3 Months + .00	2 Months .00	1 Month .00	Current 110.00			Total 110.00

Figure 5.2

Blackman Software Ltd High Street Wincarton Wessex		Account 0300 T/Over	10,500/Feb	11 Feb 1990 Cr.Lim 5,000		
Date	Type	Reference	Status	Debit	Credit	Balance
11.02.90	Invoice	0000000006		12,000.00		
16.02.90	Adjust	DISCOUNT			1,000.00	
21.02.90	Receipt	CHQ 1231			10,500.00	
21.02.90	Discnt	CHQ 1231			500.00	
3 Months + .00	2 Months .00	1 Month .00	Current .00			Total .00

Figure 5.3

The aged debtors list might look something like Figure 5.4

At this stage, examine the reports and accounts as a way of appreciating what has happened. Most of the detailed information generated has been omitted to reduce lengthy explanations.

When examining much of the information, try to avoid printing everything; instead, inspect much of it on the screen.

Before progressing on with the Purchase Ledger, you might find it worthwhile entering some of your own transactions and possibly

			Pegasus User Enterprises			
11.02.90			Aged Debtors List			
A/c	3 Months +	2 Months	1 Month	Current	Total	Cr.Limit
0001 A J Amber	.00	.00	.00 Personal Account	400.00	400.00	900
0002 P M Bluesdale	.00	.00	.00 Personal Account	1,020,00	1,020,00	1,500
0100 K K Schwarz	.00	.00	.00 Personal Foreign	110.00	110.00	1,500
0101 A P Klingen	.00	.00	.00 Personal Foreign	600.00	600.00	1,000
0200 Wessex County Council	.00	.00	.00 Local Authority	11,715.00	11,715.00	
0303 Microchip Hardware Supplies	.00	.00	.00 Business Account	50.00	50.00	10,000
0400 Connells Enterprises Inc.	.00	.00	.00 Foreign Business	1,120.00	1,120.00	6,500
	.00	.00	.00	15,015.00	15,015.00	
Total	.00	.00	.00	15,015.00	15,015.00	

Figure 5.4

creating some new customer accounts. At a later stage in this chapter you will be shown how this information can be automatically posted to the nominal accounts.

As a final point, the VAT analysis available from the main Sales Ledger menu in option 3 (Analysis) shows how the system has kept details on all VAT invoiced to customers. Also, when a credit note is issued, the VAT on the amount credited must be taken off the total VAT collected from customers. For most businesses, VAT due to Customs and Excise will be the amount invoiced to the customers, not the amount actually collected.

PURCHASE LEDGER FUNCTION

The next stage is to progress to the Purchase Ledger. However, if you are unclear about the transactions used earlier, experiment with the Sales Ledger until you are clearer about what is going on. As with the Sales Ledger, you will be required to create the parameters first. The following is a suggested parameter setting to get us started:

Purchase Parameters

Company Name		Pegasus User Enterprise
	Address Line 1	100 High Street
	Address Line 2	Newtown
	Address Line 3	Wessex
	Address Line 4	
	1st Tel No.	01 001 0001
	2nd Tel No.	
	Telex No.	
	VAT Reg No.	
Printer Type		0
	TOF Code	12
	Columns	80
	Lines/Page	66
Option No. 1		Y
Option No. 2		Y
VAT Code for Analysis		VAT1
Option No. 3		Y
Option No. 4		Y
Option No. 5		N
Option No. 6		N
Option No. 7		Y
Purchase Analysis 1	– Sequence	12/3456
	– Narrative	Supplier/Stock Type
Purchase Analysis 2	– Sequence	3456/12
	– Narrative	Stock Type/Supplier
Purchase Analysis 3	– Sequence	
	– Narrative	
Cheque Format Details	– Lines/Chqe	
Date Position	– Line/Col	
Payee Position	– Line/Col	
Amnt Position	– Line/Col	
10000 Position	– Line/Col	
1000 Position	– Line/Col	
100 Position	– Line/Col	
10 Position	– Line/Col	
1 Position	– Line/Col	
Upper Cheque Limit		

The cheque format can be used to automate the production of cheques when paying suppliers. Arranging the format of a cheque is dependent upon the stationery used. This involves a good deal of trial and error but once set up will be automatic.

As with the sales parameters, you can always return to this and make any required alterations in the future.

Using Purchase Ledger 'ledger processing' (option 1), you will need to create some suppliers to trade with. The a/c name and address update should be used. Below are some supplier details:

A/c Number	Supplier Name and Address	Account Details
0001	Williams and Sons Stationery Supplies Ltd 101 Nottingham Road Wessex	30 1.00% 60 .50% 90 Days Code S1 Type O Cr.Limit 4,500 T/Over

A/C Number	Supplier Name and Address	Account Details	
0002	Kramer & Kramer Supplies 24 London Square Wilmington-On-Sea Wessex	 Code S1 Type O Cr.Limit 1,000 T/Over	30 Days
0003	Peaky Paper Supplies Jason Avenue Littelston Wessex	30 1.50% Code S4 Type B Cr.Limit 7,000 T/Over	
0100	Accounts Software Inc 123 Street New York U.S.A.	 Code O1 Type O Cr.Limit 7,000 T/Over	60 Days
0200	V J Schmidt 20 Weissel Str. Dusseldorf W. Germany	30 1.00% Code O5 Type O Cr.Limit 3,000 T/Over	60 Days
0400	Albany Office Supplies 12 High Street Forringdon Herts	30 2.00% 45 1.50% Code S8 Type O Cr.Limit 2,000 T/Over	90 Days

The terms as set up in the accounts above refer to settlement terms. In the case of 0400 Albany Office Supplies, for example, the terms are; if payment is made within 30 days a 2.00% discount can be claimed, and within 45 days a 1.50% discount can be claimed, and the invoice WILL NOT BE settled until 21 days has lapsed. Suppliers codes stated will be used at a later stage in conjunction with the purchase analysis.

The next stage is to perform some transactions on the accounts by recording a range of the following transaction types:

I   Invoices from suppliers
P   Payments to suppliers
A   Adjustments of invoices
C   Credit notes from suppliers
F   Refunds from suppliers
X   Allocations

Table 5.12 giving transaction records, is an attempt at using most of the ledger posting types. It is important to bear in mind that this activity **will not** update the Nominal Ledger, only the Purchase Ledger. Making postings to the Nominal Ledger is an activity that is done at a later stage. Because purchases, can be for a varied number of accounts, I have simplified each purchase by having just one analysis code associated with each purchase. Each analysis code is the same as the nominal code so that postings can be made easily later on.

Table 5.12

A/c	Date	Type	Reference	Value	Goods	VAT	Analysis Code	Period
0001	11.02.90	I	CHQ	1,200.00	1,000.00	200.00	P101	
0002	11.02.90	I	CHQ	500.00	500.00	0.00	P102	
0003	11.02.90	I	CHQ	5,400.00	5,000.00	400.00	P103	
0100	11.02.90	I	CHQ	980.00	900.00	80.00	P102	
0200	11.02.90	I	CHQ	500.00	500.00	0.00	F101	
0400	11.02.90	I	CHQ	450.00	400.00	50.00	Q103	
0002	11.02.90	I	CHQ	400.00	360.00	40.00	Q102	
0003	14.02.90	I	CHQ	1,300.00	1,300.00	0.00	P101	
0200	15.02.90	I	CHQ	7,300.00	6,570.00	730.00	Q105	
0003	16.02.90	C	RETURNS	−400.00	−380.00	−20.00	R102	
0001	20.02.90	P	CHQ 123221	−1,050.00				
0001	20.02.90	D	CHQ 123221	−150.00				
0003	21.02.90	A	DISCOUNT	300.00				2

Listing invoices and credit notes and receipts and adjustments from the above transactions will reveal the following totals:

Total Discounts	−150.00		
Total Payments	−1,050.00		
Total Refunds	0.00		
Total Adj – Contras	0.00		
Total Adj – Write Offs	0.00		
Total Adj – Misposts	0.00		
Total Adj – Discounts	300.00		
Total Adj – Sundry	0.00	(VALUE)	(VAT)
Total Invoices	18,030.00	16,530.00	1,500.00
Total Cr.Notes	−400.00	−380.00	−20.00

With this information, enter each of the transactions to match the table of transaction records given. After doing this, produce from the ledger processing the following reports:

1 List of Invoices and Credit Notes   (option 3)
2 List of Receipts and Adjustments   (option 4)
3 Account Enquiries on some accounts   (option 5)
4 A set of Suppliers Account Status reports (option 6)
5 An Aged Creditors List   (option 7)

Figure 5.5 is an example account belonging to one of the Supplier Accounts on the Purchase Ledger that will reflect the transactions carried out.

Peaky Paper Supplies Jason Avenue Littelston			Account 0003			11 Feb 1990	
		T/Over		5920/Feb		Cr.Lim 7,000	
Date	Type	Reference	Status	Debit		Credit	Balance
11.02.90	Invoice	CHQ				5,400.00	
14.02.90	Invoice	CHQ				1,300.00	
16.02.90	Cr. Note	RETURNS		400.00			
21.02.90	Adjust	DISCOUNT	Feb			300.00	
3 Months +	2 Months	1 Month	Current				Total
0.00	0.00	0.00	6,600.00				6,600.00

Figure 5.5

The aged creditors list might look something like Figure 5.6.

		Pegasus User Enterprises				
11.02.90			Aged Creditors List		Page 1	
A/c	3 Months +	2 Months	1 Month	Current	Total	Cr.Limit
0001	0.00	0.00	0.00	0.00	0.00	4,500
Williams & Sons Stationery			30 1.00% 60		.50% 21 Days	
0002	0.00	0.00	0.00	900.00	900.00	1,000
Kramer & Kramer Supplies					30 Days	
0003	0.00	0.00	0.00	6,600.00	6,600.00	7,000
Peaky Paper Supplies			30 1.50%			
0100	0.00	0.00	0.00	980.00	980.00	7,000
Account Software Inc					20 Days	
0200	0.00	0.00	0.00	7,800.00	7,800.00	3,000 ***
V J Schmidt			30 2.00% 45		1.50% 21 Days	
0400	0.00	0.00	0.00	450.00	450.00	2,000
Albany Office Supplies			30 2.00% 45		1.50% 21 Days	
Total	0.00	0.00	0.00	16,730.00	16,730.00	

Figure 5.6

At this stage, examine the reports and accounts as a way of appreciating what has happened. Again, most of the detailed information generated has been omitted to reduce lengthy explanations.

When examining much of the information, try to avoid printing everything; instead inspect much of it on the screen.

Before progressing on with the automatic postings, you might find it worthwhile entering some of your own transactions and possibly creating some new supplier accounts.

As a final point, the VAT analysis available from the main Sales Ledger menu in option 3 (Analysis) shows how the system has kept details on all VAT invoiced by suppliers. Also, when a credit note is issued, the VAT on the amount credited must be taken off the total VAT paid to suppliers. For most businesses, VAT that can be claimed from Customs and Excise will be the amount invoiced by suppliers, not the amount actually paid.

A useful exercise might be to place some supplier invoices in dispute. This is done by placing a **D** in the last place in the reference box.

AUTOMATIC POSTINGS

By now you should have gained a reasonable understanding of the Purchase Ledger in order to proceed to the next stage. You should experiment with all three ledgers until you feel confident that you understand how they are working.

The next stage is to attempt to post all the figures to the Nominal Ledger. At the beginning of the text the parameters were set such that the two 'MASKS' were left blank. On inspection, the masks will show:

Nominal Parameters

Sales A/c Mask	********
Purchase A/c Mask	********

The effect of this will be to post ALL sales to the sales analysis codes assigned to each sale. If the sale has an analysis code that is not matched by a nominal code, then postings will be made to the debtors suspense. Likewise, exactly the same applies to the Purchase Ledger except that, when an analysis code has no matching nominal code, it is posted to the creditors suspense account.

If, say, the masks were:

Sales A/c Mask	S101
Purchase A/c Mask	P101

then ALL Sales would be posted to nominal account S101 and all purchases to nominal account P101.

From the main Nominal Ledger menu use:

3 Analysis of Sales and Purchases

From this the following menu will appear:

1 Sales Invoices/Credits
2 Purchase Invoices/Credits
3 Sales Receipts/Adjustments
4 Purchase Receipts/Adjustments

Run ALL FOUR, then terminate. You will be asked if you want output to the printer. Bear in mind that postings of the above transactions **can only happen once.**

The effect is to post all transactions, in turn, to the relevant nominal account. Because of the way the masks have been set, ALL sales transactions are posted to SL01.

In the sales parameter, the VAT is to be posted to nominal account SVAT, which was set up in the sales parameters. Also, VAT paid through purchases will be posted to PVAT.

The following is an explanation through an example of the kind of listings generated by a posting:

1 Nominal analysis of sales invoices and credit notes

S101 Sales – Hardware					
11.02.90	Inv	0000000001	0001	-190.00	A J Amber
11.02.90	Inv	0000000002	0002	-390.00	P M Bluesdale
11.02.90	Inv	0000000004	0101	-550.00	A P Klingen
11.02.90	Inv	0000000006	0300	-8,500.00	Blackman Software Ltd
11.02.90	Inv	0000000007	0303	-7,300.00	Microchip Hardware Supplies
11.02.90	Inv	0000000010	0200	-30,000.00	Wessex County Council
13.02.90	Inv	0000000011	0400	-5,000.00	Connells Enterprises Inc.
14.02.90	C/Note	C1	0002	80.00	P M Bluesdale
14.02.90	C/Note	C2	0303	100.00	Microchip Hardware Supplies
				-51,750.00	

Figure 5.7

Figure 5.7 shows all those invoices and credit notes where the analysis code was S101.

S102 Sales – Software					
11.02.90	Inv	0000000001	0001	-100.00	A J Amber
11.02.90	Inv	0000000002	0002	-100.00	P M Bluesdale
11.02.90	Inv	0000000005	0200	-100.00	Wessex County Council
11.02.90	Inv	0000000006	0300	-1,000.00	Blackman Software Ltd
11.02.90	Inv	0000000010	0200	-15,000.00	Wessex County Council
13.02.90	Inv	0000000011	0303	-400.00	Microchip Hardware Supplies
				-16,700.00	

Figure 5.8

In the case illustrated in Figure 5.8, the Nominal Ledger S102 is updated. In many cases the invoice number that appears on this account also appeared on the S101. This is because these invoices had both analysis codes on them.

```
S103  SALES – CONSULTANCY

11.02.90   Inv      0000000002    0002      -360.00    P M Bluesdale
11.02.90   Inv      0000000003    0100      -100.00    K K Schwarz
11.02.90   Inv      0000000006    0300    -1,000.00    Blackman Software Ltd
11.02.90   Inv      0000000008    0400      -100.00    Connells Enterprises Inc.
12.02.90   Inv      0000000009    0001       -80.00    A J Amber
11.02.90   Inv      0000000010    0200    -5,000.00    Wessex County Council
                                          _____
                                         -6,640.00
                                          _____
```

Figure 5.9

Again, nominal account S103 has also been updated in the same way. (*See* Figure 5.9.)

```
S193  Nominal Account Not on File **** Posted to Suspense ****

11.02.90   Inv      0000000004    0101      -100.00    A P Klingen
                                          _____
                                           -100.00    *** To Suspense ***
                                          _____
```

Figure 5.10

In the instance illustrated in Figure 5.10, an attempt was made to post an item to nominal account S193, for which there is no nominal account. As a result the posting is made to the debtors suspense account. Later on, this figure will have to be posted to an appropriate account. It may be the case that S193 is missing from the nominal header file, in which case it will need to be added.

```
SVAT  VAT COLLECTED THROUGH SALES

11.02.90   Inv      0000000001    0001       -30.00    A J Amber
11.02.90   Inv      0000000002    0002      -140.00    P M Bluesdale
11.02.90   Inv      0000000004    0101      -150.00    A P Klingen
11.02.90   Inv      0000000005    0200       -15.00    Wessex County Council
11.02.90   Inv      0000000006    0300    -1,500.00    Blackman Software Ltd
11.02.90   Inv      0000000007    0303    -1,200.00    Microchip Hardware Supplies
11.02.90   Inv      0000000008    0400       -20.00    Connells Enterprises Inc.
12.02.90   Inv      0000000009    0001       -18.00    A J Amber
11.02.90   Inv      0000000010    0200    -6,900.00    Wessex County Council
13.02.90   Inv      0000000011    0303       -50.00    Microchip Hardware Supplies
14.02.90   C/Note   C1            0002        10.00    P M Bluesdale
                                          _____
                                         -10,013.00

                    Total Posted          -85,103.00
                    Total Suspense           -100.00
                                          _____
                                         -85,203.00    Entry No. 10
                                          _____
```

Figure 5.11

All VAT from sales has been posted to SVAT. (*See* Figure 5.11.)

2 Nominal analysis of purchase invoices and credit notes

Figure 5.12 shows how purchase invoices and credit notes are posted across to the nominal accounts in exactly the same way.

F101 CLOTHING – FACTORY STAFF

11.02.90	Inv	CHQ	0200	500.00	V J Schmidt	OVERALLS FOR FACTORY STAFF
				500.00		

P101 PURCHASES – RAW MATERIALS

11.02.90	Inv	CHQ	0001	1,000.00	Williams & Sons Stationery	RAW MATERIALS
14.02.90	Inv	CHQ	0003	1,300.00	Peaky Paper Supplies	PAPER MATERIAL
				2,300.00		

P102 PURCHASES – COMPONENTS

11.02.90	Inv	CHQ	0002	500.00	Kramer & Kramer Supplies	COMPONENTS FOR STOCK
11.02.90	Inv	CHQ	0100	900.00	Account Software Inc	RAW MATERIALS
				1,400.00		

P103 PURCHASES – SERVICES

11.02.90	Inv	CHQ	0003	5,000.00	Peaky Paper Supplies	SERVICES
				5,000.00		

Q102 PLANT & MACHINERY

11.02.90	Inv	CHQ	0002	360.00	Kramer & Kramer Supplies	MACHINE COMPONENT
				360.00		

Q103 FURNITURE

11.02.90	Inv	CHQ	0400	400.00	Albany Office Supplies	NEW OFFICE DESK
				400.00		

Q105 MOTOR VEHICLES

15.02.90	Inv	CHQ	0200	6,570.00	V J Schmidt	NEW CAR REG G129 PLD
				6,570.00		

Figure 5.12

```
┌─────────────────────────────────────────────────────────────────────────┐
│  R102  GOODS RETURNED – OUTWARDS                                          │
│                                                                           │
│  16.02.90  C/Note    RETURNS   0003    –380.00  Peaky Paper Supplies   GOODS RETURNED │
│                                        ────────                           │
│                                        –380.00                            │
│                                                                           │
└─────────────────────────────────────────────────────────────────────────┘
```

Figure 5.12 Continued

The VAT entry has been posted to account PVAT which was set up in the Purchase Ledger parameter file. (*See* Figure 5.13.)

```
┌─────────────────────────────────────────────────────────────────────────┐
│  PVAT  VAT PAID THROUGH PURCHASES                                         │
│                                                                           │
│  11.02.90  Inv      CHQ       0001     200.00  Williams & Sons Stationery │
│  11.02.90  Inv      CHQ       0003     400.00  Peaky Paper Supplies       │
│  11.02.90  Inv      CHQ       0100      80.00  Account Software Inc       │
│  11.02.90  Inv      CHQ       0400      50.00  Albany Office Supplies     │
│  11.02.90  Inv      CHQ       0002      40.00  Kramer & Kramer Supplies   │
│  15.02.90  Inv      CHQ       0200     730.00  V J Schmidt               │
│  16.02.90  C/Note   RETURNS   0003     –20.00  Peaky Paper Supplies       │
│                                        ────────                           │
│                                        1,480.00                           │
└─────────────────────────────────────────────────────────────────────────┘
```

Figure 5.13

3 Nominal analysis of sales receipts and adjustments

Generally, there are only four accounts (or groups) to which these postings are made.

1 Bank Account All payments are made to this account which acts as a control account. In practice, it may be desirable to use a journal entry after these postings to other bank accounts or cash accounts.

2 Discounts Given.

3 Goods Returned Inwards.

4 Debtors Suspense.

```
┌─────────────────────────────────────────────────────────────────────────┐
│  G102  BANK ACCOUNT                                                       │
│                                                                           │
│  14.02.90  Recpt   CHQ 123991   0100       96.00  K K Schwarz             │
│  14.02.90  Recpt   CHQ 222111   0200   43,000.00  Wessex County Council   │
│  15.02.90  Recpt   CHQ 232112   0303    8,500.00  Microchip Hardware Supplies │
│  15.02.90  Recpt   CASH         0400    4,000.00  Connells Enterprises Inc. │
│  21.02.90  Recpt   CHQ 1231     0300   10,500.00  Blackman Software Ltd    │
│                                        ──────────                         │
│                                        66,096.00                          │
└─────────────────────────────────────────────────────────────────────────┘
```

Figure 5.14

```
┌──────────────────────────────────────────────────────────────────────────┐
│ A111  DISCOUNTS GIVEN                                                       │
│                                                                            │
│ 14.02.90    Disc     CHQ 123991    0100        4.00  K K Schwarz           │
│ 14.02.90    Disc     CHQ 222111    0200    2,300.00  Wessex County Council │
│ 15.02.90    Disc     CHQ 232112    0303      300.00  Microchip Hardware Supplies │
│ 21.02.90    Disc     CHQ 1231      0300      500.00  Blackman Software Ltd │
│                                                                            │
│                                            3,104.00                        │
│                                            ────────                        │
└──────────────────────────────────────────────────────────────────────────┘
```

```
┌──────────────────────────────────────────────────────────────────────────┐
│ G199  DEBTORS SUSPENSE                                                     │
│                                                                            │
│ 16.02.90    Refund   DEBIT 1001    0002     -120.00  P M Bluesdale         │
│ 16.02.90    Adjust   DISCOUNT      0001       18.00  A J Amber             │
│ 16.02.90    Adjust   MISPOST       0100     -110.00  K K Schwarz           │
│ 16.02.90    Adjust   WRITE OFF     0101      200.00  A P Klingen           │
│ 16.02.90    Adjust   DISCOUNT      0300    1,000.00  Blackman Software Ltd │
│                                                                            │
│                                              988.00                        │
│                                              ──────                        │
└──────────────────────────────────────────────────────────────────────────┘
```

Figure 5.14 Continued

In the example illustrated in Figure 5.14, the adjustments have been posted to debtors suspense simply because no posting account was specified. Each of these will need to be allocated to proper accounts via journal entries.

4 Nominal analysis of purchase receipts and adjustments

These work in much the same way as that for sales receipts and adjustments with the accounts (shown in Figure 5.15) being posted to:

1 Bank Account As with sales except posted are reducing (crediting) bank balances.
2 Discounts Taken.
3 Goods Returned Outwards.
4 Creditors Suspense.

```
┌──────────────────────────────────────────────────────────────────────────┐
│ G102  BANK ACCOUNT                                                         │
│                                                                            │
│ 20.02.90    Paymnt   CHQ 123221    0001   -1,050.00  Williams & Sons Stationery │
│                                                                            │
│                                           -1,050.00                        │
│                                           ─────────                        │
└──────────────────────────────────────────────────────────────────────────┘
```

```
┌──────────────────────────────────────────────────────────────────────────┐
│ A112 DISCOUNTS TAKEN                                                       │
│                                                                            │
│ 20.02.90    Disc     CHQ 123221    0001     -150.00  Williams & Sons Stationery │
│                                                                            │
│                                             -150.00                        │
│                                             ───────                        │
└──────────────────────────────────────────────────────────────────────────┘
```

Figure 5.15

C199 CREDITORS SUSPENSE					
21.02.90	Adjust	DISCOUNT	0003	300.00	Peaky Paper Supplies
				300.00	

Figure 5.15 Continued

CONCLUSIONS

Having figures posted to suspense accounts can prove a nuisance. It is important, therefore, to set up the appropriate accounts to avoid unnecessary journal entries.

As a result of all this activity, the trial balance will change quite significantly to reveal the sales, purchases, VAT and other transactions. Table 5.13 is an example of a brief trial balance. If you inspect a detailed trial balance you will be able to see more clearly the effect of the nominal analysis.

Table 5.13

		Pegasus Users Enterprises Summary Trial Balance	
		Dr	Cr
G 104	DEBTORS	132,670.00	
C 101	CREDITORS		25,730.00
G 105	DEBTORS RESERVES/PROVISIONS	16,000.00	
G 101	CLOSING STOCK	21,000.00	
A 111	DISCOUNTS GIVEN	3,104.00	
A 112	DISCOUNTS TAKEN		150.00
K 102	PROFIT and LOSS		12,000.00
G 102	BANK ACCOUNT	84,899.01	
G 199	DEBTORS SUSPENSE	888.00	
C 199	CREDITORS SUSPENSE	300.00	
S 101	SALES – HARDWARE		163,750.00
S 102	SALES – SOFTWARE		132,681.89
S 103	SALES – CONSULTANCY		84,640.00
P 101	PURCHASES – RAW MATERIALS	45,300.00	
P 102	PURCHASES – COMPONENTS	35,900.00	
P 103	PURCHASES – SERVICES	7,650.00	
R 101	GOODS RETURNED – INWARDS	3,350.00	
R 102	GOODS RETURNED – OUTWARDS		4,780.00
W 101	FACTORY WAGES	20,000.00	
W 102	ADMINISTRATION WAGES	6,000.00	
W 103	SALARIED STAFF	12,000.00	
F 101	CLOTHING – FACTORY STAFF	2,700.00	
F 102	CLEANING – FACTORY	1,520.00	
F 103	DEPRECIATION OF MACHINERY		10,000.00
F 104	DISTRIBUTION	1,200.00	
F 105	ELECTRICITY – FACTORY	936.99	
K 101	SHARE CAPITAL		500,000.00
K 103	DEBENTURES		200,000.00
C 102	SHORT TERM BANK LOAN		10,000.00

Table 5.13 Continued

Pegasus Users Enterprises
Summary Trial Balance (continued)

		Dr	Cr
Q 101	PROPERTY	253,000.00	
Q 102	PLANT and MACHINERY	120,360.00	
Q 103	FURNITURE	121,400.00	
Q 104	FIXTURES and FITTINGS	154,000.00	
Q 105	MOTOR VEHICLES	96,570.00	
G 103	CASH IN HAND		258.11
P VAT	VAT PAID THROUGH PURCHASES	1,480.00	
S VAT	VAT COLLECTED THROUGH SALES		10,013.00
F 106	DEPRECIATION OF FIXTURES	12,000.00	
G 106	PETTY CASH	.00	
F 107	BAD DEBTS		1,655.00
F 108	SUNDRY EXPENSES	580.00	
F 109	ENTERTAINMENT ALLOWANCES	850.00	
Grand Totals		1,155,658.00	1,155,658.00

In comparison to the trial balance prior to the nominal analysis there has been a significant change in many of the figures.

The next exercise is to do something about the two suspense accounts:

		Dr	Cr
G 199	DEBTORS SUSPENSE	888.00	
C 199	CREDITORS SUSPENSE	300.00	

Essentially, figures in a suspense account come about in one of many ways, such as:

1   Entry errors are made when sales or purchase analysis codes are entered on the invoice details. Later in the book, we will examine ways of reducing the likelihood of this occurring.

2   Entries have been made correctly, with sufficient details to ensure all transactions are posted to the correct nominal account. However, the nominal account may not have a correct header because it was omitted in error.

3   It was intended. In other words, an operator may well be instructed to enter a certain analysis code if they are unable to determine where the transaction is to be posted. This allows checks to be made on batch and prevents the holding up of processing work. Even if a transaction does not have the required analysis code, it can still register a sale or purchase and give important analysis information.

4   A nominal code defined in the parameter file does not correctly match the code set up as a header. From the parameter file, the set of control accounts defined with codes must be set up as headers with exactly the same code, although the header can have a different name.

Some of these errors can be easily corrected so that they will not occur again at the next nominal analysis of sales and purchase. Whatever the error, suspense posting will have to be transferred to other nominal accounts.

The first example of a suspense posting occurred at nominal analysis of sales invoices and credit note. In this instance illustrated in Figure 5.16, an analysis code of S193 was entered for which there was no nominal account.

Entry 14	22.02.90 ALLOCATE SALES INVOICE FROM SUSPENSE			
		Dr	Cr	
S102	SALES – SOFTWARE		100.00	SUSPENSE
G199	DEBTORS SUSPENSE	100.00		S102
Input by DR		100.00	100.00	

Figure 5.16

The sale has been removed from the suspense account and credited to the sales account in the normal way.

The next occurrence was with the nominal analysis of sales receipts and adjustments as shown in Figure 5.17. In this case, a refund and four adjustments have had no nominal account to post to, so were sent to debtors suspense.

Entry 15	22.02.90 ALLOCATE SALES RECEIPTS/ADJ FROM SUSPENSE			
		Dr	Cr	
G104	DEBTORS		230.00	SUSPENSE
A111	DISCOUNTS GIVEN	1,018.00		SUSPENSE
F107	BAD DEBTS	200.00		SUSPENSE
G199	DEBTORS SUSPENSE		988.00	TRANSFERS
Input by Dr		1,218.00	1,218.00	

Figure 5.17

The correction here was to take the refund and *mispost* adjustment (£120 and £110 respectively) which were credited to the debtors suspense and credit them instead to the *debtors* account.

Again the two *discount* adjustments (£18 and £1,000) were debited to the suspense account and need to be debited to the discounts given account instead.

Finally, a *write off* was debited to the suspense and has been debited to the bad debts account instead.

In practice, it is often not obvious where such adjustments should go and advice from another individual or department may have to be sought.

The third posting to suspense account was made with the nominal analysis of purchase receipts and adjustments. In the instance shown in Figure 5.18, a *discount* adjustment was posted to the creditors suspense.

Entry 16	22.02.90	ALLOCATE CREDITORS SUSPENSE TO ACCOUNTS		
			Dr	Cr
F108	SUNDRY EXPENSES		300.00	SUSPENSE
C199	CREDITORS SUSPENSE		300.00	F108
Input by Dr			300.00	300.00

Figure 5.18

The correction was to debit the amount to sundry expenses instead. It may well be the case that the amount should be debited to the discounts taken rather than sundry. Again, each re-posting will have to be examined about its nature to determine where the posting should go.

Table 5.14

	Summary Trial Balance	
	Dr	Cr
G 104 DEBTORS	132,440.00	
C 101 CREDITORS		25,730.00
G 105 DEBTORS RESERVES/PROVISIONS	16,000.00	
G 101 CLOSING STOCK	21,000.00	
A 111 DISCOUNTS GIVEN	4,122.00	
A 112 DISCOUNTS TAKEN		150.00
K 102 PROFIT & LOSS		12,000.00
G 102 BANK ACCOUNT	84,899.01	
G 199 DEBTORS SUSPENSE	.00	
C 199 CREDITORS SUSPENSE	.00	
S 101 SALES – HARDWARE		163,750.00
S 102 SALES – SOFTWARE		132,781.89
S 103 SALES – CONSULTANCY		84,640.00
P 101 PURCHASES – RAW MATERIALS	45,300.00	
P 102 PURCHASES – COMPONENTS	35,900.00	
P 103 PURCHASES – SERVICES	7,650.00	
R 101 GOODS RETURNED – INWARDS	3,350.00	
R 102 GOODS RETURNED – OUTWARDS		4,780.00
W 101 FACTORY WAGES	20,000.00	
W 102 ADMINISTRATION WAGES	6,000.00	
W 103 SALARIED STAFF	12,000.00	
F 101 CLOTHING – FACTORY STAFF	2,700.00	
F 102 CLEANING – FACTORY	1,520.00	
F 103 DEPRECIATION OF MACHINERY		10,000.00
F 104 DISTRIBUTION	1,200.00	
F 105 ELECTRICITY – FACTORY	936.99	
K 101 SHARE CAPITAL		500,000.00
K 103 DEBENTURES		200,000.00
C 102 SHORT TERM BANK LOAN		10,000.00

Table 5.14 Continued

		Dr	Cr
	Summary Trial Balance (continued)		
Q 101	PROPERTY	253,000.00	
Q 102	PLANT & MACHINERY	120,360.00	
Q 103	FURNITURE	121,400.00	
Q 104	FIXTURES & FITTINGS	154,000.00	
Q 105	MOTOR VEHICLES	96,570.00	
G 103	CASH IN HAND		258.11
P VAT	VAT PAID THROUGH PURCHASES	1,480.00	
S VAT	VAT COLLECTED THROUGH SALES		10,013.00
F 106	DEPRECIATION OF FIXTURES	12,000.00	
G 106	PETTY CASH	.00	
F 107	BAD DEBTS		1,455.00
F 108	SUNDRY EXPENSES	880.00	
F 109	ENTERTAINMENT ALLOWANCES	850.00	
Grand Totals		1,155,558.00	1,155,558.00

As a conclusion to this chapter, the trial balance, illustrated in Table 5.14, now confirms that the suspense have now been transferred to other nominal accounts.

The use of nominal analysis to post both sales and purchase transactions can be used as many times during a period as you wish.

It is a good idea to run the analysis activities frequently in order to make the task of tidying up more manageable.

In addition to transferring suspense account figures, there may also be a need to transfer figures from other control accounts. For example, all sales receipts and purchase payments are posted to a single bank account. In practice, this may have to be transferred to a number of company bank or cash accounts. Another example is the need to transfer petty cash to other nominal accounts, albeit it cash.

The next chapter will examine reporting capabilities of the package and the end-of-period activities. Before progressing to this chapter, experiment further by entering more transactions, performing nominal analysis to post to nominal accounts and use journal entries to tidy up accounts.

6 End-of-period and Reporting

A good deal of the ledger activity has been left until now in order to ensure you gain a good understanding of how to process ledger transactions and extract basic reports. This chapter will concentrate more on the analysis of transactions and ending a period of accounts (a month end in our example). A good deal of activity in this chapter will require you to investigate accounts and reports rather than entering transactions in the way required of you in the previous chapter.

The end-of-period routine is a common requirement in all accounting systems, whether computerised or not. At the end of each period, all nominal accounts will be cleared of transactions, with only the **net balance** being carried to the next period. In the case of both Sales and Purchase Ledger accounts all balanced accounts will be cleared in exactly the same way. With open item accounts, all transactions will be cleared except any unpaid or partially paid invoices which are carried to the next period. In a practical situation, all transaction files should be backed up.

This chapter will take you through further worked examples based on the data generated in the previous chapter as a way of developing understanding. The data used is limited and is simply designed to offer a speedy way of learning. As before, you should expand on the suggestions if you feel confident.

Most of the activities covered in this chapter will require you moving between the ledgers.

ANALYSING SALES

As a starting point, it is worth examining the analysis on sales available which can be found in option 3, Analysis, of the Sales Ledger.

Of the options available, the VAT analysis is the only one that will appear when the package is set up. The others are dependent on the sales parameter file. The VAT analysis will reveal the following (which is only an extract and **includes** all sales input). It was generated using the data in the previous chapter and is illustrated in Figure 6.1.

			Pegasus User Enterprises			
22 Feb 90			Sales Analysis Input			
Code	Type	VAT	Value	A/c	Date	Reference
P1SVAT	I	0	30.00	0001	11.02.90	00000000001
P1S101	I	1	190.00			
P1S102	I	1	100.00			
P1SVAT	I	0	140.00	0002	11.02.90	00000000002
P1S101	I	1	390.00			
P1S102	I	1	100.00			
P1S103	I	1	360.00			
P3S103	I	E	100.00	0100	11.02.90	00000000003
P3SVAT	I	0	150.00	0101	11.02.90	00000000004
P3S101	I	1	550.00			
P3S193	I	1	100.00			
L1SVAT	I	0	15.00	0200	11.02.90	00000000005
L1S102	I	1	100.00			
B1SVAT	I	0	1,500.00	0300	11.02.90	00000000006
B1S101	I	1	8,500.00			
B1S102	I	1	1,000.00			
B1S103	I	1	1,000.00			
B1SVAT	I	0	1,200.00	0303	11.02.90	00000000007
B1S101	I	1	7,300.00			
B5SVAT	I	0	20.00	0400	11.02.90	00000000008
B5S103	I	1	100.00			
P1SVAT	I	0	18.00	0001	12.02.90	00000000009
P1S103	I	1	80.00			
L1SVAT	I	0	6,900.00	0200	11.02.90	00000000010
L1S101	I	1	30,000.00			
L1S102	I	1	15,000.00			
L1S103	I	Z	5,000.00			
B1SVAT	I	0	50.00	0303	13.02.90	00000000011
B1S102	I	1	400.00			
B5S101	I	Z	5,000.00	0400	13.02.90	00000000011
P1SVAT	C	0	−10.00	0002	14.02.90	C1
P1S101	C	1	−80.00			
B1S101	C	1	−100.00	0303	14.02.90	C2

Figure 6.1

The VAT analysis will ask if you want a listing of all input. If you answer 'Y' to this, then a report as shown above will be listed first, showing all transactions entered in invoice sequence. The transactions are grouped in invoices showing analysis code breakdown on each invoice. In the code column, the code shows the first two digits of the customer code that appeared in the customer header record when the account header was created. The four digits that follow this are the analysis codes that appear on each invoice or credit note.

The VAT column indicates the category of VAT associated with each sales item.

SVAT code appears on each group of sales and represents the amount of total VAT for that invoice or credit note and has a VAT of 0.

This breakdown is one form of sales analysis which, as we shall see later, can be manipulated into different groupings.

The point to observe is that the VAT analysis shows how the VAT was collected (or returned in the case of credit notes) from the customers. When extracting a VAT statement it is important to account for VAT on each invoice issued.

Such a list can be useful to trace any transactions that may have been entered wrongly or have caused problems when trying to post to the Nominal Ledger through sales and purchase analysis.

	Pegasus User Enterprises	
22 Feb 90	Sales Analysis	
VAT Code		Value
1		65,090.00
E		100.00
Z		10,000.00
Total Goods		75,190.00
VAT		10,013.00
Total		85,203.00

Figure 6.2

Figure 6.2 presents the summary to the VAT analysis report which gives totals for goods sold and sub-totals for each category of VAT. In addition, it shows total sales value and VAT collected through sales. From this it can be seen that:

(a) £65,090.00 worth of sales were made with standard rate (1) of VAT.

(b) £100.00 worth of sales were made that were exempt of VAT.

(c) £10,000.00 worth of sales were made with zero rate of VAT.

(d) Total sales valued £75,190.00 exclusive of VAT.

(e) Total VAT collected was £10,013.00.

Such a report is sufficient to meet the requirements of VAT returns required by Customs and Excise. In practice, the VAT collected from sales will be passed on to Customs and Excise along with such a report. Please note, this is not the only source of VAT; for many firms, **cash sales** will also involve the collection of VAT which do not necessarily get posted to the Sales Ledger. A final VAT statement, therefore, may have to be left until later.

The next report available, illustrated in Figure 6.3, appears in option 1 of the sales analysis (transaction/customer), which **excludes** all sales input. If you request such a report with all sales input, then you will get a copy of the breakdown in invoices and credit notes that also appeared in the VAT analysis. This report reveals the sales input over the period in the same way as that for VAT. The bottom portion of the analysis gives a breakdown of the sales in a different way.

The report was generated by information set up in the sales parameters file and will require some careful thought and experimentation to see exactly what is happening.

Pegasus User Enterprises		
22 Feb 90	Sales Analysis	
Customer	Transaction	Value
B1	S101	15,700.00
B1	S102	1,400.00
B1	S103	1,000.00
B1	SVAT	2,750.00
B1	Total	20,850.00
B5	S101	5,000.00
B5	S103	100.00
B5	SVAT	20.00
B5	Total	5,120.00
L1	S101	30,000.00
L1	S102	15,100.00
L1	S103	5,000.00
L1	SVAT	6,915.00
L1	Total	57,015.00
P1	S101	500.00
P1	S102	200.00
P1	S103	440.00
P1	SVAT	178.00
P1	Total	1,318.00
P3	S101	550.00
P3	S103	100.00
P3	S193	100.00
P3	SVAT	150.00
P3	Total	900.00
Total		85,203.00

Figure 6.3

The customer code (e.g. P3) is the code entered when generating the headers in order to create the accounts. The transaction code is the four-digit sales analysis code entered on the ledger postings when recording an invoice to the ledger.

In the report, the only figures of interest are the sales figures (inclusive of VAT) and the groups of customer to whom they were sold.

Total sales amounted to £85,203.00, which matches the same total in the VAT analysis.

This report is based on the parameters set out in sales parameters which read as follows:

Sales Parameters – { Date }   (extract)

Sales Analysis 1	– Sequence	12/3456
	– Narrative	Customer/Transaction
Sales Analysis 2	– Sequence	3456/12
	– Narrative	Transaction/Customer
Sales Analysis 3	– Sequence	
	– Narrative	

Pegasus User Enterprises		
22 Feb 90	Sales Analysis	
Transaction	Customer	Value
S101	B1	15,700.00
S101	B5	5,000.00
S101	L1	30,000.00
S101	P1	500.00
S101	P3	550.00
S101	Total	51,750.00
S102	B1	1,400.00
S102	L1	15,100.00
S102	P1	200.00
S102	Total	16,700.00
S103	B1	1,000.00
S103	B5	100.00
S103	L1	5,000.00
S103	P1	440.00
S103	P3	100.00
S103	Total	6,640.00
S193	P3	100.00
S193	Total	100.00
SVAT	B1	2,750.00
SVAT	B5	20.00
SVAT	L1	6,915.00
SVAT	P1	178.00
SVAT	P3	150.00
SVAT	Total	10,013.00
Total		85,203.00

Figure 6.4

As this was Sales Analysis 1, the headings became Customer and Transaction respectively. The sequence numbers instruct what should go into each column. Numbers 1 and 2 are always the customer code as entered in the account header while 3, 4, 5 and 6 are the four digits in the sales analysis code entered on the invoices.

The choice set out in the parameters can be arranged in any permutation of the codes (1 to 6) and can be mixed. In addition to this, the report will reveal the transactions in alphabetic and/or numeric order with sub-totals determined by the first element within the parameter.

The other report, Transaction/Customer, reveals the opposite. (*See* Figure 6.4.)

Before proceeding any further, experiment with the Sales Analysis reports by altering the parameters and inspecting the result. This is not an easy aspect of the package to get to grips with, so give yourself ample time with it.

ANALYSING PURCHASES

From the Purchase Ledger menu, option 3, Analysis, produces exactly the same type of analysis as with sales analysis. As shown in Figure 6.5, the VAT analysis (without all purchase inputs) reveals that:

1   £15,650 worth of goods are standard rated.
2   £500 worth of sales is zero rated.
3   VAT paid out is £1,480.
4   Value of goods sold is £16,150.

Pegasus User Enterprises	
22 Feb 90 Purchase Analysis Page 1	
VAT Code	Value
1	15,650.00
Z	500.00
Total Goods	16,150.00
VAT	1,480.00
Total	17,630.00

Figure 6.5

Along with the VAT on sales analysis, a complete VAT picture on this period of VAT is available with respect to the Sales and Purchase Ledgers. When these figures are included with any journal entries of VAT (often resulting from cash sales and purchases) the VAT picture is complete. For a final VAT picture, VAT accounts will be set up in the Nominal Ledger with all Sales and Purchase Ledger VAT being posted to it along with journal entries. This complete picture will offer the basis of VAT returns for H.M. Customs and Excise.

Again, the other analysis reports will be dependent on the parameter settings. Experiment with the purchase analysis reports by altering the parameters and inspecting the result in the same way as you did with the sales analysis. A good understanding of this aspect of reporting will prove a useful and powerful analytical tool.

SALES LEDGER SPECIAL REPORTS

The objective of this part of the package is to prompt our customers (or politely remind them) for settlement of accounts. The principle is simple. We input a number of standard letters that each correspond to a length of time a debt has been outstanding. We can then send a letter reminding the customer of the situation.

Collecting debt will always be an important job for firms selling goods and services on a credit term basis. While a debtor is in a position of owing us money, this money cannot be employed for profitable purposes. For example, if £100,000 is owing to a firm by its debtors, this money cannot be put to use. Placing this money in a building society or a deposit account with a bank will still earn far more for the business than having it 'tied up' with debtors. Also, if debt is not checked and controlled, the occurrence of bad debts will be more frequent. One of the benefits of a computer is to control such financial matters and help to reduce funds being tied up unnecessarily.

The Special Reports appears as option 5 of the Sales Ledger menu and has the following options:

1 Amend/Create Debtors Letters. This allows us to set up three letters covering differing ages of debt outstanding. Normally, the longer the time a debt has been left unpaid, the stronger will become the letter.

2 Print Debtors Letters. This automatically prints the letters to customers as set up in option 1 of this menu. The system searches through all customer statements to see how long debt has been outstanding and prints a letter accordingly.

When you use these activities for the first time, you will be required to use option 1, amend/create debtors letters, to create the letters.

As an example, the debtors letters illustrated in Figure 6.6 were set up. The first part to be filled in informs the package of our requirements.

Paper Depth is the number of lines per letter.

Enquiry Print If this is set to 'Y' then a customer enquiry giving details about the state of the customer account will be produced with each of the letters.

Lower Limit here is set at £100. Any accounts with less than £100 still owing will not receive a letter.

No. of Days Before Letters has been set so that all customers still owing money after 30 days, but less than 60 days, will receive the first letter. Customers still owing money after 60 days, but less than 90 days, will receive the second letter. Customers still owing money after 90 days will receive the third letter.

```
        Paper Depth    :66:          No. of Days Before   1st Letter  : 30:
        Enquiry Print  :N:                                2nd Letter  : 60:
        Lower Limit    :100:                              3rd Letter  : 90:
    :Customer Account Number:     @1
    :
    :Date                         @2
    :
    :Account Balance:             @4
    :
    :Dear Customer
    :
    :I am writing to inform that the above balance has had no settlement for
    :over 30 days. As a consequence of this, I have to inform you that no
    :discount can be offered on this occasion.
    :
    :I look forward to receiving payment and hope you will take advantage
    :of our cash discount scheme in the future.
    :
    :
    :
    :
    :
```

Figure 6.6

Figure 6.6 is an example of a letter entered as the first letter. This letter contains in it a number of codes, namely:

@1 Extracts and places the customer ACCOUNT NUMBER here.

@2 Prints the date here.

@4 Extracts and places the amount owed by the customer for more than 30 days but less than 60.

Other codes can also be used; there are seven in all. The others are:

@3 Amount owing LESS THAN first number of days.
@4 Amount owing LESS THAN second number of days but more than the first.
@5 Amount owing LESS THAN third number of days but more than the second.
@6 Amount owing MORE THAN third number of days.
@7 Total balance on customer account.

When starting the second letter, simply press the down arrow key until the bar along the bottom of the screen indicates you are about to enter details of the second letter. (*See* Figure 6.7.)

It has come to our notice that settlement of your account has not been paid and now exceeds 60 days. I would like to remind that we now require a payment of 9999.99 as settlement of your account.

If you have any queries regarding this account, then please contact us to clear any possible problems.

If payment is not forthcoming, then we will feel obliged to take action on this matter.

Yours faithfully

K Waitnomore

Figure 6.7

The appearance of 9999.99 in the printout is where @4 would go. It should be clear that, with a little patience, letters can be printed giving exact figures and information related to each specific customer. Such letters would typically be printed on letter-headed paper.

Again, when starting the third letter, simply press the down arrow key until the bar along the bottom of the screen indicates you are about to enter details of the third letter. At this stage, enter a third letter of your choice. When you have finished, keep pressing the down arrow key until it is confirmed that the letter has been accepted by the computer.

Using 'print debtors letters' will print a letter to all those debtors who have outstanding debts within the categories outlined in the parameters stated in the letters above.

Figure 6.8 shows the customer enquiry on an account.

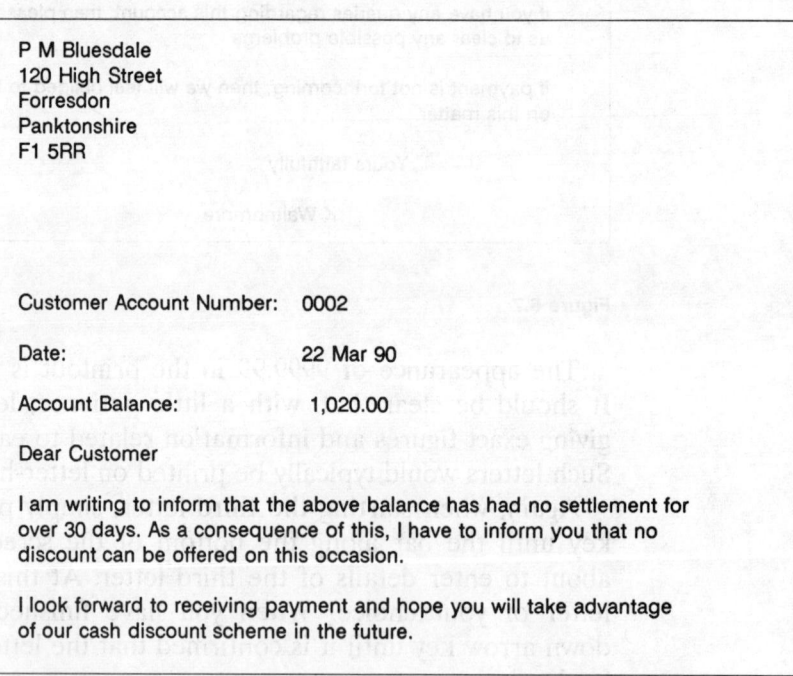

P.M. Bluesdale			Account 0002	22nd March 1990		Page 1
Date	Type	Reference	Status	Debit	Credit	Balance
11.02.90	Invoice	00000000002		990.00		
14.02.90	Cr. Note	C1			90.00	
16.02.90	Refund	DEBIT 1001		120.00		
	90 + Days	60 + Days		30 + Days	Current	Total
	.00	.00		1,020.00	.00	1,020.00

Figure 6.8

When using option 2 of the special reports, print debtors letters, it produced the letter set out in Figure 6.9.

P M Bluesdale
120 High Street
Forresdon
Panktonshire
F1 5RR

Customer Account Number: 0002

Date: 22 Mar 90

Account Balance: 1,020.00

Dear Customer

I am writing to inform that the above balance has had no settlement for over 30 days. As a consequence of this, I have to inform you that no discount can be offered on this occasion.

I look forward to receiving payment and hope you will take advantage of our cash discount scheme in the future.

Figure 6.9

At this point, the only part of the Sales Ledger not covered is that of report generator, a topic dealt with in Chapter 13.

PURCHASE LEDGER SPECIAL REPORTS

The first option here is Dispute/Release Transactions. The option allows an operator the chance to place Purchase Ledger invoices in dispute until satisfied that the transaction is either complete or is correct. Placing an invoice in dispute can also be achieved by placing a '**D**' in the right-most part of the reference box when entering invoice details to the ledger postings part of the Purchase Ledger. The purpose of doing this is to remind the operator of such transactions, especially at the end of a month or other specified periods.

The option allows you to place a transaction in dispute after it has been entered (but before it has been posted to the Nominal Ledger).

Automatic payments can be made to suppliers. To do this you will need:

1 Special stationery in the form of cheques as continuous stationery for your printer.
2 The parameters set up correctly in the Purchase Ledger parameters (a 'fiddly' but important job).

If you do not have the required stationery, there is no reason why automatic payments cannot be made, with the actual cheque production being done manually. In other words, details are printed with all relevant postings being made, followed up by the writing and distribution of cheques.

A list of cheques produced can be extracted at any time.

The final option here generates a list of suggested payments by ranking them in order of benefit to the firm. The suggested list takes into account the deadlines for payment of suppliers as well as the best discounts offered by suppliers. Again, this report is available at any time.

At this point, the only part of the Purchase Ledger not covered is that of report generator, a topic dealt with in Chapter 13.

NOMINAL REPORTS

This part of the package is available as option 5 of the Nominal Ledger menu and has just two choices. Setting up report parameters is a complicated activity, but is required if the Profit and Loss account and Balance Sheet are to be presented in the correct format.

It is important that if this section is to be used correctly, you distinguish clearly between a Balance Sheet item, and a Profit and Loss item when you create the Nominal Accounts Headers. All Profit and Loss items must have a secial report code prefixed with a 'P' and followed by two-number digits. The listing in the Profit and Loss accounts will be in number order. It may be that the headers will have to be amended to get the correct output.

All balance sheet items must have a special report code prefixed with a 'B' and followed by two-number digits. The next stage is to Create Report Parameters using option 5 from the Nominal Ledger, amend/create report parameters.

Entering the parameters requires all numeric parts of the special codes to be grouped. For example, all P02 codes will be grouped as PURCHASES.

Figures 6.10 and 6.11 are samples of parameters entered.

Profit & Loss Report Parameters	
TRADING ACCOUNTS	
Sales	R01
Purchases	L02
Goods Returned	L03
Cost of Goods	R81
GROSS PROFIT	D91
EXPENSES AND OVERHEADS	
WAGE & SALARIES	L04
FACTORY COSTS	L05
ADMINISTRATION	L06
DISCOUNTS GIVEN	L07
DISCOUNT TAKEN	A08
TOTAL EXPENSES	R81
NET PROFIT	C80

Balance Sheet Report Parameters	
LIABILITIES	
LONG TERM LIABILITIES	L01
SHORT TERM LIABILITIES	L02
	L06
PROFIT & LOSS	L80
	L81
ASSETS	
FIXED ASSETS	R03
CURRENT ASSETS	R04
	R05
VAT	R11
	R91

Figure 6.11

Figure 6.10

When you use option 1 from the special reports, amend/create report parameters, you will be confronted with a blank screen of two empty columns. The first screen will be the parameters for the profit and loss account which can run into two pages.

You are required to enter the parameter details with an **END** in the first column to indicate this part is done. When you 'end' Profit and Loss, you are then required to enter the Balance Sheet parameters in exactly the same way.

The first column contains the narrative that is to appear on the reports, while the second column instructs the system what figures are to appear on the report.

In the examples opposite, the profit and loss codes work as follows:

Sales **R01** – all P01 are grouped, totalled and displayed to the right.

Purchases **L02** – all P01 are grouped, totalled and displayed to the left.

Goods Returned **L03** – all P01 are grouped, totalled and displayed to the left

Cost of Goods **R81** – 'R' indicates the figure is to go on the right and 81 indicates the figure is to be the sum of all figures on the left-hand side since the last appearance of 81 or the start of the report if there is no 81 before this.

GROSS PROFIT **D91** – 'D' indicates the figure is to go on the right, but if the amount is a debit item (LOSS) it becomes bracketed. 91 indicates the figure is to be the sum of all figures on the right-hand side since the last appearance of 91 or the start of the report if there is no 91 before this.

All the expense items are to appear on the left with their respective groupings. The presence of A08 indicates that if this figure is a credit item (GAIN), then it stays on the left but is bracketed. The use of:

TOTAL EXPENSES **R81** – 'R' indicates the figure is to go on the right and 81 indicates the figure is to be the sum of all figures on the left-hand side since the last appearance of 81, which was the figure that calculated cost of goods sold.

NET PROFIT **C80** – 'C' indicates the figure is to go on the left but in brackets if normally a credit (LOSS) item and 80 is especially reserved for storing the value of the NET PROFIT that also has to appear on the balance sheet.

The Balance Sheet works in almost the same way, but uses all the B nominal codes.

All liabilities are set up to appear on the left, including their totals, while assets appear on the right, including their total. The use of number 80 allows the net profit to be carried across from the Profit and Loss account.

The result of the parameters set is shown in Figures 6.12 and 6.13.

Profit & Loss Account for Period Ended 22 Feb 1990		
TRADING ACCOUNTS		
Sales		381,172
Purchases	109,850	
Goods Returned	1,430	
Cost of Goods		108,420
GROSS PROFIT		272,752
EXPENSES & OVERHEADS		
WAGE & SALARIES	38,000	
FACTORY COSTS	8,632	
DISCOUNTS GIVEN	4,122	
DISCOUNT TAKEN	(150)	
TOTAL EXPENSES		50,604
NET PROFIT		222,148

Figure 6.12

Balance Sheet for Period Ended 22 Feb 1990		
LIABILITIES		
LONG TERM LIABILITIES	712,000	
SHORT TERM LIABILITIES	35,730	
PROFIT & LOSS	222,148	
	969,878	
ASSETS		
FIXED ASSETS		745,330
CURRENT ASSETS		233,081
VAT		8,533
		969,878

Figure 6.13

Setting up the parameters can be a long, tedious job. However, once done, the results are effective. When using this, you are asked if you require a nominal extraction. If you answer 'Y' to this, a much more detailed and informative breakdown of the Profit and Loss and Balance Sheet is given, showing how each group total is arrived at.

In summary the codes for the parameters are as follows:

Letter Code	Function
L	Figure on left column.
R	Figure on right column.
A	Figure on left column assumed debit, but bracketed if a credit value.
B	Figure on right column assumed credit, but bracketed if a debit value.
C	Figure on left column assumed credit, but bracketed if a debit value.
D	Figure on right column assumed debit, but bracketed if a credit value.

Numbers

| 0 – 79 | Grouping given in special report codes on nominal headers. |
| 80 | Net profit for appearing in both sets of reports. |

END-OF-PERIOD RUNS

This next section allows you to perform many of the requirements needed at the end of each month as well as investigating the effects they have on the accounts.

One of the first requirements will be to complete all Sales Ledger and Purchase Ledger transactions. A good deal of time is spent chasing up lost receipts, invoices and other documents – a fact of accounting life that the computer cannot always help you with.

Once the transactions have been entered, it is a good idea to back up all ledger files in case of any future mishaps; this routine **must** become second nature to anyone operating a computerised accounting system.

In the previous chapter, you discovered that when you used the Nominal Ledger to perform an **analysis of sales and purchases** to post Sales and Purchase Ledger transactions to the Nominal Ledger, many transactions ended up in the debtors suspense accounts and the creditors suspense accounts because some accounts had not been prepared with account headers. One of the first jobs is to add any known nominal headers that are required for the purpose of posting transactions.

The end-of-period run will, typically, involve the following activities being undertaken. You are advised to work through most of them in order to set accounts in all ledgers to the next period:

1 Use the Journal Entries to convert all data in the suspense accounts to other more representative accounts, often a result of not setting up the accounts correctly. It is worth noting that in any business situation, you will be confronted with these kind of 'teething' problems. Over time you will be able to iron them out.

2 Add any new accounts to the Nominal Ledger that will allow postings from sales and purchases to be done without sending large amounts of transactions to suspense accounts. You may have to alter some parameters to achieve this.

3 Finish posting any remaining Sales and Purchase Ledger transactions and ensure that all purchase invoices still in dispute are rectified and ready for posting. For your own benefit, invent some new transactions to simulate these activities.

4 From the Nominal Ledger, use Analysis of Sales and Purchases to post all remaining transactions.

5 Produce part of an audit trail consisting of:

(a) A list of all invoice, credit notes, adjustments and allocations for both the Sales and Purchase Ledgers.

(b) Prints of customer statements of account.

(c) Prints of ALL analysis reports for both the Sales and Purchase Ledgers.

(d) Produce Aged Debtors and Aged Creditors Reports for both the Sales and Purchase Ledgers.

6 Run the end-of-period programs for both the Sales and Purchase Ledgers.

7 Now do a further tidy up of nominal accounts for such accounts as suspense, petty cash, etc., using the Journal Entries facility.

8 Use Nominal Ledger Special Reports and amendments to the nominal special codes (through the nominal Headers Update) to produce a better profit and loss account and balance sheet.

9 Complete the audit trail by producing the following:

(a) A detailed trial balance.

(b) Profit and Loss account and Balance Sheet with extractions.

10 Run the nominal end-of-period program.

11 Now investigate the effect on the accounts and reports of the above transactions.

BANK RECONCILIATION

The following functions within the Nominal Ledger programs are for carrying out a bank reconciliation, checking your payments and receipts against your bank statement.

By selecting option 6 from the Nominal Ledger menu, a sub-menu will be displayed:

> **Post Presented Receipts**
> **Post Presented Payments**
> **Print Receipts**
> **Print Payments**
> **Enquiries**
> **Reconciliation Statement**

Post Presented Receipts

You would use this facility to post to the system those receipts that you have presented to the bank from your customers. A form will be displayed listing the receipts available for presenting. To post a presented receipt, use the cursor key to locate the arrow alongside the receipt and type 'P'. A tick will appear in the right-hand column and an asterisk show alongside the receipt. There is a facility to scroll through the receipts if there are more than can be displayed on the screen at one time.

To cancel a presented receipt, locate the arrow alongside the receipt and type 'C': the tick will be removed from the right-hand column, and the asterisk will disappear.

Post Presented Payments

This routine works in an identical fashion to posting receipts.

Print Receipts

This function provides a printout of payment details, and you can include all receipts, or only those presented or not presented as you wish.

Print Payments

This function operates as described for printing receipts.

Enquiries

This function provides an enquiry for the bank account much like normal account enquiries. You can print a 'hard copy' of the enquiry if you wish. Presented receipts or payments are highlighted by an asterisk.

Reconciliation Statement

This function provides a reconciliation statement printout which summarises the presented transactions, showing bank balance details and brought forward amounts for helping you to reconcile your bank statement.

7 Sales Invoicing and Sales Order Processing

INTRODUCTION

The objective of a sales invoicing and processing system is to produce invoices and process sales, as its title implies. Until now, we have been processing sales in a somewhat unusual manner, namely that invoice details have been directly entered to the Sales Ledger with all invoice details required, but with no invoices! One of the principal objectives of this chapter, therefore, is to produce invoices automatically, extracting all the customer information from the Sales Ledger and performing all calculations such as totals and VAT automatically. Ultimately, we will want the computer to update the Sales Ledger automatically, rather than post the invoices one at a time ourselves through the Sales Ledger. Consequently, this part of the Pegasus package will require an operational Sales Ledger.

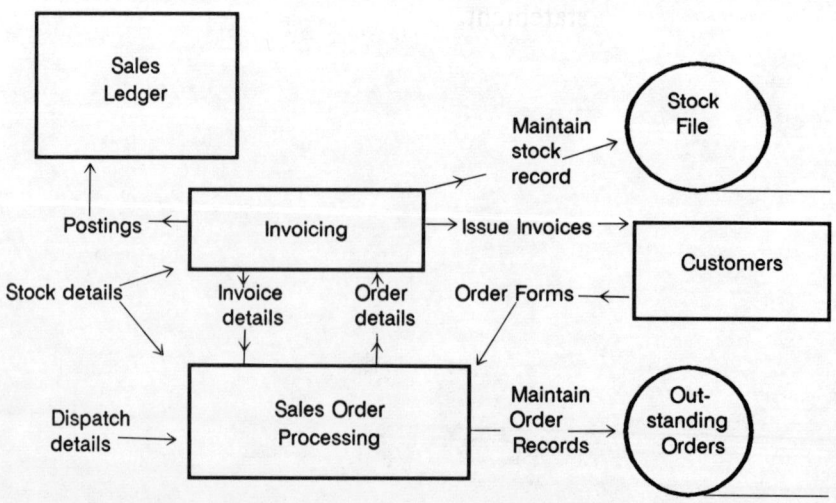

Figure 7.1 Invoicing and Sales Order Processing functions

Figure 7.1 depicts the way the invoicing and sales order processing functions are integrated with other functions. In addition to integrating with the Sales Ledger, there is the option of integrating with the stock control system. The purpose of this would be to extract from the stock file details about the stock being sold as well as subsequently updating stock files. For the purpose of this chapter, it is assumed that the stock system is not being used, which will mean us keeping a product file in order to run the system.

The product file will be used to extract stock details for the invoice, such as the unit price, VAT code, stock description, analysis code and discount terms. Such a file makes invoice production both quick and efficient. However, such a product file will involve some maintenance.

Another function covered in this chapter is Sales Order Processing. When customers place an order with the firm, processing of the form will involve:

(a) Checking to see if stock is available.

(b) Logging the sales order in a file called an **outstanding orders file**.

(c) Subsequently dispatching the goods, issuing an invoice and releasing the order from the outstanding orders file.

(d) Ensuring the stock availability is constantly updated.

GETTING STARTED

As with the ledgers, we will have to set up parameters before going any further. From option 3 of the Sales Invoicing menu the following is a parameter file set up (with explanations):

Invoicing Parameters

Company	Name	Pegasus Users Enterprises
	Address Line 1	100 High Street
	Address Line 2	Newtown
	Address Line 3	Wessex
	Address Line 4	
	1st Tel No.	01 001 0001
	2nd Tel No.	
	Telex No.	
	VAT Reg No.	

This will be used for invoice information in much the same way as that for the Sales Ledger where this information was needed for the customer statements of account.

Printer	Type	0
	TOF Code	12
	Columns	80
	Lines/Page	66

Such printer details need to be set to match the stationery that might be used. Invoice stationery may differ from other stationery.

Option No. 1   **N**

This will suppress a column on the invoice that states invoice terms. This will be purely a policy for a particular company. If discounts are common practice then this column is useful.

Option No. 2   **Y**

This will allow an overall invoice discount to be made. An entry of **1** will prevent this, but line discounts will be added and indicated as a total on the invoice. An entry of **2** allows both line discounts and overall invoice discounts to be added to create a total invoice amount.

Basically, discounts are normally used when:

(a) Dealing with special customers. For example, traders will often get discounts where individuals do not.
(b) As a way of promoting a product.
(c) To help clear stock.
(d) As an incentive to customers to make early payment. Such discounts will be allowed if a payment is made within a stated number of days.

Whatever the reason, such discounts will normally be indicated on the invoice.

Option No. 3   **Y**

This indicates that we are not integrating with the Stock Control system. Because no stock files will be available, we will be required to maintain a product file. In the next chapter we will examine the stock control system which will mean the invoices can get their stock information from the stock file maintained by the stock control function.

Option No. 4   **N**

If this was set to Y then a percentage can be added to the invoice as a surcharge, allowing for such events as the customer not paying promptly. The percentage to charge is set later on in these parameter settings.

Option No. 5   **N**

This will prevent over-riding of percentage for settlement discounts on data entry display to the invoice. If set to Y then the operator has the chance of changing the settlement discounts for any invoice, with the settings becoming defaults.

Option No. 6   **Y**

This sets the number of decimal places on the price to 3. When linked with the Stock Control function, stock prices must also be set to 3 places of decimal.

Option No. 7   **Y**

This ensures factor quantity is printed as a whole number. Later on we shall see that the product file requires a factor, the number of items per box, crate or whatever. If this is set at 5 then and the quantity required by the customer is 2/3, then it reads as:

2 lots of 5 plus 3 units = 13 units.

The number 13 is printed on the invoice.

Had the option been set at N, the figure on the invoice would have remained as 2/3.

The purpose of having a factor is to allow the selling of goods in parts rather than always as a whole.

VAT Rate		
	1	15.00
	2	0.00
	3	0.00

This allows up to 3 rates of VAT. In the UK at the time of writing, the only rate was that of 15%. This rate is used when posting to the Sales Ledger. The other two VAT values are not required here, but are:

Z – For zero rated.
E – For exempt from VAT.
X – For export, where VAT is not charged.

Settlement Discount Period 1	30
% 1	1.50
Period 2	60
% 2	.50

In this example, if payment is made within 30 days, the customer can take 1.5% off the invoice as discount. If payment is made after 30 days but within 60 days, the customer can take 0.5% off the invoice as discount.

No. of Invoice Lines   **12**

In this example this limits the number of items on an invoice to 12.

Surcharge Rate   **0.00**

As mentioned before this sets the percentage to be added to the invoice as a surcharge, allowing for such events as the customer not paying.

Option No. 8   **Y**

Invoice total calculations method showing total goods, VAT and total, being total goods less VAT.

Option No. 9	**N** Relates to non-UK VAT
Option No.10	**Y**
Option No.11	**Y**
Surcharge Analysis Code	**SUR1**

This will be the nominal code to which all surcharges eventually get posted. It means the nominal header is required if this function is to be integrated with the Nominal Ledger.

Surcharge VAT Code   **1**

The next two sections, shown in Figures 7.2 and 7.3, relate to the format that an invoice should take. Designing the invoice with these parameters will take a considerable degree of time and skill. In practice, a company may call upon outside experience to set it up, but if you can do it yourself, it will save your firm money and, more important in the long run, offer a good degree of flexibility in that alterations can be easily made for differing styles, stationery and changes in regulations.

The narrative section indicates what has to go on the invoice. That is, the details that are common to all invoices.

```
Narratives

 1     To:
 2     Date:
 3     Inv No.
 4     Order No.
 5     Account No.
 6     Product
 7     Qty            Description              Code        Price
 8     Total Goods
 9
10     VAT
11     Total
12     --------------------
13     Payment due within 90 days
14
```

Figure 7.2

The remainder is used:

(a) To indicate where on the invoice the above narratives should go.

(b) To show where on the invoice the stock, VAT, price, quantities, totals, terms should go.

Each line stated here will be used to match a line on an invoice. Hence, if the line is blank, then a blank line appears on the invoice. Much of this is in coded form, and an appendix appears at the end of this chapter listing what codes are available.

The manual specifies a list of codes that need to be studied and, with patience and care, used to build up the invoice. As an example, I shall explain three of the lines.

```
┌─────────────────────────────────────────────────────┐
│ Invoice Format Lines                                │
│ G1:          1/98:  2/22:  79/99                    │
│ :                                                   │
│ G0:          1/23:  48/27                           │
│ G0:          1/24:  48/28                           │
│ G0:          1/25:  48/29                           │
│ G1:          1/26:  41/30                           │
│ :                                                   │
│ G1:          1/1 :  30/98: 31/79: 79/99             │
│ G0:          1/35:  40/2 : 48/44                    │
│ G0:          1/36:  40/3 : 50/45                    │
│ G0           1/37:  34/4 : 35/46                    │
│ G0:          1/38:  34/5 : 45/43                    │
│ G0:          1/39                                   │
│ G0:          1/40                                   │
│ :                                                   │
│ G0:          43/6                                   │
│ G1:          1/7                                    │
│ :                                                   │
│ D3:          1/83:  11/81: 41/80:  54/84:  64/85    │
│ :                                                   │
│                                                     │
│ G0:          39/8:  64/57                           │
│ G0:          39/10: 64/59                           │
│ G0:          64/12                                  │
│ G0:          39/11: 64/60                           │
│ G6:          64/12                                  │
│ G7:           1/13                                  │
│ :                                                   │
│ :                                                   │
└─────────────────────────────────────────────────────┘
```

Figure 7.3

The first line contains:

G1: 1/98: 2/22: 79/99

Codes are   G1:   G is a General line (done just once) and 1 indicates skip 1 line.

1/98   Print item 98 (see manual code) starting at the 1st character position on the line. 98 turns on enhance mode **ON**.

2/22   Print item 22 (see manual code) starting at the 2nd character position on the same line. 22 is the company name.

79/79   Print item 99 (see manual code) starting at the 79th character position on the same line. 98 turns on enhance mode **OFF.**

The 9th line contains:

G0: 1/35: 40/2 : 48/44

Codes are   G0:   G is a General line (done just once) and 0 indicates do not skip a line, just to next line.

1/35   Print item 35 (see manual code) starting at the 1st character position on the line. 35 is 1st line of customer name and address label.

40/2   Print 2nd narrative at 40th character position.

48/44   Print item 44 (see manual code) starting at the 48th character position on the same line. 44 is current date.

The 19th line contains:
D3: 1/83: 11/81: 41/80: 54/84: 64/85

Codes are   D3:   D is a detail line printed once, limited to a maximum of 12 as set out in the earlier parameter. The 3 indicates that 3 lines are skipped before each detail line is written.

1/83   Print item 83 (see manual code) starting at the 1st character position on the line. 83 is the quantity of items.

11/81   Print item 81 (see manual code) starting at the 11th character position on the line. 81 is the product description.

41/80   Print item 80 (see manual code) starting at the 41st character position on the line. 80 is the product code.

54/84   Print item 84 (see manual code) starting at the 54th character position on the line. 84 is the unit price.

64/85   Print item 85 (see manual code) starting at the 64th character position on the line. 85 is the price sub-total.

Clearly, some time may have to be spent on this before skills have been developed. Pegasus does supply a grid to make invoice preparation easier.

In addition to the invoice, other documents are also printed in the same form, namely:

Credit Notes

A record of owing the customer money for goods returned, over-pricing, refunds, etc.

Pro-Forma Invoices

This does not issue an invoice for any accounting purposes but is a way of indicating how much a customer would have to pay if they were to receive the goods. Once the goods have been dispatched, a proper invoice should be issued. Consequently, these are not posted to the Sales Ledger.

Quotations

Similar to the pro-forma invoice, but offers an option to the customer to take up a purchase. An invoice must be formerly dispatched in the normal way.

Order Acknowledgement

Simply acknowledges that an order has been received.

In conclusion, the invoice that would be produced from the above would look something like Figure 7.4.

```
    Pegasus Users Enterprises

100 High Street                          01 001 0001
Newtown
Wessex


To:                      INVOICE

     ****************************    Date:        DD.MM.YY
     ****************************    Inv No.      **********
     ****************************    Order No.    **********
     ****************************    Account No.  X999
     ****************************
     ****************************

     Qty        Description          Product        Code      Price

     99999999  ****************************  XX9999999999   99999.999   99999.99
     99999999  ****************************  XX9999999999   99999.999   99999.99
     99999999  ****************************  XX9999999999   99999.999   99999.99
     99999999  ****************************  XX9999999999   99999.999   99999.99
     99999999  ****************************  XX9999999999   99999.999   99999.99
     99999999  ****************************  XX9999999999   99999.999   99999.99
     99999999  ****************************  XX9999999999   99999.999   99999.99
     99999999  ****************************  XX9999999999   99999.999   99999.99
     99999999  ****************************  XX9999999999   99999.999   99999.99
     99999999  ****************************  XX9999999999   99999.999   99999.99
     99999999  ****************************  XX9999999999   99999.999   99999.99
     99999999  ****************************  XX9999999999   99999.999   99999.99

                              Total Goods              99999.99
                              VAT                      99999.99
                              Total                    99999.99
```

Figure 7.4

The invoice here simply acts as a way of showing you the format of a finished invoice. The * symbol indicates where the text will be positioned. Likewise, the **9** indicates where the numbers will go. **DD.MM.YY** shows where the date will appear.

If the invoice is not quite as required, then you should take this opportunity to go back into the parameters and alter them accordingly.

PRODUCT FILE MAINTENANCE

This part of the module is required in order to produce an invoice. Basically, it holds all product information required to generate a transaction. In order to use the invoice processing part of the system the product file will have to be set up. In practice, this can be a long and tedious job because there are often hundreds of product codes and details to place on the file before invoicing can commence.

Table 7.1 illustrates the structure of a product file which contains details of a number of suggested records.

Table 7.1

PRODUCT CODE	DESCRIPTION	ANALYSIS CODE	FACTOR	UNIT DESCRIPTION	SELLING PRICE	V.A.T. RATE CODE	PRODUCT DISCOUNTS 1	2	3
0010	Adjustable Computer Desk	S101			388.000	1	2.00	1.00	.50
0020	Hand Scanner	S101			320.000	1			
0100	Bar Code Reader	S101			450.000	1	2.00		
0110	Floppy Disk holder (4 × 50)	S101	4	Case	13.000	1			
0120	Multi Port Transceiver	S101			998.000	1	2.00	1.00	.50
1010	Enterprises Word Processor	S102			180.000	1			
1030	Enterprises Database	S102			300.000	1			
1040	Enterprises Spreadsheet	S102			200.000	1			
1100	Enterprises Office Planner	S102			250.000	1			
1200	Enterprises Language Gener	S102			300.000	1	1.00		
1220	Enterprises Integrated Gener	S102			500.000	1	1.00		
2010	Pegasus Training Course	S103	5	CRSE	950.000	1			
2100	Telephone Service Contract	S103	12	Year	300.000	1	1.00		

Before proceeding with the product file it is worth examining the way all this fits into the overall structure of this module. Product file maintenance is available as option 2 from the main Invoicing and Sales Order Processing menu and has a structure as shown in Figure 7.5.

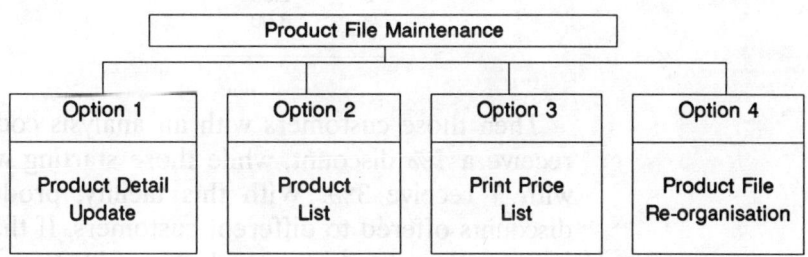

Figure 7.5

1 Product Detail Update

This is used to create a new set of product details. As is common with other files, each product is represented in the product file as a record.

With this, products can be added, deleted or information on them altered. When creating a product or amending an existing product, you will need to observe the following field information:

Product code This is a unique field in that each product has to have a different product code. It will serve as the only way Pegasus can reference a stock item. Such a technique should be familiar to you when reading catalogues, for which goods each have a different reference number or stock code or product code.

Analysis code This will be used for sales analysis so that integration with the Sales Ledger can be made. When invoices are produced, the goods sold to a customer can be used to automatically update the Sales Ledger, of which sales analysis forms the basis of a transactions record. At a later date, the Nominal Ledger can be updated using the analysis of sales invoices and credit notes.

Factor The number of items sold in a unit of sale. For example, per pack, box, crate or dozen. This has the advantage of you being able to sell products as part units. If eggs, say, are sold in boxes of 6 then 3/5 would read 3 boxes and 5 eggs.

Unit description This describes the unit sold. In the example of the eggs above, a suitable description may be **BOX**.

VAT code either 1, 2, 3, Z, X or E, as discussed earlier.

Discount code Up to three discount codes can be used with the invoice production. If the following discounts were entered:

Discount Codes	
1	1.00
2	2.00
3	3.00

Then those customers with an analysis code that starts with **1** will receive a 1% discount, while those starting with a **2** receive 2% and with **3** receive 3%. With this facility, products can have different discounts offered to different customers. If this facility is used, then it is normally a good idea to allow a column on the invoice to advertise this fact.

2 Product List & 3 Print Price List

This simply lists all products on the product file. Table 7.2 is a list of suggested products that appeared in Table 7.1 as an example of a set of product records.

Table 7.2

	Pegasus Users Enterprises		
25.02.90		Price List	
Product	Description	Unit Desc	Price
0010	Adjustable Computer Desk		388.000
0020	Hand Scanner		320.000
0100	Bar Code Reader		450.000
0110	Floppy Disk holder (4 × 50)	Case	13.000
0120	Multi Port Transceiver		998.000
1010	Enterprises Word Processor		180.000
1030	Enterprises Database		300.000
1040	Enterprises Spreadsheet		200.000
1100	Enterprises Office Planner		250.000
1200	Enterprises Language Generator		300.000
1220	Enterprises Integrated Genius		500.000
2010	Pegasus Training Course (Days)	CRSE	950.000
2100	Telephone Service Contract	Year	300.000

It is worth noting that many customers will want to use such a price list. In many cases, such a price list could be placed on to a floppy disk and posted to the customer who can then use such a price list to update their computer system. The method of doing this will be discussed more fully in Chapter 13.

When extracting a price list, you can print a portion of it by stating a starting product reference and a finishing one.

At this point, your product price list will appear in the same order that goods were entered into the computer. This order can be altered to be stored in product reference order.

4 Product File Re-organisation

As mentioned before, the order of products is the order they were entered. You can use the product re-organisation option to re-arrange these in product order.

When using this facility, the files will be re-written to another disk in case anything should go wrong. Having completed the options, the files should be copied back to the ledger disk. It is worth noting, that many customers will want to benefit by such a price list. In many cases, such a price list could be placed on to a floppy disk and posted to a customer who can then use such a price list to update their computer system. The method of doing this will be discussed more fully in Chapter 13.

In practice, companies will use product codes in such a way as to create lists of products grouped in some logical way. For example, in a department store all products relating to foodstuffs may start with **FD**. Hence, when a product list or price list is extracted, all foodstuffs will be grouped together. Further still, all foodstuffs that refer to biscuits may have a reference starting **FDBS**, so further sub-dividing stock.

The importance of deciding on codes to be associated with products will vary from firm to firm. In most cases a good deal of attention is paid to this.

INVOICE PROCESSING

This section is in four parts, and is used to generate: Invoices, Credit Notes, Pro-Forma Invoices, or Quotations. As mentioned before, the only information that gets posted to the Sales Ledger will be that obtained from the invoices and credit notes. Figure 7.6 may help give a clear picture about the processing activity for an invoice.

Generating either document is now relatively simple, much easier than entering data direct to the invoice.

When producing an invoice, two screens of forms will need to be completed. The data required are:

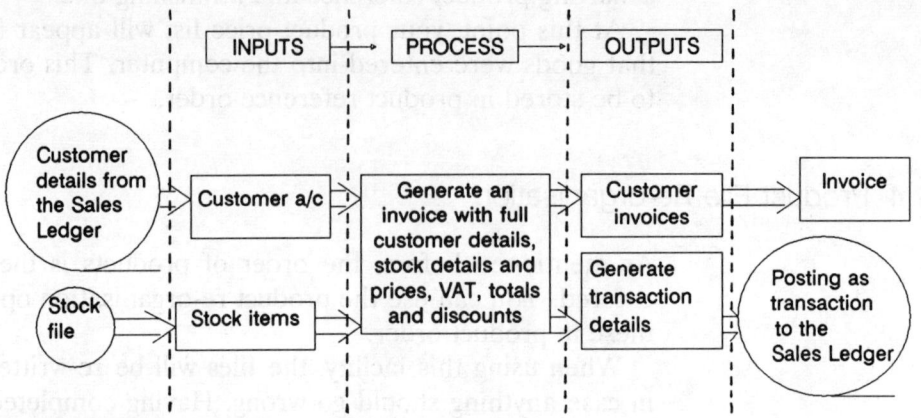

Figure 7.6

First page

The first page really concerns itself with who the invoice is to and how the goods are to be sent.

A/c No. The customer account number as it appears in the Sales Ledger. When this number is entered, the activity extracts from the Sales Ledger the customer information. It is important therefore that the customer account number exists.

Date This will automatically display the system date which can be changed.

Invoice No. For the invoices, this will be done automatically if required. Each invoice number generated is one greater than the previous number.

Customer Ref. Can be used by the company for their own purpose such as information to assist the customer.

Despatched By Can be used by the company for their own purpose and would normally be the name of the person or department responsible for the dispatch of goods.

Delivery This allows any delivery information to be entered on the invoice.

Second page

The second page now addresses itself with information on the actual goods to be sent and information about prices, VAT and the amount to be paid.

Product Product code from the product file. The activity then searches the product file to find the required details on a product.

Description This will be found automatically from the product file, but can be altered if desired.

Code Again, this will be found automatically from the product file, but can be altered if desired.

Qty The number of units required.

Price This will be found automatically from the product file, and this too can be altered if desired.

VAT Likewise, this will be found automatically from the product file.

As a useful tip, it pays to batch process much of the work in the same way as mentioned previously with respect to the ledger activity. In other words, it is always wise to produce a large number of invoices in one go rather than on an *ad-hoc* basis involving multiple visits to the computer in order to produce the required invoices. This, of course, also applies to credit notes and the other documents.

When invoices and credit notes are generated, all the postings are done for you along with calculation of VAT. Also each invoice is printed as you progress through your invoices. With parameters set, Figure 7.7 illustrates the kind of invoice that may be produced.

Pegasus Users Enterprises				
100 High Street Newtown Wessex		01 001 0001		
To:		INVOICE		
A J Amber 33 Littleston Road Wilmington Green Hiltshire		Date: 25.02.90 Inv No. 1 OAJA 9009 Account No. 0001		
Qty	Description	Product Code	Price	
1	Adjustable Computer Desk	0010	388.000	388.00
1	Bar Code Reader	0100	450.000	450.00
		Total Goods		838.00
		VAT		117.62
		Total		913.72
Payment due within 90 days				

Figure 7.7

Before moving on to Sales Order Processing, have a go at the following exercise as a way of gaining practice with invoicing and to see how this function is integrated with the Sales Ledger.

Exercises

1   Set up parameters with your own chosen options. Be careful that option 3 is set at **N** for now. This will ensure the system does not revert to the stock control system for product information.

2   Create a product file with records, making sure that the analysis codes on each record match up with a nominal code. For the more adventurous of you, enter some extra nominal codes that may be required for various items of stock.

3   Generate a few invoices and credit notes and extract the following reports:

(a)   A list of transactions from the Sales Ledger.
(b)   Statements of accounts for those customers who received invoices or credit notes.

4   From the Nominal Ledger use Analysis of Sales and Purchases in order to post all transactions held in the Sales Ledger into the Nominal Ledger.

If you have worked through these exercises then you will appreciate that, having set up both the parameters and product files, the process of producing an invoice can be quicker and more accurate than manually printing invoices and then posting them direct to the Sales Ledger ourselves. Having automated these entries of transactions, direct entry to the Sales Ledger need only concern itself with payments by customers, which often requires very little information from the operator, and adjustments of customer accounts.

SALES ORDER PROCESSING

We now arrive at a slight dilemma about where to go from here. In order to use the Sales Order Processing (**SOP**) system you will have to set up a stock file using the Stock Control system. In other words, you will not be able to progress with this function until you have worked through the next chapter on Stock Control.

For study purposes, therefore, skip to the next chapter where you will be reminded to come back to this part of this chapter.

The purpose of Sales Order Processing (SOP) is self-explanatory. Basically, an order is placed by a customer which is then processed by the firm and is later completed by the firm with the goods or services being despatched with an invoice.

When an order is received and entered into the computer, stock quantities are adjusted to indicate that certain stock have been **allocated** against an order. Stock allocation can only be achieved through the Stock Control function of the Pegasus package, thereby requiring integration with Stock Control.

There will be two stages with regard to SOP. The first is when a customer places an order. Figure 7.8 is an attempt to illustrate this.

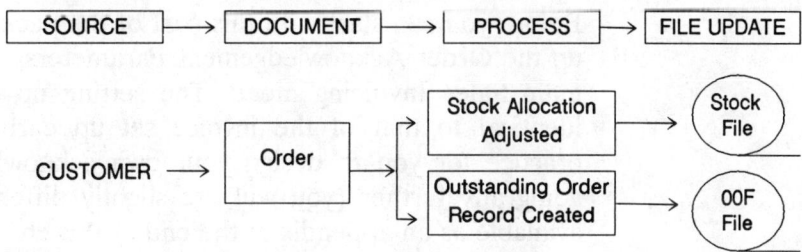

Figure 7.8

When an order is received a stock allocation is made to indicate that items of stock will be needed to meet an order. The stock file record, therefore, is updated to reflect this. As a consequence, when decisions have to made about stock, a more rational decision can be made when it is known what stock is required to meet SOP.

The second stage occurs when an order has been met, shown in Figure 7.9.

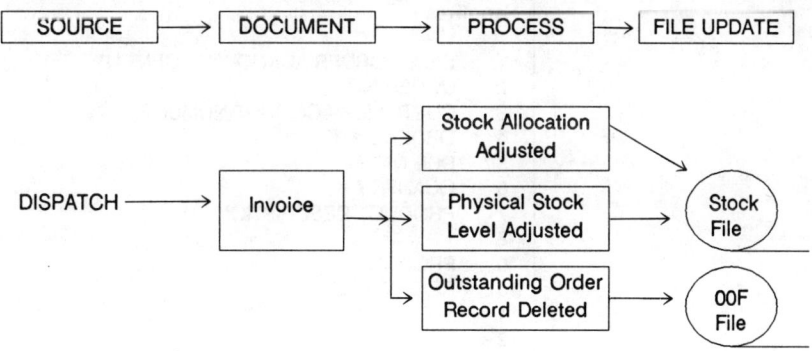

Figure 7.9

The structure of this function is shown in Figure 7.10.

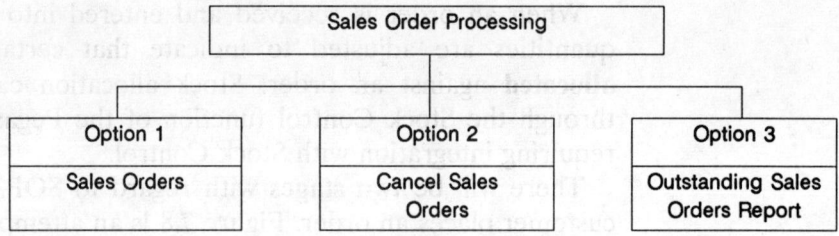

Figure 7.10

Before you can start with this part of the package you will have to set up the Order Acknowledgement Parameters, which is option 5 in the main Sales Invoicing menu. The setting up of these parameters is identical to that of the invoice set up earlier. It would be useful practice for you to design your own acknowledgement form before going any further (you will use slightly different codes for this also available as an appendix at the end of this chapter).

When an order is received from a customer the firm acknowledges receipt of the order by sending back a sales acknowledgement form. It is this form that extra parameters are required for.

The process requires two stages. The first stage is to state any narratives you want placed on to your order acknowledgement form. In many cases, a firm uses prepared pre-printed stationery, in which case very few narratives would be required. Figure 7.11 illustrates the kind of narratives that could be placed on an acknowledgement form.

```
Order Acknowledgement Parameters – 25 Feb 90

Narratives

    1    SALES ORDER ACKNOWLEDGEMENT
    2    ORDER NO.
    3    CUSTOMER ACCOUNT NUMBER
    4    ORDER DATE
    5    DUE DATE
    6    QUANTITY
    7    PRODUCT DESCRIPTION
    8
    9    PRODUCT
   10    REFERENCE
   11
   12
   13    PRICE
   14    VALUE
   15    TOTAL
```

Figure 7.11

The second screen requires details on what appears on the acknowledgement form along with where such details should appear. The setting of these parameters requires the same operation as with invoice parameters.

Figures 7.12 and 7.13 show format lines and the acknowledgement form that will result from it.

```
**************************************************
              SALES ORDER ACKNOWLEDGEMENT

CUSTOMER ACCOUNT NUMBER X999 ORDER NO.  *****
*******************************
*******************************
*******************************
*******************************
*******************************
*******************************

ORDER DATE                        DUE DATE  DD.MM.YY
```

QUANTITY	PRODUCT REFERENCE	PRODUCT DESCRIPTION	PRICE	VALUE
99999999	XX9999999999	****************	999999.99	999999.99
99999999	XX9999999999	****************	999999.99	999999.99
99999999	XX9999999999	****************	999999.99	999999.99
99999999	XX9999999999	****************	999999.99	999999.99
99999999	XX9999999999	****************	999999.99	999999.99
99999999	XX9999999999	****************	999999.99	999999.99
			TOTAL	999999.99

Figure 7.12

```
Order Acknowledgement Format Lines

G1:   20/22
G1:   25/1
G1:   1/3 : 25/31: 30/2 : 41/33
G0:   1/36
G0:   1/37
G0:   1/38
G0:   1/39
G0:   1/40
G1:   1/41
G1:   1/4 : 30/5 : 41/34
G0:   1/6 : 10/9 : 26/7 : 60/13: 70/14
G2:   10/10
D1:   1/63: 10/60: 26/61: 60/64: 70/65
G1:   45/15: 70/35
  :
```

Figure 7.13

The main objective of this part of the package is to keep a record of all orders received from customers and, if appropriate, to send to the customer an acknowledgement of the order. Consequently, an operator will, typically, be 'batch' processing a pile of order forms received from customers. Clearly, this requires integration with the

Sales Ledger in order to trace the customer details and the Stock Control system in order to extract details about stock.

If this part of the package is managed properly, effective monitoring of customer orders can be made and you can avoid failing to meet customer orders through poor data processing. Option 4 from the Sales Invoicing program will be used to process sales orders. The options will be covered in the order of this menu.

1 Sales Orders

This activity collects details of an order, updates the **outstanding orders file** and then prints an acknowledgement form to be sent to the customer.

At this point it is worth examining the details that make up a record within the outstanding orders file. (*See* Table 7.3.)

Table 7.3

Order number	Customer A/C no.	Order date	Due date	Balance outstanding	Outstanding order amount	Comment	List of stock references and Quantities	
1	0100	01/01/90	03/03/90	450	450		0100	2
2	0300	01/01/90	02/02/90	550	1,000	OVERDUE	0100	1
							1020	2
3	0303	01/01/90	01/03/90	300	300	CANCELLED	1030	3

Each order still outstanding will be represented in the file by a single record. As each order is met, then an invoice is sent to the customer and the record that relates to outstanding orders will need to be recorded as such.

A form will be displayed on the screen which is used to keep outstanding sales orders updated. The information you will need to complete the fields that make up a record are:

A/c No. The customer account number, which will have to appear in the Sales Ledger. When this is entered, customer details will appear on the screen.

Date The date will be the system date by default, which can be changed by you.

Order No. The order number will be displayed as 1 greater than the previous order processed. You may change this if you wish.

Due Date The date which you expect to meet the order. This will be important for future monitoring.

Product This will be the product code from the stock file.

Qty The quantity of an item required.

Price The price will be found in the product file (or stock file if using stock control) and may be altered at this point.

When entering order details, insertion of **END** in the product column will end this entry. In other words, you enter a line for each product ordered by the customer, followed by END as the product code.

2 Cancel Sales Orders

This simply reverses the process of entering a sales order by asking for the sales order number. This can be used either when the order has been met or to subsequently cancel an order by request of a customer or because the order has been entered by mistake.

3 Outstanding Sales Orders Report

This simply gives a summary of those sales orders that have not yet been fulfilled. In order to be of any real value, it is important that the outstanding orders are regularly kept updated. It is this report that will assist a firm in avoiding the problems incurred when overlooking a customer order.

When invoices are prepared and delivered, you will have the option of cancelling an order outstanding. If you do not cancel an order once it has been completed, you are in danger of inadvertently meeting the order again.

Exercises

As a conclusion to Sales Order Processing, have a go at the following exercises.

1. Create an order acknowledgement form using the Order Acknowledgement Parameter Update activity.
2. Process a number of sales orders by entering imaginary orders placed by customers for goods or services. Each entry should generate an order acknowledgement form.
3. Cancel one or two of these orders.
4. Produce an Outstanding Sales Order Report.

APPENDIX

Table 7.4 gives item numbers to be used when designing an invoice.

G A general line (done just once) and is followed by a number which indicates the number of blank lines to FOLLOW the information printed.

D D is a detail line printed once for each detail. For example, in this chapter it is used to print a line for each item of stock to invoice the customer for. It is followed by a number which indicates the number of blank lines to FOLLOW the information printed.

Each format line starts with either a G or D.

Table 7.4

Item	Description	Source of information
1-21	Narrative lines 1 to 21	Parameters
22	Company Name – Centred	Parameters
23-26	Company Address Lines 1 to 4	Parameters
27-28	Telephone numbers 1 and 2	Parameters
29	Telex Number	Parameters
30	VAT Number	Parameters
31	Settlement terms 1 (Days)	Parameters
32	Settlement terms 1 (%)	Parameters
33	Settlement terms 2 (Days)	Parameters
34	Settlement terms 2 (%)	Parameters
35	Customer's Name	Sales Ledger
36-40	Customer's Address Lines 1 to 5	Sales Ledger
41	Customer's Account Comment	Sales Ledger
42	Customer Analysis Code	Sales Ledger
43	Customer Analysis Number	Sales Ledger
44	Invoice Date	Keyed/Default
45	Invoice, Credit note, Pro-forma or Quote number	Keyed
46	Customer's Reference	Keyed
47	Dispatched by	Keyed
48-53	Delivery Address Lines 1 to 6	Keyed
54	Overall invoice discount (%)	Keyed
55-56	Invoice narratives 1 and 2	Keyed
57	Total Goods Value	Calculated
58	Overall invoice discount amount	Calculated
59	Total VAT	Calculated
60	Invoice Total	Calculated
61	VAT Analysis 1 – Rate	Calculated
62	VAT Analysis 1 – (%)	Calculated
63	VAT Analysis 1 – Goods	Calculated
64	VAT Analysis 1 – VAT	Calculated
65-68	VAT Analysis 2 – As above	Calculated
69-72	VAT Analysis 3 – As above	Calculated

Table 7.4 Continued

Item	Description	Source of information
73-76	VAT Analysis 4 – As above	Calculated
77	Settlement Discount Amount 1	Calculated
78	Settlement Discount Amount 2	Calculated
79	Invoice, Credit Note, Pro-forma or Quotation	Deduced
80	Product Code	Keyed
81	Description	Keyed/Product File
82	Analysis Code	Keyed/Product File
83	Quantity	Keyed
84	Price	Keyed/Product File
85	Goods Value (Quantity x Price)	Calculated
86	Line Discount – (%)	Keyed/Product File
87	Line Discount Amount	Calculated
88	Discounted Goods Value	Calculated
89	VAT Code	Keyed/Product File
90	VAT – (%)	Deduced
91	VAT Amount	Calculated
92	Unit Description	Product File
94	Total Taxable Goods Value (Net)	Calculated
95	Surcharge (%)	Parameters
96	Surcharge Amount	Calculated
97	Page Number	Counted
98	Printer Enhance (Large Print) ON	Program
99	Printer Enhance (Large Print) OFF	Program

Table 7.5 gives item numbers to be used when designing an order acknowledgement form.

Table 7.5

Item	Description	Source of information
1-21	Narrative lines 1 to 21	Order Acknowledgement Parameters
22	Company Name – Centred	Sales Parameters
23-26	Company Address Lines 1 to 4	Sales Parameters
27-28	Telephone numbers 1 and 2	Sales Parameters
29	Telex Number	Sales Parameters
30	VAT Number	Sales Parameters
31	Sales Account Number	Keyed
32	Order Acknowledgement Date	Keyed
33	Order Number	Keyed
34	Order Due Date	Keyed
35	Order Acknowledgement Total	Keyed
36	Sales Account Name	Sales N/A Records
37-41	Sales Account Address lines 1 to 5	Sales N/A Records

Table 7.5 Continued

Item	Description	Source of information
60	Product Code	Keyed
61	Description	Stock File
62	Unit Description	Stock File
63	Quantity	Keyed
64	Selling Price	Keyed
65	Goods Value (Quantity × Price)	Calculated
66	In Stock Quantity	Calculated
98	Printer Enhance (Large Print) ON	Program
99	Printer Enhance (Large Print) OFF	Program

8 Stock Control

INTRODUCTION

In the previous chapter, we covered invoicing and sales order processing with the aid of a product file which had to be kept up-to-date in order to make effective use of that part of the system by being able to insert product details into an invoice, credit note, ro-forma invoice or quotation automatically. However, sales order processing will need the facilities of the Stock Control module before advantage can be taken of the function. In this chapter, we shall use the Stock Control system as an alternative to the product file as well as satisfying the needs of SOP. In addition to this, we will examine many other features of Stock Control and Purchase Ordering.

The system maintains stock records in order to offer control of stock in such a way that:

1   The minimum of funds are tied up in surplus or obsolete stock.
2   A firm does not run out of any items of stock.

As an example, a firm may decide to hold very large quantities of stock because it simply does not want to either sell out or run out of an important raw material. Although this may appear to be rational, it can be costly. If a firm can reduce its stock levels by, say, £1 million, then imagine how much such a sum could earn a business if it was put to work! Even if a firm could not obviously put money to work in its own business, it could still earn a good deal in a building society or bank.

The aim of controlling stock, therefore, will be to keep stock at its lowest level without impeding either sales or production. This can be achieved only if:

(a)   Stock records are updated regularly and promptly.
(b)   Reporting techniques on stock levels are quick, efficient and timely.

Achieving this may well inflict extra costs on the business, which should not exceed the savings made by holding lower stock levels.

A stock file will hold records on stock items with each stock item having the set of fields shown in Table 8.1.

Table 8.1

FIELD NAME	FUNCTION
STOCK REFERENCE	A unique field to identify the stock item. No two stock items should have the same reference code.
STOCK DESCRIPTION	Describes the item of stock as it should appear on either an invoice to a customer or purchase request from a supplier.
SALES ANALYSIS CODE	The code that would appear in the sales analysis with the Sales Ledger. This will be used within the Sales Ledger to analyse sales and can be used to assist the posting of sales from the Sales Ledger to the Nominal Ledger
SELLING PRICE	The selling price per unit
COST CODE	This is used in conjunction with the Job Costing function. If a code here matches a code within the Job Costing function, then any movement in stock can be used to monitor the cost of a job.
FACTOR	The number of items sold in a unit of sale. For example, per pack, box, crate or dozen. This has the advantage of your being able to sell products as part units. If eggs, say, are sold in boxes of 6 then 3/5 would read 3 boxes and 5 eggs.
UNIT DESCRIPTION	This describes the unit sold. In the example of the eggs above, a suitable description may be box.
RE-ORDER LEVEL	The amount of stock level reached when goods should be re-ordered. The system will use this field value to assist in advising us when to order stock.
RE-ORDER QUANTITY	When the re-order level has been reached, this field tells us the optimum quantity to re-order.
MINIMUM STOCK LEVEL	This is the stock considered to be too low for the business.
COST PRICE	The cost price per unit.
LOCATION	This can be used by the company to code where the stock is physically held. If, however, it is an assembly which is to be used by the Bill of Materials function then its value should be ****.
SUPPLIER CODE	This is used to remind us of the normal supplier of the stock item and matches the supplier code entered in the Purchase Ledger. If option 1 in the Stock Control parameters is set at 'Y', then entry of this code is compulsory.
SUPPLIER PART NUMBER	This is the stock code that the supplier uses to identify the stock item.
SALES V.A.T. CODE	Either 1, 2, 3, Z, X or E. This code assists the invoicing and Sales Ledger functions.
3 SALES DISCOUNTS	This is used to allow different customer groups different discounts on items of stock.
3 MONTHS RECENT ISSUE HISTORY	This holds details of the stock issues over the past 3 months and serves as a useful measurement of determining the re-order level and re-order quantity.

A stock system will have to record, and report, all stock movements in and out of stock, stock allocations, de-allocations, adjustments and order details. In addition to this, a Stock Control system should produce, in the way of reports, valuations of both stock-in-hand, stock availability and goods on order with suppliers. From this, price lists can be extracted in much the same way as in the previous chapter.

Keeping a close check on goods on order is always important, to prevent such occurrences as ordering twice in error, or to make sure that suppliers meet delivery dates.

In tackling this part of the Pegasus package, it is important to note that the stock file generated will replace the product file used with Invoicing and Sales Order Processing part of the package. Apart from developing the Stock Control system, you will also have to alter the sales invoicing parameter file. In that parameter file, option 3 must be 'Y' to instruct the program to integrate with Stock Control.

GETTING STARTED

As is always the case, you will need to set up the parameters before you can start. The construction of the parameter file is similar to that of the others for the business name, address, telephone numbers and printer details. The number of P/O (purchase order) lines indicates the number of purchase detail lines on a purchase order (between 5 and 19).

Option No. 1   Y

Entry of a supplier code must match that of a Purchase Ledger supplier code.

Option No. 2   Y

This ensures sales analysis codes on the Stock Control system conform to that on the Nominal Ledger, that is, four-digit codes. Although not essential for integration, it will prove to be a very useful tool for analysis of sales at a later date.

Option No. 3   Y

This allows the system to produce purchase orders for suppliers rather than simply acting as a record of orders.

Option No. 4   N

When new stock enters stock with a different price, all the old stock will be given the new price for the purposes of valuation. If an option of 'Y' were entered, the new stock would be valued at cost, with each unit being an average of the total paid for that stock.

Option No. 5   Y

Expected profit is recorded on items entering stock and leaving stock.

Option No. 6   **N**

The selling price is recorded to 2 decimal places rather than 3.

Option No. 7   **1**

Sub-totals for stock valuation reports to be based on the first character of the stock reference only.

Option No. 8   **Y**

This integrates with Invoicing and Sales Order Processing.

Option No. 9   **N**

This avoids (for this chapter) integrating with Job Costing.

Option No. 10   **N**

This serves no purpose in this version of Pegasus.

The next two sections of the parameters deal with the design of the purchase order, and are designed in exactly the same way as for invoice layout. The purpose of a purchase order is to place an order for goods or services with a supplier. In some cases, the supplier will require us to complete one of their forms or will take an order by telephone. Whatever method is used, the recording of the purchase must be made, as this will be reflected in the stock file. In addition to this, we will need to keep a close check on what has been ordered, so we can prevent ordering more than once in error.

The first page, shown in Figure 8.1, is a list of all the text that is required to enter on to the purchase order, while the two pages that follow are used to set the invoice layout. The following is an example of such parameters followed by a sample purchase order form.

When setting up parameters do not use the 'ESC' key at any point. You must use the down arrow key in order to get to the next page. **Keep using the down arrow key until you are prompted to enter purchase order format lines.**

Figure 8.2 represents the second page which will require you to enter purchase order format lines. When entering these codes, the use of 'G' and 'D' is the same as that for the Invoices. The other codes are shown as an appendix to this chapter.

You should take the opportunity to investigate these format lines by examining the codes at the end of this chapter and experimenting with your own settings.

The sample invoice format in Figure 8.3 indicates how a final purchase order might look. The * shows where text would appear, the **9** where numbers would appear and **DD.MM.YY** where the date would appear.

Before moving on, it is useful to see how the Stock Control function, illustrated in Figure 8.4, is structured.

```
Narratives

 1   To:
 2   From:
 3   Vat Reg. No.
 4   Date:
 5   Order No.
 6   Stock ref.
 7   Description
 8   Quantity
 9   Cost Price
10   Totals
11   Purchase Order Total
12   Delivery Instructions
13
```

Figure 8.1

```
Purchase Order Format Lines

G1:   1/98:   2/22:  60/99
G1:   1/1 :   45/2
G0:   1/36:   45/23
G0:   1/37:   45/24
G0:   1/38:   45/25
G0:   1/39:   45/26
G0:   1/40
G0:   1/41:   45/27
G2:   1/3 :   15/30:  45/4 :  50/32
G1:   1/5 :   10/33
G2:   2/6 :   15/7 :  55/8 :  65/9 :  75/10
D1:   1/51:   15/52:  55/53:  65/54:  75/55
G3:   30/11:  75/50
G1:   1/12
G0:   1/42
G0:   1/43
G0:   1/44
G0:   1/45
G0:   1/46
G0:   1/47
```

Figure 8.2

```
                          Pegasus User Enterprises

To:                              From

******************************   100 High Street
******************************   Newtown
******************************   Wessex
******************************
******************************
******************************   01 001 0001
Vat Reg. No.                     Date: DD.MM.YY

Order No. ******
```

Stock ref	Description	Quantity	Cost Price	Totals
XXXXXXXXXXX	******************************	99999999	999999.99	999999.99
XXXXXXXXXXX	******************************	99999999	999999.99	999999.99
XXXXXXXXXXX	******************************	99999999	999999.99	999999.99
XXXXXXXXXXX	******************************	99999999	999999.99	999999.99
XXXXXXXXXXX	******************************	99999999	999999.99	999999.99
XXXXXXXXXXX	******************************	99999999	999999.99	999999.99
XXXXXXXXXXX	******************************	99999999	999999.99	999999.99
XXXXXXXXXXX	******************************	99999999	999999.99	999999.99
XXXXXXXXXXX	******************************	99999999	999999.99	999999.99
XXXXXXXXXXX	******************************	99999999	999999.99	999999.99
XXXXXXXXXXX	******************************	99999999	999999.99	999999.99
XXXXXXXXXXX	******************************	99999999	999999.99	999999.99

	Purchase Order Total			999999.99

```
Delivery Instructions

******************************
******************************
******************************
******************************
```

Figure 8.3

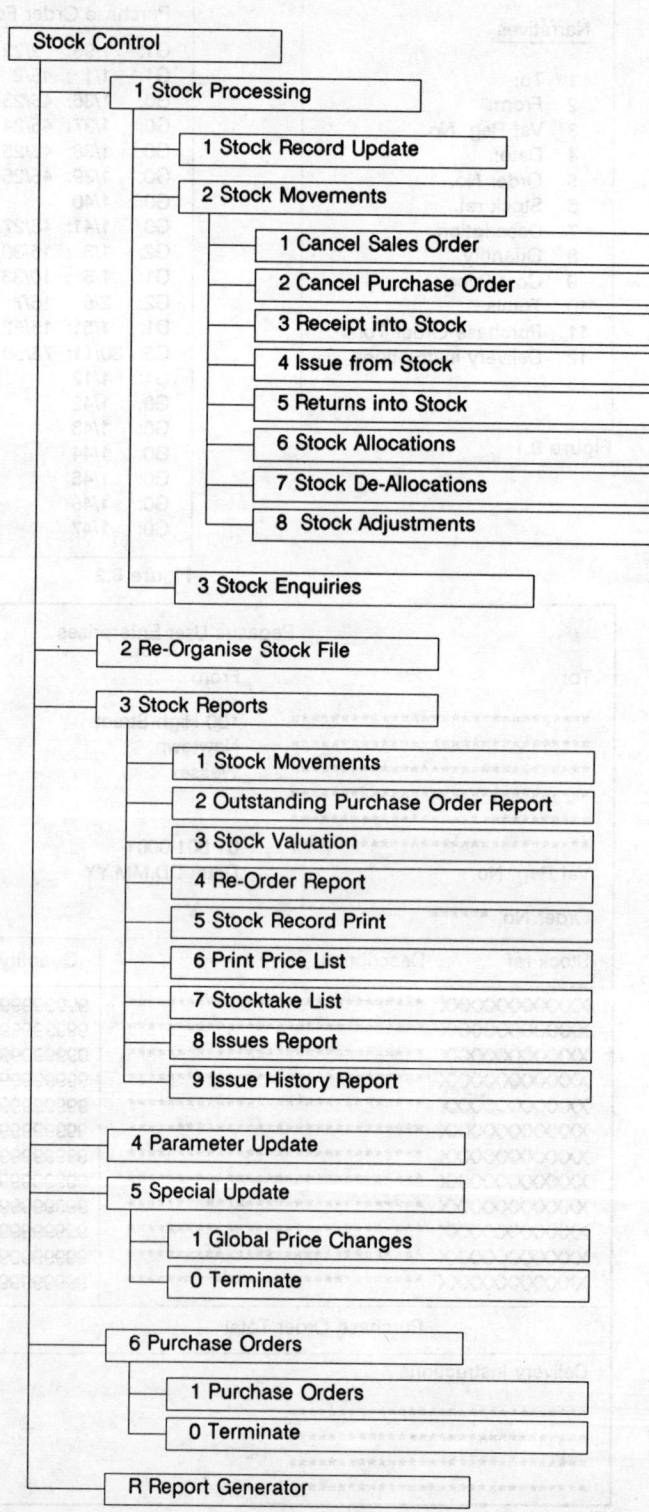

Stock Control

1 Stock Processing

1 Stock Record Update

2 Stock Movements

1 Cancel Sales Order

2 Cancel Purchase Order

3 Receipt into Stock

4 Issue from Stock

5 Returns into Stock

6 Stock Allocations

7 Stock De-Allocations

8 Stock Adjustments

3 Stock Enquiries

2 Re-Organise Stock File

3 Stock Reports

1 Stock Movements

2 Outstanding Purchase Order Report

3 Stock Valuation

4 Re-Order Report

5 Stock Record Print

6 Print Price List

7 Stocktake List

8 Issues Report

9 Issue History Report

4 Parameter Update

5 Special Update

1 Global Price Changes

0 Terminate

6 Purchase Orders

1 Purchase Orders

0 Terminate

R Report Generator

Figure 8.4

From observation of the activities within the Stock Control function, it can be seen that much of the work will be done within the stock processing part with the stock reports producing most of the reports about stock situations.

From this, Figure 8.5 depicts the kind of information flow that might be typical of Stock Control:

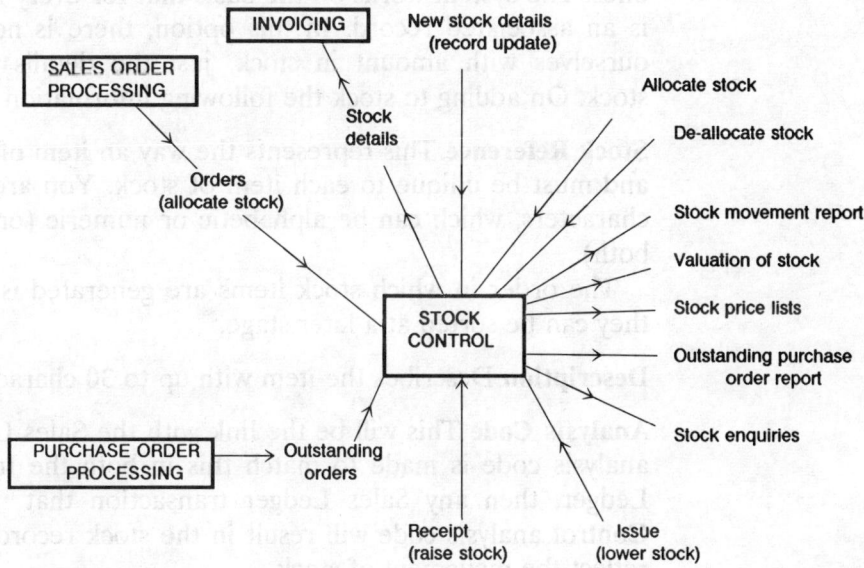

Figure 8.5

Figure 8.5 shows how three other functions integrate with Stock Control. **Sales Order Processing** will process orders sent in by customers and allocate certain stock to those customers. **Purchase Orders** will ensure that stock records are flagged with details about what is on order. Also, stock details are sent to **Invoicing** giving such details as price, VAT code, analysis code and description of stock.

The reports that can be extracted from stock records can only be informative if stock records are kept up to date and accurate. This is very much a problem of logistics and business organisation, which is not wholly dependent on the computer.

Although stock may be on the shelves in the warehouse, it is important to record within a stock file what stock, and how much, has been allocated to a particular job or sale. Although any stock item can be de-allocated, the point of the exercise is to ensure that stock is not inadvertently issued when it is needed elsewhere.

STOCK PROCESSING

Much of the work in Stock Control will be processing stock records, option 1 from the Stock Control menu. Such activities will include updating the stock file, recording stock movements, issuing purchase orders and making stock enquiries.

1 Stock record update

This will allow you to add new stock records as well as amend existing ones. The system works on the basis that for every item of stock there is an associated record. In this option, there is no need to concern ourselves with amount in stock, just the details about an item of stock. On adding to stock the following information may be required:

Stock Reference This represents the way an item of stock is identified and must be unique to each item of stock. You are allowed up to 12 characters, which can be alphabetic or numeric (or a combination of both).

The order in which stock items are generated is not important, as they can be sorted at a later stage.

Description Describes the item with up to 30 characters.

Analysis Code This will be the link with the Sales Ledger. If the sales analysis code is made to match this in both the Invoicing and Sales Ledger, then any Sales Ledger transaction that matches the Stock Control analysis code will result in the stock record being updated to reflect the movement of stock.

Selling Price You will have to refer back to option 6 in the parameter file. This will be useful if you are integrating with the Invoicing part of Pegasus.

Cost Code This will only be used if integrated with Job Costing.

Factor The case may arise where stock is not sold in decimal notation (e.g. 12.6 means 12 and 6 tenths), but is sold in blocks of 12. If 12 is entered in this box, then 12/6 reads 12 and 6 individual parts.

Unit Description This helps the documentation by using words to express how units are measured (e.g. box, ton or dozen).

Re-Order Level This is the stock level that, when reached, demands that a purchase order be placed. This is going to be crucial for assisting a firm in keeping a check that adequate stocks are maintained. One of the reporting facilities will want to establish what should be ordered at any given time. If this is left blank, the re-order level check will not be performed.

Re-Order Qty The amount that is normally ordered per order once the re-order level has been reached.

Minimum Stock Level This can be used to warn you that a certain level has been reached when making the stock movement. This warning takes precedence over the re-order quantity.

Cost Price The cost price that has to be entered will depend on what was entered in option 6 of the parameters.

Location Codes can be entered here to indicate where the stock is physically stored. They will appear on your stock lists if used.

Supplier Code This can be used to indicate who normally supplies the stock item. It is only mandatory if option 1 in the parameter is set to 'Y'.

Suppliers Part No. This is optional.

VAT Code This is used to integrate with the Invoicing and Sales Ledger. The code will consist of one digit (e.g. Z, E, 1, 2 or 3) and will automate the entry to the invoice every time the stock item is entered.

Discount Code Up to three discount entries are allowed here. The code is then used by the Invoicing system to automatically discount goods issued to certain customers. For example,

A   1%
B   2.5%
C   5%

means customer codes prefixed with A (such A8) will receive 1% discount off the selling price of goods issued, while those prefixed with B will receive 2.5% and those with C will receive 5%.

Qty Issued this gives you the opportunity to enter the stock quantity issued during each of the previous three periods. These figures are updated on each re-organisation of the stock run.

If you wish to enter some stock quantities then you should use receipt into stock, which is available as a Stock Movement Option (option 2) from the Stock Processing menu.

If you wish to DELETE a stock item from the record, then enter DELETE as the first characters in the description field of the stock record to be deleted. The record will be physically deleted after file re-organisation.

Having entered stock details for the first time, it is often a good idea to extract stock lists and check that they are complete. Such lists will show stock appearing in the same order as they were entered to the computer. It is not until file re-organisation that they will be sorted into stock reference order.

3 Stock enquiries

At this point some practice would be useful. The stock records in Figures 8.6 and 8.7 illustrate the kind of details needed by the system.

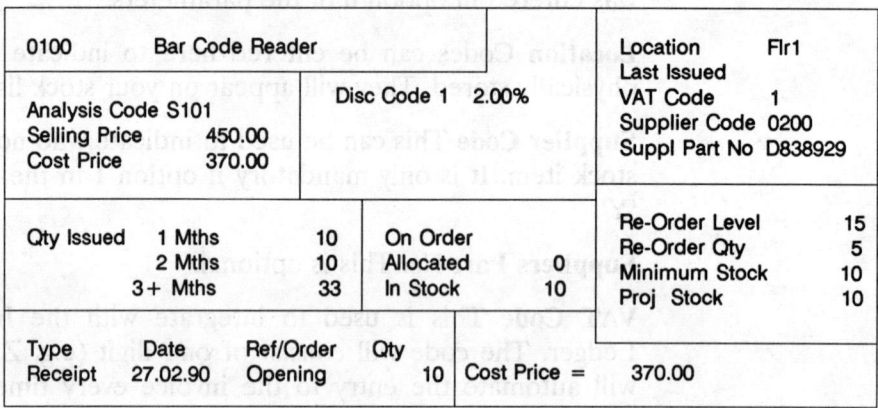

0100	Bar Code Reader		Location	Flr1
			Last Issued	
Analysis Code S101	Disc Code 1 2.00%		VAT Code	1
Selling Price 450.00			Supplier Code 0200	
Cost Price 370.00			Suppl Part No D838929	
Qty Issued 1 Mths 10	On Order		Re-Order Level	15
2 Mths 10	Allocated	0	Re-Order Qty	5
3+ Mths 33	In Stock	10	Minimum Stock	10
			Proj Stock	10
Type Date Ref/Order Qty				
Receipt 27.02.90 Opening 10	Cost Price =	370.00		

Figure 8.6

2100	Telephone Service Contract		Location	
			Last Issued	
Analysis Code S103	Disc Code 1 1.00%		VAT Code	1
Selling Price 300.00			Supplier Code 0000	
Cost Price 220.00			Suppl Part No	
Qty Issued 1 Mths	On Order		Re-Order Level	
2 Mths	Allocated	0	Re-Order Qty	
3+ Mths	In Stock	10	Minimum Stock	
			Proj Stock	10
Type Date Ref/Order Qty				
Receipt 27.02.90 Opening 10	Cost Price =	220.00		

Figure 8.7

In both cases, the record was entered as a stock record update using the option **'Stock processing'**. Details of the stock record were extracted using the option **'Stock enquiries'** from the same menu. As can be seen from such enquiries, a reasonable knowledge of the stock system is required to understand what the fields represent.

In both cases it can be seen how much stock is in hand and what exactly it cost. The **'Proj Stock'** is an attempt to project how much stock is likely to be issued in this period based on what has been issued in the past months.

The stocktake list in Figure 8.8 was adapted from the product file stock details used as an example in the previous chapter, but with more detail as required by Stock Control.

27.02.90			Price List								Page 1	
					<—————— Discounted Prices ——————>							
Stock Ref	Description	Price	Per									
0010	Adjustable Computer Desk	388.00		1	2.00%	380.24	2	1.00%	384.12	3	.50%	386.06
0020	Hand Scanner	320.00										
0100	Bar Code Reader	450.00	Case	1	2.00%	441.00						
0110	Floppy Disk Holder (4 x 50)	13.00										
0120	Multi Port Transceiver	998.00		1	2.00%	978.04	2	1.00%	988.02	3	.50%	993.01
1010	Enterprises Word Processor	180.00										
1030	Enterprises Database	300.00										
1040	Enterprises Spreadsheet	200.00										
1100	Enterprises Office Planner	250.00										
1200	Enterprises Language Generator	300.00		1	1.00%	297.00						
1220	Enterprises Integrated Genius	500.00		1	1.00%	495.00						
2010	Pegasus Training Course	950.00	CRSE									
2100	Telephone Service Contract	300.00		1	1.00%	297.00						

Figure 8.8

The list in Figure 8.8 was extracted from 'Stock Reports' menu and is a detailed **Stock Price List** from that menu. Another report in that same menu is listed in Figure 8.9 and is the **Stocktake List**.

27.02.90		Stocktake List				Page 1
Stock Reference		Location	Stock Qty	Unit Desc	Supplier's Part No.	
0010	Adjustable Computer Desk	Flr1	10		AC10211	
0020	Hand Scanner	Flr1	10		D929388	
0100	Bar Code Reader	Flr1	10		D838929	
0110	Floppy Disk Holder (4 x 50)	Flr2	20	Case		
0120	Multi Port Transceiver	Flr1			MPT100	
1010	Enterprises Word Processor	Flr3	4			
1030	Enterprises Database	Flr3	10			
1040	Enterprises Spreadsheet	Flr3	10			
1100	Enterprises Office Planner	Flr3	10			
1200	Enterprises Language Generator	Flr3	10			
1220	Enterprises Integrated Genius	Flr3	1			
2010	Pegasus Training Course			CRSE		
2100	Telephone Service Contract		10			

Figure 8.9

STOCK MOVEMENTS

The next step is to examine stock movements. The stock movement option in the stock processing menu will not be the only source where stock movements are recorded. If integrated with the Invoicing and Sales Order Processing, then an issue of an invoice will result in automatic adjustment of stock, thereby avoiding the need to record a stock movement in this section. In addition to altering stock quantity, you will be informed about the **free stock** available while you are preparing the invoice. Also, when goods are received after a purchase order has been issued, the acknowledgement of this must be recorded both as a stock movement and within the purchase order system – a topic to be covered shortly.

At this point you should distinguish the difference between **in-stock, allocated** and **free** stock quantities:

(a)   **In-stock quantity** refers to the physical presence of stock that should be on the premises of the firm.

(b)   **Allocated quantity** refers to those stock items that have been allocated for sale.

(c)   **Free quantity** refers to stock available for issuing and is:
         In-stock quantity LESS Allocated quantity.

Stock that has been allocated for a purpose can, at any time, be de-allocated. Conversely, more stock can be allocated. An important source of stock allocation other than sales order processing is Bill of Materials. If an order requires the assembly or manufacture of a finished product, then all the materials that are used to make the finished product must also be allocated, thereby reducing the free stock available.

Stock movement is an option available within the stock processing option from the Stock Control menu and shows the screen illustrated in Figure 8.10 to be completed.

Stock Ref	Date	Type	Reference	Quantity

Figure 8.10

When recording a stock movement the first entry must be the stock reference (number). Brief stock record details will be shown below the entry boxes. The date will then appear with the current date as default; this may be altered if required.

The system then prompts you for 'Type' of stock movement to be recorded in much the same way as the ledger posting in the Sales and Purchase Ledgers required you to identify the type of transaction. For this a single code will be required with one of the following:

1 = Cancel sales order

This allows you to cancel a previously issued sales order, thereby increasing the allocated stock level while leaving the in-stock quantity the same. When cancelling an order, you will be required to enter the sales order number. If integrated with sales order processing, the order number will have been generated in that section.

2 = Cancel purchase order

This allows you to cancel a previously issued purchase order. When cancelling an order, you will be required to enter the purchase order number. This order number will have been generated when issuing a purchase order, to be covered later.

3 = Receipt into stock

This simply allows you the facility of recording an increase in stock. Some documentation should be available somewhere for future audit trails. When receiving goods you will be required to enter the cost price. In addition to this, the system asks whether the goods were received against a purchase order. If the answer is yes, you will be required to enter each purchase order number which the receipt is to be set against. This will be required at a later stage to indicate whether purchase orders have been met.

4 = Issue from stock

This decreases 'in-stock' quantity but will be automatically used if integrated with the invoicing facility of the previous chapter. The system asks whether the goods are to be issued against a sales order. If the answer is yes, you will be required to enter each sales order number which the receipt is to be set against. The sales order will have been created in the sales order processing system in the previous section. Also, if the issue exceeds the free allocated stock available, you will be warned about this and asked if you still wish to proceed.

5 = Returns into from stock

This increases 'in-stock' quantity but, as before, will be done automatically if integrated with the Invoicing facility of the previous chapter.

6 = Stock allocations

This increases stock availability but will be done automatically if integrated with the Sales Order Processing facility of the previous chapter and will not appear as an option. However, option 8 in the parameters file must be set at 'Y'. Allocations will only affect the 'free stock' rather than the 'in-stock' figure.

7 = Stock de-allocations

This decreases stock availability and again will be automatically used if integrated with the Sales Order Processing facility of the previous chapter and will not appear as an option. Again, option 8 in the parameters file must be set at 'Y'. De-allocations will only affect the 'free stock' rather than the 'in-stock' figure.

8 = Stock adjustments

Allows the alteration of 'in-stock' quantities and is often used after a stocktaking exercise in order to match the computer records with actual physical stock levels which can often 'drift' apart over time. This figure can be positive or negative.

The reference that is asked for should be meaningful to the firm and has no direct effect on the stock records.

When starting off a stock system for the very first time, a firm will have to:

(a)   Use stock record update to create stock records for every item of stock held.

(b)   Use stock movements to create stock levels. Entering a positive stock adjustment for each item would be the most straightforward way of doing this.

(c)   Enter ALL outstanding purchase order details (see later on in chapter how to do this).

(d)   Enter ALL outstanding sales order details.

Consequently, this can be a marathon job often taking weeks of effort to collate the figures, enter the details to the computer and then checking them (by which time your stock details may be already out of date). When doing this job in practice it is vital that it is well planned. Once the stock records have been made up, it will be important to enter the stock adjustment quickly in one go and then start operating the computer system almost immediately in order to avoid another batch update of figures. (Staff must, therefore, be well trained before starting on this kind of venture.)

Figure 8.11 shows a stock record enquiry from the stock processing menu showing the effect when a number of stock record movements have been entered.

0020	Hand Scanner			Location	Flr1
				Last Issued	
Analysis Code S101				VAT Code	1
Selling Price	320.00			Supplier Code 0200	
Cost Price	244.00			Suppl Part No	D929388
				Re-Order Level	15
Qty Issued	1 Mths	10	On Order	6	Re-Order Qty	5
	2 Mths	12	Allocated	5	Minimum Stock	10
	3+ Mths	32	In Stock	10	Proj Stock	10
Type	Date	Ref/Order	Qty		
Receipt	27.02.90	Opening	10	Cost Price =	244.00

Figure 8.11

Exercises

At this point you should attempt the following exercises as a way of gaining required practice.

1   If you have not already done so, set up the Stock Control parameters as suggested in this chapter making sure you have integrated with Invoicing and Sales Order Processing functions.

2   Try to make certain you have an adequate purchase order form for later in this chapter.

3   Set up some stock records using the stock record update activity from the stock processing menu.

4   Enter some stock quantities to start the records using stock movements to create stock levels by entering a positive stock adjustment for each stock item.

5   Enter a number of stock movements as described earlier in this chapter. In doing this, try to use as many movements types as possible, and enter a total of about fifty transactions in all.

6   Use the **Invoicing** function described in Chapter 7 in order to produce, say, twenty invoices for a varied number of customers. Make sure that the parameters in the Invoicing function are set for integration with Stock Control. This can be done by making sure **option 3 is set to Y**.

7   Now use the **Sales Order Processing** function in order to generate orders from customers. You should take this opportunity to reflect back to the Sales Order Processing section in Chapter 7. It will prove good practice to keep working between the functions while they are all integrated in this manner.

8   After this experiment with the following reports from the stock reports option of the Stock Control menu:

1   Stock Movements Report
3   Stock Valuation
5   Stock Record Print
6   Print Price List
7   Stocktake List
8   Issues Report
9   Issues History Report

9   Use the enquiries option from the stock processing menu in order to investigate the effect your transactions have had on the stock records.

PURCHASE ORDERS

By now you should have a good idea of what stock control is largely about in terms of maintaining stock records, entering stock movements and extracting reports. The final stage is to cover purchase orders which will make use of the purchase form layout in the parameters file to issue orders to suppliers.

In addition to issuing orders, this aspect of Stock Control will have an effect on the stock available to be issued and, when a receipt of stock has been recorded against a purchase, will affect the in-stock quantity.

A purchase order will be issued and sent to a supplier. In some cases, we may have to send orders to certain suppliers on their purchase order forms. However a purchase order is sent, a record must be made and details of the order stored in the stock file. Each stock record will contain details of what is on order so that any reference to a stock record will give us stock information. When stock levels are low, it is important to know whether any more is on order, if only to avoid ordering stock more than once.

In addition to keeping stock records updated with what is on order, an outstanding purchase order file will also need to be kept so that we are able to keep track of orders placed and report on those orders that are late being met by suppliers. Such a file will have the record structure illustrated in Figure 8.12.

Supplier Code	Date Sent	Date Due	Order No.	Originator	Deliver By	Stock Ref(s)	Quantities

Figure 8.12

There will be a record held in the file for each purchase order still outstanding.

Issuing a purchase order can be done through option 3 of the main Stock Control menu. Two pages will have to be completed. The first page requires the following:

Supplier The supplier code is entered here and the supplier details will be found in the Purchase Ledger and displayed in the Suppliers Name and Address box. If the entry is left blank, you will have to enter purchaser details yourself.

Date The date appears with the current date as default which can be altered.

Order No. The system will do this for you by making each order no. 1 greater than the previous one issued. This, again, can be changed by you.

Originator Normally the name of the person who has authorised the purchase.

Deliver By A delivery date required by you. This will often be negotiated with the supplier.

The rest of this screen should be self-explanatory. When completing this screen you will be shown another screen requesting purchase details.

Stock Ref This will have to match a stock reference held in the stock file. When you enter a valid reference, the stock description will be entered to the order form automatically.

Quantity By entering the quantity required, the rest of the details will be calculated for you.

In order to keep the stock file and outstanding purchase orders updated properly, it is important to use the activity in stock movements that cancels outstanding orders. Exactly the same principle applies to keeping sales orders updated.

Exercise

As a conclusion to Stock Control, produce about a dozen purchase orders based on your supplier and stock information available and produce the following reports from option 3 of the main Stock Control menu:

(a)   Outstanding P/Orders Report.
(b)   Re-order Report.

Record some movements that record receipt of stock against some of your orders.

APPENDIX

Table 8.2 gives the item numbers to be used when designing purchase orders

G   A general line (done just once) and is followed by a number which indicates the number of blank lines to FOLLOW the information printed.

D   D is a detail line printed once for each detail. For example, in this chapter it is used to print a line for each item of stock to invoice the customer for. It is followed by a number which indicates the number of blank lines to FOLLOW the information printed.

Each format line starts with either a G or D.

Table 8.2

Item	Description	Source of Information
1-21	Narrative lines 1 to 21	Parameters
22	Company Name – Centred	Parameters
23-26	Company Address Line 1 to 4	Parameters
27-28	Telephone numbers 1 and 2	Parameters
29	Telex Number	Parameters
30	VAT Number	Parameters
31	Supplier Code	Keyed
32	Purchase Order Date	Keyed/Default
33	Order Number	Keyed
34	Originator	Keyed
35	Delivery Date	Keyed
36-41	Supplier's Address Lines 1 to 5	Keyed

Table 8.2 Continued

Item	Description	Source of Information
42-47	Delivery Instructions	Keyed
48-49	Narrative 1 and 2	Keyed
50	Purchase Order Total	Calculated
51	Stock reference	Keyed
52	Description	Keyed/File
53	Quantity	Keyed
54	Cost Price	Keyed/Stock File
55	Quantity x Price	Calculated
56	Supplier's Part Number	Keyed/Stock File
57	Unit Description	Stock File
98	Printer Enhance (Large Print) ON	Program
99	Printer Enhance (Large Print) OFF	Program

9 Payroll (Setting Up the System)

This lengthy section on Payroll is split into two chapters and deals with the whole process of running a payroll system, that is, paying people.

This is a long and demanding section that attempts to cover most practical aspects of running and maintaining such a system using the Pegasus package. In order to cover the topic properly, some explanation will be given about certain issues, such as the workings of PAYE. If you are already familiar with PAYE, this section can be read through speedily; otherwise you will find it well worth your while going through it slowly.

The chapter begins by defining the inputs that are required to run a Payroll system. Some effort is then made to explain how the parameters are set up – a major task in this module. Setting up parameters requires details about such things as: tax bands under PAYE, National Insurance rates, SSP and other stoppages. Also this section covers payslip design, cheque design, pay periods, salaried v. weekly paid staff.

Time is spent explaining how to maintain employee records and how they are used during payroll runs as well as supplying useful personnel details. The next chapter examines how a user can get the best out of a Payroll system in the form of enquiries, reports and automatic postings to the Nominal Ledger and, of course, producing a Payroll run.

THE NEED FOR COMPUTERISED PAYROLL

Payroll, as an application, was one of the earliest business tasks a computer was used for. Typically, many firms used, and still do, an outside agency (such as Computer Bureaux) to batch process a Payroll run on a weekly or monthly basis. A firm would send details of employees' work and sickness for each payment period along with details of any new employees and information on those employees leaving. After a short period of time the firm would receive back payment details for each employee. Even with an outside agency operating a company Payroll system, work is still required in order to get details to the agency. Such agencies are often well geared to a large variety of Payroll systems and can often offer a cheaper solution to the Payroll problem than a firm can achieve by running its own.

Firms with a large number of employees found that running a payroll was a long, time-consuming and expensive process. Firms who pay staff on a weekly basis will often employ one or more staff simply to operate a Payroll system. Paying all staff on a monthly basis will reduce the cost of operating a Payroll system.

The essence of Payroll is to pay staff a wage or salary in much the same way as paying for any other commodity or service. In fact, wages and salaries are treated as an expense to the firm and, as with any other business expense, will appear within the Nominal Ledger accordingly. In terms of the Nominal Ledger, such details will often appear in a number of accounts such as: directors' salaries, office salaries, maintenance staff wages, factory staff wages, and so on. For each group of staff, it is normal practice to keep a separate set of data and process each set one at a time – a point that will be returned to.

Computerising Payroll can, without doubt, save a vast amount of processing time and improve the efficiency by which salaries and wages are paid, controlled and monitored. The amount of time saved as a result of computerisation will, in general, increase as the size of the Payroll increases. For example, a firm with a complex pay and staff structure employing over 1,000 staff can expect a big saving in time and cost by computerising Payroll, whereas a small firm employing only 5 staff on a straightforward salary basis can expect little, if any, saving in time and cost. Consequently, the costs and benefits to a firm computerising Payroll will vary from firm to firm, and is not simply measured by the size of its Payroll.

One thing which affects the extent to which a computerised payroll system benefits a firm is the way it is set up and the efficiency with which it is run. A good deal of this is dependent upon how the parameters are set up in order to match the computerised Payroll to the firm's needs.

SETTING UP THE PARAMETERS

As in previous chapters, nothing can be done until these have been set. Setting up these parameters should be a 'one-off' job with only minor alterations being required in the future. Consequently, time and care should be taken at this stage. From the Payroll menu you will see the following menu options on your screen:

Payroll	
1	Payroll Processing
2	Calculation
3	Payroll Reports
4	Departmental Analysis
5	Nominal Analysis
6	Payroll Update
7	Parameter Update
8	Special Update
9	Special Reports
R	Report Generator

At this stage, it is worth examining the structure of the Payroll function illustrated in Figure 9.1.

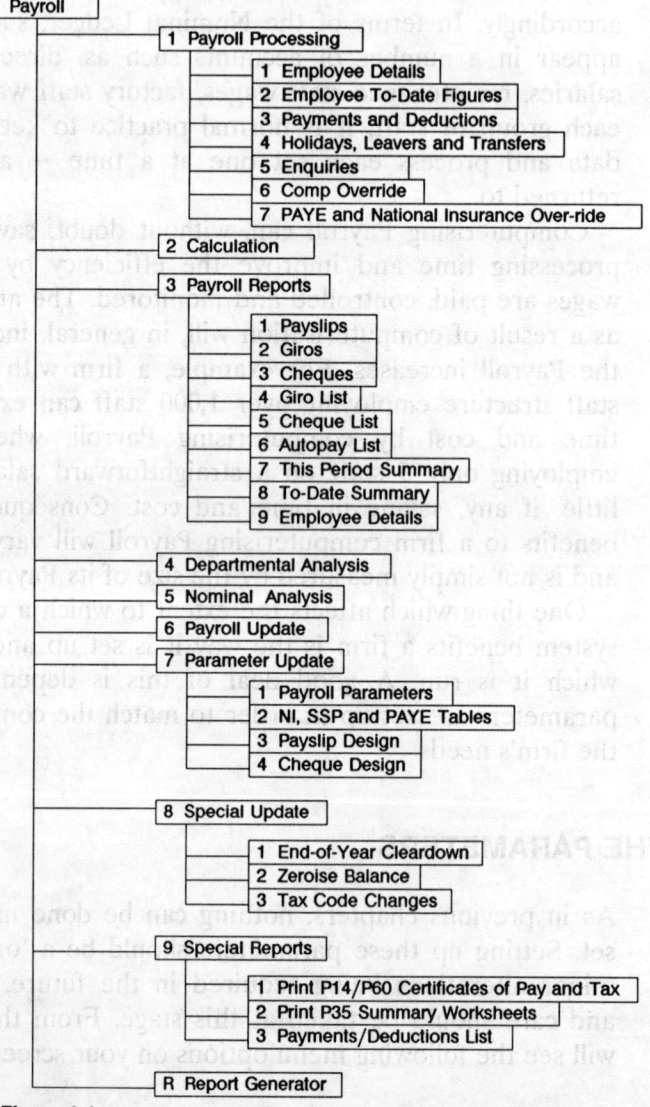

Payroll

1 Payroll Processing
  1 Employee Details
  2 Employee To-Date Figures
  3 Payments and Deductions
  4 Holidays, Leavers and Transfers
  5 Enquiries
  6 Comp Override
  7 PAYE and National Insurance Over-ride

2 Calculation

3 Payroll Reports
  1 Payslips
  2 Giros
  3 Cheques
  4 Giro List
  5 Cheque List
  6 Autopay List
  7 This Period Summary
  8 To-Date Summary
  9 Employee Details

4 Departmental Analysis

5 Nominal Analysis

6 Payroll Update

7 Parameter Update
  1 Payroll Parameters
  2 NI, SSP and PAYE Tables
  3 Payslip Design
  4 Cheque Design

8 Special Update
  1 End-of-Year Cleardown
  2 Zeroise Balance
  3 Tax Code Changes

9 Special Reports
  1 Print P14/P60 Certificates of Pay and Tax
  2 Print P35 Summary Worksheets
  3 Payments/Deductions List

R Report Generator

Figure 9.1

This chapter and the next will attempt to cover ALL Payroll options but it is worth spending time and effort on option 7 from this menu, '**parameter update**'. You will be asked if this is to be a new file (Enter 'Y' or 'N'). If you are attempting this for the first time you will probably enter 'Y' in response to this. If you are amending an existing set of parameters, then make sure the existing data is mounted on your system and enter 'N'.

You will be required to enter a password in the usual way, after which the following menu will appear:

1	**Payroll Parameters**
2	**NI, SSP & PAYE Tables**
3	**Payslip Design**
4	**Cheque Design**
0	**Terminate**

Each of these will be covered in the above sequence, and ALL will be required.

1 Payroll Parameters

The following payroll parameters have been set up to illustrate how they are set up and used, with explanations.

Payroll Parameters – { Date }

Company	Name	Pegasus User Enterprise
	Address Line 1	100 High Street
	Address Line 2	Newtown
	Address Line 3	Wessex
	Address Line 4	

The above details are required when printing payslips and statements, as will become apparent later.

Bank	Name	National Wessex plc
	Branch	Newtown
	Sort Code	00-01-99

The bank details will be needed if paying employees by cheque, or direct into an employee's account through the autopay method.

PAYE	Reference	223 P 9999
	Tax District	Wessex

This information is required by all employers and is obtainable from the local Department of Social Security office.

Printer	Type	0	These parameters are
	TOF Code	12	the same as in previous
	Columns	80	chapters for defining our
	Lines/Page	66	printer details

A list of options appear from 1 to 7.

Option No. 1   Y

This instructs the system to integrate with the Nominal Ledger system.

Option No. 2

This option allows you to enter a '1' which will instruct the system to calculate tax on the gross pay after national insurance contribution has been deducted and to change the coinage analysis to cater for dollars and cents in units of 1, 2, 5, 10, 25 and 50 cents, and 5, 20, and 100 dollar bills. Net pay rounding (pence) will be changed to net pay rounding (cents). This option has application for West Indian payrolls.

Option No. 3

If you wish to operate a contracted-out money purchase (comp) pension scheme, this option should be set to 'Y'.

Option No. 4

This option is not in use at the present time.

Option No. 5

If you wish to use the password that you enter for access to the parametres in other areas of the payroll module, enter a 'Y' here. When items are selected from the Payroll menu, the user will be prompted for entry of the password before being allowed to proceed.

The following nominal codes are for integrating the Payroll with the nominal system. The idea is that when the nominal analysis routine is activated, pay details are posted to the account codes indicated.

Nominal code N.I.'ERS Cost   **NI01**

Employer's National Insurance Contribution which is accumulated on the Nominal Ledger and, as implied, is paid by the employer. The amount has to be settled at the end of the financial year with the Department of Social Security.

N.I.'ERS+'EES   **NI02**

This National Insurance is deducted from the employee's pay and will have to be paid to the Department of Social Security.

P.A.Y.E.   **PAYE**

This is income tax (under Pay As You Earn) deducted from the employees' pay and will have to be paid to the Inland Revenue.

Wages Control   **W111**

This will be used to hold the total net pay made to employees in the current pay period. Having been made as a DEBIT entry to this account, the system will also make the required CREDIT entry on the bank account.

Comp 'ers Cost

Enter the account code for which the value of the employer's comp contributions will be accumulated on the Nominal Ledger to year end.

Comp 'ers and 'ees

Enter the account code for which the value of the employer's and the employee's comp contributions will be accumulated on the Nominal Ledger to year end.

Not Used   **0000**

This field is not used at the present time.

Wages Suspense   **W110**

It is important to note that all codes indicated above must have account headers with these same codes in the Nominal Ledger. This was something that was encountered when first setting up the Nominal Ledger. Getting this accurate can be a big time-saver. The actual header names can be made to reflect more precisely what is being held in them.

Pay Period   (W,2,4,M)   **M**

Pay periods can be set as 'W' for weekly, '2' for fortnightly, '4' for 4 weekly and 'M' for monthly. It is worth noting at this point that each differing group of paid staff must have separate sets of data.

Hours Decimal or Minutes   **M**

Hours can be expressed either as 42.5 (42-and-a-half hours) or as 42 hours 30 minutes.

Coinage Largest Note   **20**

This indicates that the largest note to be issued is that of £20.

Minimum One Pound Coins   5

This sets the number of £1 coins issued to a minimum of 5, guaranteeing employees a certain amount of small change.

Net Pay Rounding (Pence)   10

Wages are rounded to the nearest 10p.

Scheme Contracted-Out Number

Under new regulations, employees can opt out of the state pension scheme whereby they contribute a proportion of their salary or wage to invest in a future pension. Instead they can use a private scheme. If employees have opted out, then a 9-figure contracted out number issued by the Department of Social Security should be issued here.

No. of Payments for Hol Pay

If you require holiday entitlement to be calculated as a percentage of gross pay, you may use this option to tell the system which pay entitlements are to be used in calculating this figure. For example, if you have called your first payment type BASIC and you wish your employees' holiday credits to be calculated as a percentage of this payment type only, you should enter '1' for this option.

Company Code for Nominal

This allows you to enter the company identifier of the Nominal Ledger to which Payroll information is to be transferred.

Number of SSP Weeks

Enter the maximum number of weeks currently in force for which statutory sick pay may be paid.

	Payment	Tax	Nominal		Deduction	Bal	Nominal
1	:GROSS	:T:	:W101:	1	:PENSION	:P:	:W201:
2	:O/TIME 1.5	:T:	:W112:	2	:	: :	:
3	:O/TIME 2.0	:T:	:W113:	3	:INSURANCES	: :	:W202:
4	:O/TIME 3.0	:T:	:W114:	4	:CAR LOAN	:R:	:W203:
5	:	: :	:	5	:HEALTH INS	: :	:W204:
6	:BONUS	:T:	:W115:	6	:CHARITY	:N:	:W205:
7	:	: :	:	7	:	: :	:
8	:MORT/SUBS	:T:	:W116:	8	:UNION SUB	: :	:W206:
9	:COMMISSION	:T:	:W117:	9	:	: :	:
10	:EXPENSES	:T:	:W118:	10	:S.A.Y.E.	:A:	:W207:
11	:	: :	:	11	:	: :	:
12	:S.S.P.	:S:	:W119:	12	:	: :	:
13	:	: :	:	13	:	: :	:

Figure 9.2

The remaining page, shown in Figure 9.2, lists all payments and deductions that are to be made on employees' payslips in addition to the standard ones that appeared above. With the list must also appear the nominal code to which postings are to be made. The idea is that when the nominal analysis routine is activated, ALL pay details are posted to the account codes indicated below in exactly the same way as for those above.

As can be seen, up to 17 additional payments and 17 deductions can be made, easily sufficient for the vast majority of Payroll systems.

On the payments side there appears a tax code which indicates the status of the payment made to an employee in terms of taxation. The codes are:

N   When payment is NOT TAXABLE.
T   When payment is TAXABLE.
S   If the payment is for STATUTORY SICK PAY (SSP).
H   If the payment is for HOLIDAY PAY which conforms to the rules set down for the construction industry. Under this system holiday pay is taxable like other income, but no National Insurance is paid on it, by either employer or employee.

On the deductions side, employers will deduct pay from employees for differing purposes, all of which will either be passed on to some other body or used for a specific purpose. The 'bal' column is required to enter any special code (if required) for handling such deductions in terms of taxation, pension or some other special requirement.

P   If the deduction is for the employee to contribute to a pension fund (a way of saving for a future pension).
X   Here a deduction for a pension contribution is to be made on a proportion of gross pay AFTER deducting the lower earnings limit.
N   Deduction is taken from gross pay BEFORE income tax and National Insurance is calculated. Some schemes where employees pay a regular sum to certain charities qualify for this treatment.
R   Here the deduction is to be used to reduce a designated balance. Such a scheme would be typical if a company made a loan or advanced a mortgage to an employee.
A   Here the deduction has an accumulating effect on a balance. An example of this would be a scheme where an employee paid into a company saving scheme for extra holiday pay.

H This has the same effect as 'A' and is used to accumulate holiday pay. The difference is that no money is actually stopped from the employee's pay. The result of this is to build up a number of paid holiday days to an employee.

In conclusion to this section, it may often be the case that a different set of parameters is set up for each group of employees within a firm. The easiest way of achieving this is for each group of employees to have a different company identifier (which appears at the beginning of the program when first loaded). It will become clear later that even with different company identifiers for the Payroll groups, all groups can still have relevant totals posted to the same Nominal Ledger system.

2 NI, SSP & PAYE Tables

NI   = National Insurance
SSP   = Statutory Sick Pay
PAYE = Pay As You Earn

The tables in this section are set up to replace tables that are supplied by the Inland Revenue and Department of Social Security. In order to get these correct on a 'live' payroll system, it is essential that up-to-date figures are acquired from these offices. It is also important to note that the figures will often change, usually once a year following the Chancellor of the Exchequer's annual Budget. Again, in a practical situation, information must be sought from the respective offices as to what the changes are and the time in the year when any changes should be implemented. The person(s) responsible for managing the Payroll will often also be responsible for this.

From the parameters menu, choosing the option NI, SSP & PAYE Tables will reveal a table that needs to be completed that sets out the National Insurance rates payable by both employer and employee. Figure 9.3 is an example of the figures that could be entered. It is important to note that they are not designed to reflect the current rates but to offer an illustration to help you understand how the system works.

An understanding of how National Insurance works will enable an operator to make changes as they are required in just a few minutes and avoid the cost of employing someone to come in and make the required alterations.

National Insurance is paid by both employer AND employee, not always equal in size. Both employer and employee contributions must be passed on to the Department of Social Security.

NI, SSP & PAYE Tables – 27 Feb 90									
National Insurance									
Limits Earnings Below				Employers		Employees			
L = U =	LEL UEL	Weekly	Monthly	Non-C/O	C/Out	Non-C/Out		C/Out	
						Std	Reduced	Std	Reduced
				A TO E	D, E	A	B	D	E
1	L	39.00	169.00						
2		65.00	282.00	5.00	3.50	5.00	3.85	3.50	3.85
3		100.00	434.00	7.00	5.00	7.00	3.85	5.00	3.85
4		150.00	650.00	9.00	6.50	9.00	3.85	6.50	3.85
5	U	295.00	1279.00	10.45	7.50	9.00	3.85	6.50	3.85
6				10.45	7.50	9.00	3.85	6.50	3.85
7									
8									
9									
10									
UEL on Employers – N									

Figure 9.3

If a firm has an occupational pension scheme that satisfies certain conditions set down by the Department of Social Security, then the employer can contract their employees out of part of the state scheme, thereby reducing the amounts paid by both employer and employee. It is important that firms do not contract their employees out until they receive a certificate from the **Occupational Pensions Board**.

In calculating the National Insurance contributions for both employer and employee whether contracted out or not is a complicated business that, in a manual system, requires a set of tables issued by the Department of Social Security. In the example there are up to 10 **bands** available, of which 6 have been used. In the first column there is an **L** in row 1 and a **U** in row 5 indicating where the Lower limit starts and the Upper limit ends for employee contributions.

The extract below shows that, from row 1, if an employee earns less than £39 per week (or £169 per month) then NO National Insurance is paid by either employer or employee.

Limits Earnings Below			Employers		Employees			
LEL UEL	Weekly	Monthly	Non-C/O	C/Out	Non-C/Out Std Reduced		C/Out Std Reduced	
			A TO E	D,E	A	B	D	E
1 L	39.00	169.00						

Row 2 shows that if an employee earns less than £65 in a week (or £282 in a month) then the following applies:

2	65.00	282.00	5.00	2.85	5.00	3.85	2.85	3.85

The employer pays:

(a) If NOT CONTRACTED out 5% of the gross employee income as National Insurance.

(b) If CONTRACTED OUT then 5% of the first £39 (i.e. £1.95) plus 2.85% of the remainder of this income.

In the case of the employee, the same amount is paid, and stopped from their wages as that of the employer, unless the employee is on the reduced rate of National Insurance (which must be supported by a declaration from the Department of Social Security), in which case 3.85% of income is paid.

I shall now show three worked examples to illustrate how the system works.

NI Example 1 : An employee earns £130 in one week and is not contracted out.

From the table he earns a level on **row 4** which shows that the employer contribution is 9%.
This amounts to £11.70 (£130 × 9/100).
The employee contribution is also 9%, and they too must pay £11.70.
Hence, a total of £23.40 is paid to the Department of Social Security in respect of this employee for the week.

NI Example 2 : An employee earns £890 in one month and is contracted out.

From the table he earns a level on **row 5** which shows that the employer contribution is 6.5% for contracted-out National Insurance. This amounts to £57.85 (£890 × 6.5/100).
The employee contribution is also 6.5%, and they too must pay £57.85.
Hence, a total of £115.70 is to be paid to the Department of Social Security in respect of this employee for the month.

N.I. Example 3 : An employee earns £1400 in one month and is NOT contracted out and pays National Insurance at the lower rate.

From the table he earns a level on **row 6** which shows that the employer contribution is 10.45% for non-contracted-out National Insurance and has to be based on ALL income under the National Insurance Contribution rules. This amounts to £146.30 (£1400 × 10.45/100).

Meanwhile, the employee pays 9% on £1279 only, which again conforms to the National Insurance Contribution rules. This amounts to £114.75.

The total contribution to be paid on this employee now amounts to £261.05 (£146.30 + £114.75) which is passed on to the Department of Social Security.

Although there is no need to be fully aware of how to calculate National Insurance contributions in order to operate a Payroll system, a reasonable understanding of the principles involved will assist you in being able to maintain the tables properly. The number work in arriving at these figures will, of course, be done by the computer. When a firm has (say) 500 employees all being paid different wages, it is not difficult to see that determining the National Insurance Contributions for both employer and employee can be a mammoth task if done manually, even though tables are available to take the 'number-crunching' work away. Once the tables are set up, no working out of the contributions is required by the operator.

Some exercises exist at the end of this chapter for you to have a go at if you are interested in mastering this.

PAYE					SSP	
	Rate %	Cumulative Bandwidth	Rate %	Cumulative Bandwidth	Rate	Range
1	25.00	20000	11			40.00
2	40.00		12		35.00	60.00
3			13		45.00	80.00
4			14		60.00	
5			15			
6			16			
7			17			
8			18			
9			19			
10			20			
Base Rate 1						

Figure 9.4

The second table in this section covers both PAYE and SSP. Figure 9.4 is again designed to help you understand how the system works and is not designed to reflect the current rates but to offer an illustration.

PAYE : From the figure it can be seen that only two rates of PAYE exist (25% and 40%). Each employee will receive from the Inland Revenue a tax code. Such a code determines an employee's tax allowance, an amount that can be earned in one complete financial year before any income tax has to be paid.

All tax codes are numbers followed by one letter. Only the number part is of concern to us. If an employee is issued with the code 300H, then his or her tax allowance becomes £3,000 (in other words it is the number part times £10). This means that if this person earns less than this amount over a complete financial year, they will pay no income tax.

Under PAYE, the employer is required to collect income tax from their employees and pass this on to the Inland Revenue. Equipped with each employee's tax code and the PAYE table set up in the parameters, the computer will have enough information to calculate income tax to be paid by an employee. In practice, it will not be known exactly how much an employee will earn in any financial year until it has been completed. Rather than an employee settling his or her tax bill at the end of the financial year (as is the case in some countries), they will be required to pay income tax as they earn it, if working for an employer (i.e. not self-employed).

I will explain how PAYE works by offering three worked examples.

PAYE Example 1 : An employee earns £130 in one week and has an income tax code of 400H.

From the tax code it can be seen that the annual tax allowance is £4,000. Because we are to pay the employee on a weekly basis this figure must be converted to a weekly allowance; i.e. £4,000 divided by 52, which equals £76.92.

If he earns £130 and has an allowance of £76.92, it means he has earned £53.08 over this allowance. It is this figure that will be taxed.

From the PAYE table it can be assumed that the tax bandwidth of £20,000 means that if the employee earns less than £20,000 in one year, then any **taxable income** will be taxed at 25%. Anything over this is taxed at 40%. £20,000 over one year is equal to £384.62 in one week (£20,000 divided by 52).

In our example, the employee earns £130, well below £384.62 that would take the income into the next tax bandwidth). From this, the taxable income was found to be £53.08 which is taxed at 25%; total income tax to be stopped is £13.27 (25% of £53.08).

PAYE Example 2 : An employee earns £400 in one week and has an income tax code of 520H.

From the tax code it can be seen that the annual tax allowance is £5,200. Because we are to pay the employee on a weekly basis this figure must be converted to a weekly allowance; i.e. £5,200 divided by 52 which equals £100 (rather convenient!!).

If he earns £400 and has an allowance of £100, it means he has earned £300 over this allowance. It is this figure that will be taxed.

In our example, the employee earns ABOVE the £384.62, taking a part of the income into the next tax bandwidth. As £400 was actually earned, it can be seen that £15.38 over the bandwidth has now been earned. The total tax due is calculated as shown in Table 9.1.

Table 9.1

WAGE	TAX RATE	TAX
£100.00	NO TAX	£00.00
£284.62	@ 25%	£71.15
£ 15.38	@ 40%	£ 6.15
TOTAL £400.00		£77.30

The employee will have £77.30 of their income stopped for income tax. **Please note that when an employee earns an amount over the tax band of 25%, not all of it is taxed at 40%.**

PAYE Example 3 : An employee earns £1,400 in one month and has a tax code of 360H.

From the tax code it can be seen that the annual tax allowance is £3,600. Because we are to pay the employee on a MONTHLY basis this figure must be converted to a MONTHLY allowance, i.e. £3,600 divided by 12, which equals £300.

If he earns £1,400 and has an allowance of £300, it means he has earned £1,100 over this allowance for this month. It is this figure that will be taxed.

From the PAYE table it can be seen that the tax bandwidth of £20,000 means that if the employee earns less than £20,000 in one year, then any **taxable income** will be taxed at 25%. This works out as £1,667 in any month. Anything over this is taxed at 40%.

As the amount earned is below the top tax band, the tax due is

25% of £1,100. That is, £275 (25% of £1,100).

SSP : This allows employees the right to Statutory Sick Pay while they are not at work, which can be 'topped up' by private insurance schemes with the company. As the title suggests, Statutory Sick Pay sets a minimum. Under the rules of SSP, there is a limit to the amount of days sickness permitted, which should be checked with the Department of Social Security.

Table 9.2

	SSP	
Rate	Range	
	40.00	
35.00	60.00	
45.00	80.00	
60.00		

From Table 9.2 we can determine that:

(a) An employee earning less than £40 weekly equivalent will receive NO SSP.

(b) An employee earning less than £60 but more than £40 weekly equivalent will receive £35 per week of SSP.

(c) An employee earning less than £80 but more than £60 weekly equivalent will receive £45 per week of SSP.

(d) An employee earning more than £80 weekly equivalent will receive £60 per week of SSP.

Any SSP made by an employer can be claimed back from the Department of Social Security and is normally deducted from the National Insurance Contributions passed on by the employer.

3 Payslip Design

We now move on to designing the payslip. The principle of this works in exactly the same way within Pegasus as designing invoices and order forms as covered in previous chapters. If you mastered it at that stage, you will find this section relatively straightforward.

As before, this may be a tedious and long job requiring a good deal of time and patience in order to get a payslip design that is both suitable to the firm's Payroll and that matches any pre-printed stationery that may have been produced for the Payroll. However, once done, it should last for some time.

Payslip Design – 27 Feb 90	Payslip Format Lines
Narratives	G2: 21/22:
	G1: 1/1 : 30/27
1 Employee Name	G0: 1/2 : 30/25:
2 Payroll Number	G0: 1/3 : 30/28:
3 Personal Tax Code	G0: 1/4 : 30/31:
4 National Insurance Number	G0: 1/5 : 30/30:
5 National Insurance Rate	G2: 1/6 : 30/32:
6 Bank Code	G0: 1/7 :
7 Payment Details for this period	G1: 1/8 : 25/27: 40/58: 53/59:
8 Hours Worked/Rate/Value	G1: 1/9 : 30/38:
9 Total Payments this period	G0: 1/10:
10 Deduction details this period	G2: 1/11: 21/60: 45/61:
11 Description/Value	G1: 1/12: 40/55:
12 Total deductions (Exc. NI & PAYE)	G1: 1/13: 40/40:
13 Tax this period	G0: 1/14: 40/42:
14 Nat Ins this pay (employee contr')	G0: 1/15: 40/54:
15 TOTAL DEDUCTIONS	G0: 1/16: 40/41:
16 NET PAY THIS PERIOD	G0: 1/17: 40/50: 55/36:
17 Gross Taxable Pay to Date/Tax to Date	G0: 1/18: 40/46:
18 Nat Ins paid to date	:
19	

Figure 9.5   **Figure 9.6**

There are two screens that need to be completed for this section. The first screen, **Narratives**, states what text you want to appear on the payslip and the second screen, **Payslip Format Lines**, states where such text should appear on a payslip and where employee, pay and stoppage details should appear.

Figure 9.5 is an example of the Narratives that would appear on a payslip. While filling in this screen it is not important at this stage to indicate WHERE on the payslip the text is to appear.

The payslip format lines in Figure 9.6 concentrate on WHAT appears on a payslip and WHERE on the payslip it is to appear.

Before explaining in some detail what these payslip format lines will do, it is worth stating the **sources of information** where the payroll system must get its information from in order to produce a payslip:

1 **Company Parameters** In the payslip parameters (from option 1 of the Payroll parameter update) we identified the company name which is to appear on payslips.

2 **Payslip Parameters** This contains the narratives that will appear on the payslips.

3 **Keyboard** When running the payroll, the operator will be required to enter information during the processing of the payroll, some of which can appear on the payslips.

4 **Personal Employee Records** The Payroll system maintains personal records on each employee. These records will have to be maintained by the operator and the Payroll system and is a major topic to be covered in the next chapter.

5 **Transaction File** A file containing details for this pay period such as, payment hours, payment rate and deduction value. Again, this will be covered in the next chapter.

6 **Computer Calculations** Some figures such as total deductions will be calculated by the program during processing.

In order to produce the payslip format lines, you will need to consult the appendix at the end of this chapter to enter the correct codes that are used to:

(a) Determine the line spacing on the payslip.
(b) Identify the SOURCE of information.
(c) Determine where on a line information should appear on the payslip.

From the format lines earlier, the following explains what they do:

Line	Contents		Purpose
1	G2: 21/22:	G2 –	Prints 2 blank lines between this line and the next.
		21/22 –	Prints code 22 (which is the company name) at position 21 on the line.
2	G1: 1/1 :30/27:	G1 –	Prints 1 blank line between this line and the next.
		1/1 –	Prints Line 1 of the narrative at position 1. Line 1 of the narrative is 'employee name'.
		30/27 –	Prints code 27 (which is the employee name to be found in their personal record) at position 30 on the line.
3	G0: 1/2 :30/25:	G0 –	Prints NO blank line between this line and the next.
		1/2 –	Prints line 2 of the narrative at position 1. Line 2 of the narrative is 'payroll number'.
		30/25 –	Prints code 25 (which is the employee number to be found in their personal record) at position 30 on the line.

4   G0: 1/3 : 30/28:   G0 –   Prints NO blank line between this line and the next.

                                   1/3 –   Prints line 3 of the narrative at position 1. Line 3 of the narrative is 'personal tax code'.

                             30/28 –   Prints code 28 (which is the tax code of the employee to be found in their personal record) at position 30 on the line.

5   G0: 1/4 :30/31:   G0 –   Prints NO blank line between this line and the next.

                                   1/4 –   Prints line 4 of the narrative at position 1. Line 4 of the narrative is 'National Insurance Number'.

                             30/31 –   Prints code 31 (which is the employee National Insurance Number to be found in their personal record) at position 30 on the line.

Study the codes in the manual against what has been done for the remaining format lines and it should become clear how the system works. From these parameters appears the payslip shown in Figure 9.7.

```
Employee Name                    *********************************

Payroll Number            X999
Personal Tax Code         9999X
National Insurance Number XX-99-99-99-X
National Insurance Rate   *
Bank Code                 CHEQUE


Payment Details for this period
Hours Worked/Rate/Value ****************        99.9999        9999.99

Total Payments this period      9999.99

Deduction details this period
Description/Value *************                 9999.99


Total deductions (Exc. NI & PAYE)              9999.99

Tax this period                                9999.99 R

Nat Ins this pay (employee contr')             999.99
TOTAL DEDUCTIONS                               9999.99
NET PAY THIS PERIOD                            9999.99
Gross Taxable Pay to Date/Tax to Date          99999.99       99999.99
Nat Ins paid to date                           9999.99
```

Figure 9.7

When writing the parameters, narratives and format lines within the Pegasus system DO NOT press the **ESC** key unless you want to abandon the parameters altogether.

4 Cheque Design

This final part of setting up the parameters file works in much the same way as that for designing payslips. It allows a firm the option of printing cheques to its employees automatically, that is, using special stationery.

Set up carefully, this can also be a major labour-saving facility. As before, a good deal of trial and error may be required in order to get the information in exactly the right place on the cheques.

All cheques will be on pre-printed stationery which has to be arranged between the firm and their bank or the Post Office if printing Girocheques. Consequently, most information will already appear on the cheque, leaving just the date, payee, and amount left. The settings in Figure 9.8 are an example of parameter settings.

```
Cheque Design – 27 Feb 90

Cheque   Format  Details          – Lines/Chqe    20
         Date    Position         – Line/Col     3/30
         Payee   Position         – Line/Col      7/ 5
         Amnt    Position         – Line/Col    10/35
         10000   Position         – Line/Col    12/ 5
         1000    Position         – Line/Col    12/15
         100     Position         – Line/Col    12/25
         10      Position         – Line/Col    12/35
         1       Position         – Line/Col    13/ 5
         Upper Cheque Limit                     2500
```

Figure 9.8

CREATING EMPLOYEE RECORDS

The next step in setting up a Payroll is to enter, for each employee, a record of their details. As mentioned earlier, it may well be the case that there are a number of groups of employees on the system requiring, for each group, a separate set of parameters and set of employees. In other words, the whole of this process must be done for each set of employees.

Setting up new employees can be done from the Payroll menu option 1, **payroll processing**. From here another menu will appear in which option 1, **employee details**, will be used to create an employee record and option 2, **employee-to-date** figures, will be used to enter all payments and deductions to date, which may not be required if an employee is new to the firm and has no information on payments and receipts to date available.

Employee details

From this option, you will have to complete a form for each employee that is to appear on the Payroll. The details required, with explanation, are:

Employee Each employee must have a **unique** number by which the computer can identify their record. The first character of the number will normally be used to identify the classification of employee or the department they work in. For example, in a department store M091 may signify that the employee works in the men's clothing department, while P002 signifies the employee works in the pharmaceutical department. Clearly, such coding has to be decided by the firm in question. The important thing at this stage is to ensure that no two employees in this part of the Payroll have the same code.

Code This is to be a numeric analysis code which will be used at a later stage for departmental, or cost centre, analysis. Basically all employees working with a certain department or cost centre will receive the same code. The effect of this will be examined later.

Name Using first name first followed by surname, we enter the employee's name; e.g. Mr Fred Bloggs is valid, while Bloggs Fred is not (it causes problems in printing tax documents for the employee at a later stage).

Sex Either 'M' or 'F'.

Birth Date The date of birth is used to allow the system to warn us of such instances where staff are reaching retirement age or approaching 18.

Cost Centre This can be left blank, but is used to categorise staff into their respective cost centres. This may be of special use when attempting to cost certain jobs in (say) the construction industry.

Tax Code This will appear on an employee's **P45** and indicates their tax allowance. The code is in the form of a number suffixed with a letter normally **H, L, P, T or U**. If a code is not available, then an emergency code is supplied by the Inland Revenue which must be used until the employee produces a P45 indicating this code or the firm is notified by the Inland Revenue.

WK/MTH1 If an employee is to be taxed on a weekly or monthly basis then 'Y' is entered, otherwise 'N' is entered. In most situations where employees are permanent members of staff this will be 'N'.

N.I. Rate Normally A, B, C, D or E, which will have an effect on the National Insurance charged on employees and employer. Each employee must supply a National Insurance number where this is indicated. A further code of 'X' is available that exempts certain employees from paying National Insurance, such as some construction workers who make their own arrangements.

N.I. No. Each employee must supply a National Insurance number. If one is not supplied, then it must take the following format:

TN221066M   where the 221066 is the employee's date of birth (22nd Oct, 1966 in this example).

Pay Method This will be one of the following:

C   Employee to be paid by **CASH**.
Q   Employee to be paid by **CHEQUE**.
A   Employee to be paid by **AUTOPAY**.
G   Employee to be paid by **GIRO**.

Autopay is where the employee is to be paid direct from the firm's bank account into the employee's.

SSP Qual Days Basically, this defines the number of days in a working week for the purpose of determining the SSP entitlement. If left blank, 5 days is assumed.

Previous Gross For employees joining the firm part the way through the tax year, we must enter the accumulated gross earned prior to working for the firm and since the start of the financial year. The figure here must also appear in the figures to date, covered in the next section of this chapter.

Previous Tax For employees joining the firm part the way through the tax year, we must enter the accumulated tax paid prior to working for the firm and since the start of the financial year. The figure here must also appear in the figures to date, covered in the next section of this chapter.

Bank Details If the payment method is by giro, cheque or autopay, then details of the employee's bank account must be inserted here. This covers **bank name**, **branch**, **payee name** (as would appear on their cheque), **bank sort code** and **account number**.

Autopay If the employee is being paid by autopay, then the bank will advise the firm on this code which is then entered here.

Exercise

At this point, have a go at creating some employee records using as many of the facilities as possible. Creating about 12 employees will be enough to supply some useful test data for the next chapter, as well as serving the purpose of helping you to get to grips with creating employee records.

Once the records have been created, amendments to them can be made at any time by using the same option and entering an existing employee number in the appropriate box.

Figure 9.9 represents just two examples of employee records generated and was obtained by using option 5, **Enquiries**, which is in the Payroll Processing menu where the records were first created.

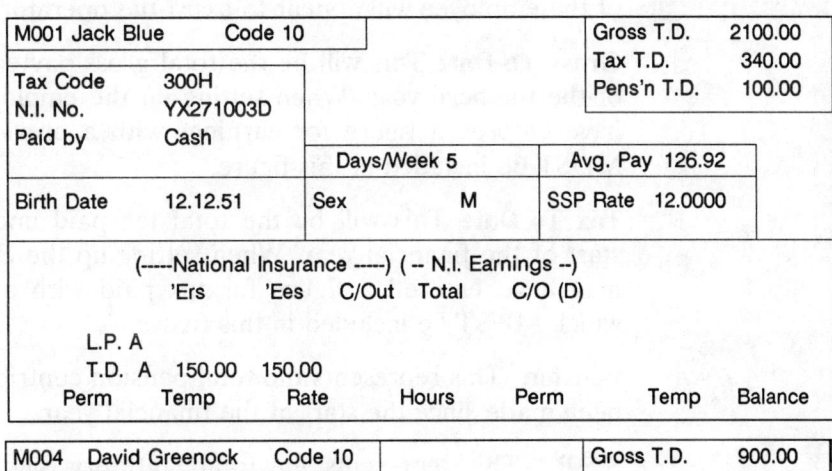

Figure 9.9

The final stage in the initial setting up of the payroll in this chapter is to enter the **to-date** figures for each employee. The requirement for this is when an employee starts part of the way into the financial year, we are required to enter all earnings received, payments made and amounts received since the start of the financial year. This will also be required for every employee within the firm if we are setting up the Pegasus system for the first time. If a firm is nearing the end of a financial year, then it may well be prudent to set up the system in preparation for the next financial year, but carry on using the manual system until the start of the financial year. Doing this may also offer the possibility of a practice run before starting the computerised payroll system.

Placing employee to-date figures can be found in option 2 of the payroll processing. When running this, the screen displays a form with the following information required:

Employee As mentioned earlier, this is the only way of accessing any specific employee record. When a valid number is picked, the name of the employee will appear to assist the operator.

Gross To-Date This will be the total gross pay earned since the start of the financial year. When setting up the employee record, you may have entered a figure for earnings with a previous employer, which MUST be included in this figure.

Tax To-Date This will be the total tax paid under PAYE since the start of the financial year. When setting up the employee record, you may have entered a figure for tax paid with a previous employer, which MUST be included in this figure.

Pension This represents the total pension contribution that may have been made since the start of the financial year.

S.S.P. This represents the total Statutory Sick Pay that may have been paid out to the employee since the start of the financial year.

SMP This applies to women who have been on Maternity Pay.

S.S.P. Days This represents the total number of SSP days actually paid since the start of the financial year.

Round B/F If the system were set up to round the amount of net pay to employees to (say) the nearest £1, then the amount either lost or gained will be carried forward to the next pay period. If an amount is still to be carried forward from the previous pay period, then this amount should be entered here.

N.I. To-Date The amount of National Insurance paid to date should be entered here along with the employee code at which this was paid.

Previous Pay If employees are paid weekly then the last 8 weeks' gross pay is required. If paid monthly, then the last 2 months' gross pay is required.

The reason for requiring this is for the purpose of calculating Statutory Sick Pay (SSP). When calculating SSP, the system has to find the average pay for the last 8 weeks of employment. This forms the basis under which SSP is paid and can be found from the SSP table in the payroll parameters set earlier in this chapter.

In fact, if Pegasus is being used for the first time at the beginning of the financial year, then this is the only set of data required on each employee in order to run the Payroll (In other words, this is a compulsory need when creating a new employee record.)

Exercise

At this point, complete a set of employee to-date figures for the employees generated when you used the employee details option. From this produce from the enquiries activity, records of all employees.

From observation, it should become clear that the records now offer a fuller account of the employees with the to-date figures now added; records that will become even fuller as we progress through the next chapter of the book.

Exercises

If you feel unsure about NI, PAYE and SSP, then have a go at the following exercises which involve you trying to arrive at the answers that appear in brackets at the end of each question.

Question 1

An employee earns £188 in one week, has a tax code of 300L and is not contracted out under National Insurance. Using the tables defined in this chapter calculate the amount of PAYE income tax due and National Insurance due by both employer and employee. [PAYE = £32.58 ; Employer NI = £19.65; Employee NI = £16.92]

Question 2

An employee earns £2188 in one month, has a tax code of 336L and is contracted out under National Insurance. Using the tables defined in this chapter calculate the amount of PAYE income tax due and National Insurance due by both employer and employee. [PAYE = £555.20 ; Employer NI = £164.10 ; Employee NI = £95.93]

Question 3

An employee has earned the following sums of money in the past 8 weeks; £88, £78, £89, £80, £90, £20, £70 and £85. On the 9th week he goes ill for the whole week, missing out 5 working days. Determine the amount of SSP to be received. [SSP = £45.00]

APPENDIX

Table 9.3 Codes required for payslip formats

Item	Description	Source
1-21	Narrative lines 1 to 21	Payslip Parameters
22	Company Name	Company Parameters
23	Tax Period Number	Company Parameters
24	Date	Keyed
25	Employee Number	Personal Record
26	Employee Analysis Code	Personal Record
27	Employee Name	Personal Record
28	Tax Code	Personal Record
29	Tax Basis (Week 1/Month 1)	Personal Record
30	Nat Ins. Rate	Personal Record
31	Nat Ins. Number	Personal Record
32	Payment Method	Personal Record
33	Bank Code	Personal Record
34	Bank Account	Personal Record
35	Gross Taxable Pay to Date	Personal Record
36	Tax to Date	Personal Record
37	Superannuation to Date	Personal Record
38	Total Payments this Period	Personal Record
39	Taxable Pay this Period	Personal Record
40	Tax this Period	Personal Record
41	Net Pay this Period	Personal Record
42	NI This Period (Employers)	Personal Record
43	NI This Period (Employees)	Personal Record
44	NI This Period (Contracted Out)	Personal Record
45	NI To Date (Employers)	Personal Record
46	NI To Date (Employees)	Personal Record
47	NI To Date (Contracted Out)	Personal Record
48	Rounding Brought Forward	Personal Record
49	Rounding Carried Forward	Personal Record
50	Pay to Date	Calculated
51	Payslip Coin Analysis Headings	Program
52	Payslip Coin Analysis	Calculated
53	Holiday Accrued this period	Calculated
54	Total Deductions	Calculated
55	Total Deductions (Exc N.I. & PAYE)	Calculated
56	Payment Description	Transaction File
57	Payment Hours	Transaction File
58	Payment Rate	Transaction File
59	Payment Value	Transaction File
60	Deduction Description	Transaction File
61	Deduction Value	Transaction File
62	Deduction Balance	Transaction File
63	Deduction Desc' for Balance item	Transaction File
64	Deduction Value for Balance item	Transaction File
80	Cost Centre Code	Employees Record
98	Printer Enhanced (Large Print) ON	Program
99	Printer Enhanced (Large Print) OFF	Program

Changes to National Insurance

One of the major problems with Payroll is the need for an operator to keep in touch with changes in legislation regarding taxes. This chapter has dealt in some length with changes in bands and rates. A bigger problem occurs when there is a change made in the structure of some aspect of taxation. As a result of the 1989 Finance Act, there has been a major alteration in the way employee contribution to National Insurance is made. There has been NO CHANGE IN THE WAY EMPLOYERS' CONTRIBUTION IS PAID.

As before, a limit is set at which employees pay no National Insurance. Once this limit has been reached, employees do not pay a fixed percentage on all the gross income earned. For example, if the amount was fixed at £43 per week before an employee needed to pay National Insurance and the lower band was set at 2% with the rate after £43 set at 9%, then an employee earning £143 in a week would pay:

2% of £43	=	£0.86
9% of £100	=	£9.00
Total NI	=	£9.86

This is different to the old system where an employee paid 9% of the whole £143, that is £12.87. The new system is £3.01 less than the old system demonstrated in this chapter.

When an employee has to pay National Insurance you will find that ALL employees will contribute the same fixed sum less under the new scheme compared to the old one. If you are using a version of Pegasus that assumes the older system, then you can get around the problem by DEDUCTING the fixed amount from those employees paying National Insurance. You will need to be careful to ensure that such a deduction is posted to the correct nominal account and that an employee's payslip reveals only the actual contribution stopped.

10 Payroll (Operating the System)

This second chapter on Payroll concerns itself much more with the actual operating of a Payroll than the last chapter, which addressed itself to the problems of setting up the Payroll and the concepts involved.

THE PROCEDURES

As with any operation there will need to be a systematic approach. The ultimate goal in running a Payroll system is to pay employees correctly and on time, to make recordings of all transactions and to meet the legal obligations such as the collection and payment of taxes. This chapter will attempt to take you through eleven stages of running a Payroll in the following order:

1   As a first step to performing a Payroll run we should add any new employees to the payroll and make any amendments required on existing employees, such as change of tax code.
2   Enter details of hours worked by hourly paid employees and details of any payments or deductions that have to be made. In this stage we shall see that running the Payroll for the first time will prove the most demanding. When the Payroll is run for the second time, many of the payments and deductions will remain as before, requiring only amendments, if necessary.
3   Details of any staff leaving the firm's employment should be entered. This stage will require documentation that will be required by the employee leaving.
4   Details about employees on holiday in the current pay period will have to be recorded.
5   Perform Payroll calculations.
6   Produce payslips, cheques, giros and autopay lists. Not all Payroll systems will necessarily make use of all of these methods of paying staff.

7 Produce a series of reports that may include:

(a) Period summary.
(b) Cheque and giro list.
(c) To-date summary and any required employee summaries.
(d) Departmental analysis.

8 Perform the nominal analysis, whereby the nominal accounts are updated to reflect the Payroll run.
9 Produce any special reports required.
10 Make any last-minute alterations and, if necessary, re-calculate the Payroll.
11 Perform the Payroll update.

As you work through this chapter, it may become apparent that you do not necessarily have to process the Payroll in the above order. However, the sequence of events listed here will serve as a means of acquiring the skills of performing a Payroll run. The important point to note is that this sequence of events will have to be performed for each set of employee data and at each Payroll run. Some updating of employee records may be done between Payroll runs. For monthly paid staff, this will need to be done monthly, while for weekly paid staff it will be done weekly.

1 Maintaining employee records

Little needs to be said about this stage, as it was covered in the last chapter on setting up the Payroll system for the first time. In practice, changes to employee records will be made regularly such as changes to employee tax codes, cost centres, analysis codes. Some changes may have to be made with regard to 'employee to-date' figures, although it is anticipated that much of this will be done automatically by the Pegasus Payroll system.

2 Payments and deductions

Here we will need to enter details of hours worked by hourly paid employees and details of any payments or deductions that have to be made. The actual table of payments and deductions will have been produced in the Payroll parameters section of parameter update discussed in the previous chapters.

Payments and deductions can be found in option 3 of the Payroll processing menu. At this point, there are two immediate things to note: firstly that the first employee Payroll number appears in the box at the top of the screen. If this is required, then simply press ENTER to reveal the employee name; otherwise replace the number with the one required. This allows an operator the facility of working through ALL employees systematically if required. Secondly, the screen is split up into payments on the left and deductions on the right in much the same way as appeared in the Payroll parameter file.

Figure 10.1 is an illustration of employee details for ONE SINGLE EMPLOYEE (it is important to be aware of the fact that this has to be done for all employees).

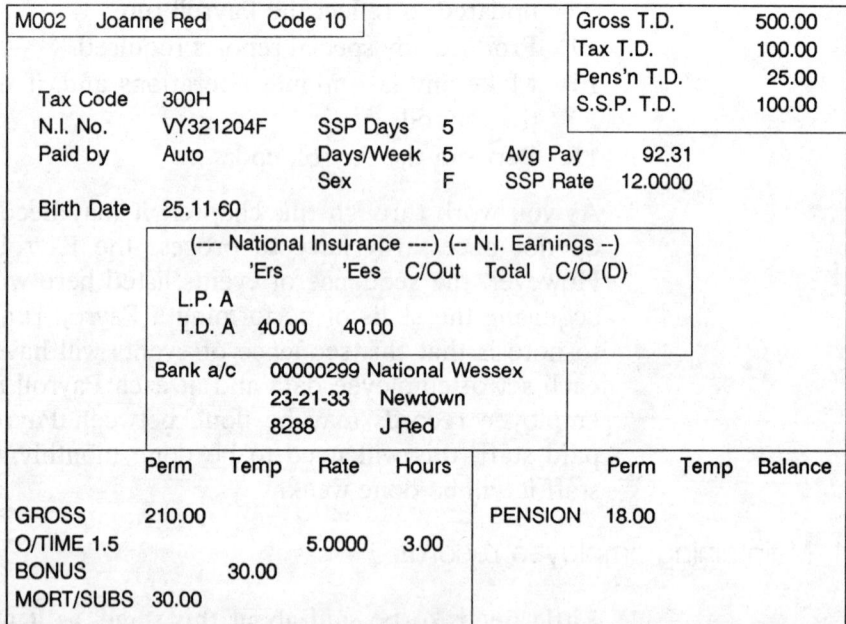

Figure 10.1

On the payments side there are four columns that appear after the payment type. They are for the following purposes:

Perm Permanent column. This figure represents a permanent feature of this employee's wage and, once entered, will remain on all future payment updates until you decide to alter it. The idea of this is to enable time to be saved from continuously entering the same information on each employee every time the Payroll is run. On each Payroll run, any figures in the permanent column can always be changed.

Temp Temporary column. This figure will apply to this pay period only and will have to be re-entered, if applicable, on the next Payroll run.

Rate Some payments require an hourly rate to be paid. It is quite feasible to have a permanent value, temporary value and hourly rate all on the same line.

Hours This is the number of hours to paid at the previous column's rate.

Once set up, Pegasus will handle the payments in accordance to the type that we set up in the last chapter in the Payroll parameters. In the case of SSP, the number of days that SSP has to be paid to an employee should be entered; the system will take over from here.

On the deductions side there are 3 columns that appear after the deduction type. They are for the following purposes:

Perm Permanent column. This figure represents a permanent feature of this employee's wage in the same way as that for payments. On each Payroll run, any figures in the permanent column can always be changed.

Temp Temporary column. This figure will apply to this pay period only and will have to be re-entered, if applicable, on the next Payroll run.

Balance In the case of deductions being made against a balance (type 'A' in parameters to indicate an accumulating balance and type 'R' in parameters to indicate a reducing balance) this column holds the balance either left or accumulated.

On the deductions side, a holiday entitlement can be set up using a type 'H' deduction in the parameters. The effect of this is to accumulate a sum of money without actually taking anything from the employee's wage.

Exercise

Produce figures for ALL employees regarding payments and deductions. Make an attempt to include as many variations as possible as a way of getting familiar with the package. If you feel confident enough at this stage, make alterations to the Payroll parameters in a way that allows extra payment and deduction types to be added such as the inclusion of 'H' type holiday pay and the establishment of a company social fund to be used at Christmas.

3 Handling the leavers of the firm

From the Payroll Processing menu, option 4, Holidays, Leavers and Transfers, you will be allowed to indicate that an employee is to leave the firm's employment. This option reveals a form that first requires the employee number. The holiday box will be left blank for this stage.

The next box for leavers should have one of the letter codes indicated below, depending on how you want to process the leaver:

L Followed by the date of leaving. A payslip will then be produced for the employee at the end of the current period for the last time.

D This will ensure that no further payslips are produced for this employee. This will, however, require the employer to produce a payslip manually and adjust the employee's record and 'to-date' totals for the purpose of end-of-year reports.

X This will delete an employee from the Payroll completely, even for end-of-year figures. This is most likely to be required when you wish to remove an employee mistakenly put on the Payroll or wish to place the employee details on to another Payroll file. In practice, use this option very carefully.

R To be used to restore an employee who has been entered as a leaver by mistake (or is re-instated after being dismissed).

If an employee is simply being transferred from one department to another, then all you need to do is to:

1 Enter the employee number.
2 Leave the holiday and leave date boxes blank.
3 Enter the new employee Payroll number in the transfer box, making sure it has not already been allocated.

Exercise

Register one of your employees as having left and transfer another employee to another department by altering their Payroll number.

4 Details about employees on holiday

From the Payroll processing menu option 4, Holidays, Leavers and Transfers, you will be allowed to indicate that an employee is about to take holiday entitlement.

This is only applicable to weekly paid staff, as salaried staff will have salaries paid monthly irrespective of whether holiday leave has been taken. The idea is a simple one. After indicating the employee Payroll number, you enter the number of weeks (up to 6) that the employee is about to go on holiday.

Entry of holiday weeks must be entered in the Payroll week **before** the employee takes the holiday. To leave it later means that the employee will have holiday pay awarded while on holiday.

PAYE and National Insurance contributions will be paid on both the normal Payroll week money and the holiday pay. When indicating that an employee is to take holiday leave, adjustments will have to be made to payments and deductions to allow the employee to receive the holiday pay.

For each of the weeks the employee is on holiday, the Payroll run will not produce payslips and maintain employee to-date figures in the correct manner.

If an employee terminates their holiday before the stated number of weeks has materialised, then a '0' entry into the holiday box will cancel the holiday and restore the employee to the Payroll run in the normal way. When inspecting the holidays, leavers and transfers for an employee on holiday, an alphabetic character will appear indicating in the following way the number of weeks holiday still remaining: **a** 1 week's holiday left, **b** 2 weeks' holiday left and so on to **f** for 6 weeks' holiday left.

5 Perform Payroll calculations

PAYE & NI override Within Payroll processing, this facility appears as option 6, allowing either PAYE or National Insurance Contributions to be set at a rate that is not compatible with the way the package will arrive at it by calculation. The option, therefore allows you to put in entries on selected employees.

If used, this option should be done prior to calculation being carried out. The option reveals a screen requiring the employee number and the amounts for tax (PAYE) and National Insurance figures (employee, employer and contracted out). Once you have done this, calculation can now go ahead.

The first four stages in this operation have dealt with preparing employee records for the batch processing of the Payroll function. The next stage is to perform the Payroll calculation in such a way that the following actions occur:

(a) Calculate all statutory deductions and determine net pay for each employee.
(b) Update each employee record with to-date figures.
(c) Re-arrange all employee records in employee number order.

To perform a Payroll calculation you will need to use option 2, Calculation, from the Payroll menu. After entering the password you will be required to enter the tax period, if this is being done for the first time.

A tax year usually starts in the first full week of April for a complete year. If the Payroll is a weekly one, there will be 52 Payroll periods in the year. Consequently, the system needs to know the week number in order to start (the system does not rely on any computer system date). If the pay period is monthly, then the period runs 1 to 12. On the next Payroll run, the system will simply add one to this number to give the next Payroll period number.

The system will now calculate pay, printing out an **exception report** as it proceeds. An exception report is a report of all those circumstances that are not regarded as normal or may need special intervention in order to be put right. Figure 10.2 is an example of such a report with an explanation to follow.

```
03.03.90                    Payroll Exceptions Report              Page 1

Tax Period = 01 Company Holiday = Weeks


M001       Jack Blue              Insufficient Pay For CAR LOAN
M001       Jack Blue              Insufficient Pay For CHARITY
M001       Jack Blue              Insufficient Pay For UNION SUB
```

Figure 10.2

Insufficient Pay For UNION SUB The net pay for the employee is not enough to pay the union sub. It is likely that pay details have not been entered or incorrectly entered for this period.

Insufficient Pay For CHARITY The net pay for the employee is not enough to pay the charity. Again, it is likely that pay details have not been entered or incorrectly entered for this period, especially as this is the same employee.

Other exception reporting messages may come up, all of which should be self-explanatory.

6 Produce payslips, cheques, giros and autopay lists

This stage will show more clearly the effect of the previous processes. This option can only be carried through after the calculation has been successfully completed. The options for the list can be carried from option 3 of the Payroll menu (Payroll Reports). The menu reveals that this stage is concerned with the first 6 options from this menu:

1	**Payslips**
2	**Giros**
3	**Cheques**
4	**Giro List**
5	**Cheque List**
6	**Autopay List**

1 Payslips Figure 10.3 is an example of a single employee payslip and shows both the effect of the preparation of the employee pay details and the way the parameters were set up.

You may, at this point, decide that the design of the payslip is not to your liking. You may, if you wish, use the parameters update to alter the payslip design and re-run the production of payslips. You can do this as many times as you like, it will not do any harm to either the final accounts or employee pay.

```
                                        Pegasus User Enterprise


  Employee Name              Joanne Red


  Payroll Number             M002
  Personal Tax Code          300H
  National Insurance Number  VY-32-12-04-F
  National Insurance Rate    A
  Bank Code                  Auto


  Payment Details for this period
  Hours Worked/Rate/Value Joanne Red                          210.00


  Total Payments this period    285.00


  Deduction details this period
  Description/Value PENSION                   10.00


  Total deductions (Exc. NI & PAYE)     10.00

  Tax this period                       31.00
```

Figure 10.3

2 Giros Option 2 of the Payroll Reports, Giros, simply prints on to pre-printed stationery girocheque information for all those employees who are to be paid by girocheque.

3 Cheques Option 3 (cheques) is exactly the same as that of option 2 (giros) except the pre-printed stationery is for cheques. With both options 2 and 3 you may decide that the design of the giro and cheque is not correct. You may, if you wish, use the parameters update to alter the designs and re-run either or both of the options. As with payslips, you can do this as many times as you like; it will not do any harm to either the final accounts or employee pay. If you do this a number of times, do not get all the produced cheques and giros signed but only the correct versions (one per employee usually).

4 and 5 Giro List and Cheque List These options simply list payments made in either of the respective ways. Such a list would act as a useful check to ensure that the Payroll is complete and accurate. It should be produced at the end of each pay run as a matter of habit, as is the case with the other lists.

6 Autopay List This list gives details about those employees who will have their pay details sent to the bank and paid through into their bank accounts automatically. Such a list is shown in Figure 10.4.

03.03.90	Autopay List			PAGE 1
Employee	Bank A/C	Sort Code	Autopay Code	Amnt
K100 Kathy Pink	33333333	33-33-33	3333	228.77
M002 Joanne Red	00000299	23-21-33	8288	224.05
			B/fwd Total	.00
			This Page	452.82
			Total	452.82

Figure 10.4

7 Produce a series of reports

There are three remaining reports available in the Payroll Report menu:

TP summary
TD summary
Employee details

These reports are well worth analysing and would prove useful in any Payroll situation.

TP Summary is This Period Summary for the current Payroll period only (e.g. current week-end or month-end). It summarises for each employee the amount paid and stopped along with totals of such amounts as tax stopped, NI stopped. Such overall stoppages are an indication of the amounts that have to be passed on to the respective organisations. The summary totals are also broken down into departments, determined in the parameters setting in our example as being the first character of the employee code.

TD Summary is a To-Date Summary for the payroll since the start of the current financial year. As such it works exactly the same as for TP Summary above. This will help the firm keep a check on the amounts paid, deducted and costs incurred since the beginning of the current financial year.

Such a summary is shown in Figure 10.5.

03.03.90			Payroll Summary (This Period)							Page 1
Emp No.	Name	Gross Pay	Gross Taxable	Tax	N.I. Emp'ee	N.I. Emp'er	Net Pay	(- N.I. Earnings -)		
								Total	C/O (D)	
K100	Kathy Pink	289.00	249.00	.00	20.23	20.23	228.77	289.00	.00	
	Total Department K	289.00	249.00	.00	20.23	20.23	228.77			
M001	Jack Blue	297.00	266.00	256.00	19.95	19.95	2.10	285.00	.00	
M002	Joanne Red	285.00	275.00	31.00	19.95	19.95	224.05	285.00	.00	
M003	Jonathan Black	223.00	161.00	-1.75	10.65	10.65	4.10	213.00	.00	
M004	David Greenock	485.00	445.00	73.50	42.75	42.75	255.80	475.00	.00	
	Total Department M	1,290.00	1,147.00	358.75	93.30	93.30	486.05			
	Total Company	1,579.00	1,396.00	358.75	113.53	113.53	714.82			

Figure 10.5

As can be seen, the report summarises all tax, National Insurance and gross pay for employees broken down into departments as well as details on each employee. A department has been identified by the Payroll function as the first character that makes an employee's Payroll number. Although the groupings are referred to as departments, the grouping could just as easily be employees working on a particular contract or job.

Employee Details offers another way of inspecting an employee's pay details, with the exception that a detailed analysis of the pay made in the current period is not given.

Figure 10.6 shows an additional report that may be required, the **departmental analysis** report. This is available as option 4 (Department Analysis) from the main Payroll menu. It gives an example for one of the departments.

Again, it takes advantage of the way codes are used against employee Payroll numbers.

The option will print such a report for each department with a final report for all employees on that particular company identifier.

If departments are not required, then ALL employees should be pre-fixed with the same number or letter.

The accumulated totals shown are for all employees for the whole of the financial year to-date, and during the financial year will grow bigger each time.

03.03.90	Departmental Payroll Analysis – Period 01		Page 2

Department M

(------------- Pay Elements ------------)   (----------- Voluntary Deductions -----------)

Payment	Type	Amount	Units	Deduction	Type	Amount	Balance
GROSS	T	809.00		PENSION	P	111.00	111.00
O/TIME 1.5	T	57.00	11.00	INSURANCES		10.00	
O/TIME 2.0	T	10.00	2.00	CAR LOAN	R	153.00	6280.00
BONUS	T	225.00		HEALTH INS		10.00	
MORT/SUBS	T	100.00		CHARITY	N	20.00	
COMMISSION	T	33.00		UNION SUB		8.00	
EXPENSES	T	56.00		S.A.Y.E.	A	40.00	1040.00

This Period Totals

Taxable Pay	1290.00	Cash Equiv	.00	Pensions	111.00
Non-Taxable	.00			Voluntary	241.00
S.S.P.	.00	Tot Taxable	1147.00	P.A.Y.E.	358.75
CI Hol Pay	.00	NI 'ERS	93.30	NI 'EES	93.30
S.M.P.	.00			True Net	485.95
Total Pay	1290.00				1290.00

Rounding		Breakdown		Coin Analysis		
True Net	485.95	Cash	257.90			
Less B/Fwd	.00	Cheque	4.10	Twenties	12	240.00
		Giro	.00	Tens	1	10.00
	485.95	Autopay	224.05	Fives	0	.00
Add C/Fwd	.10			Ones	7	7.00
		Employees		50p	1	.50
Actual Net	486.05			20p	1	.20
		Current	4	10p	2	.20
		Leavers	0	5p	0	.00
		Holiday	0	2p	0	.00
				1p	0	.00
To Date Totals						
		National Insurance				257.90
		Rate	'ERS	'EES		
Taxable	5647.00	A	433.30	433.30		
P.A.Y.E.	1198.75					
Pensions	336.00					
S.S.P.	100.00					
S.M.P.	.00					

Figure 10.6

03.03.90   Departmental Payroll Analysis – Period 01   Page 3

Company Totals

(--------------- Pay Elements -------------)				(------------ Voluntary Deductions ------------)			
Payment	Type	Amount	Units	Deduction	Type	Amount	Balance
GROSS	T	909.00		PENSION	P	151.00	151.00
O/TIME 1.5	T	57.00	11.00	INSURANCES		10.00	
O/TIME 2.0	T	10.00	2.00	CAR LOAN	R	153.00	6280.00
BONUS	T	325.00		HEALTH INS		10.00	
MORT/SUBS	T	155.00		CHARITY	N	20.00	
COMMISSION	T	55.00		UNION SUB		8.00	
EXPENSES	T	68.00		S.A.Y.E.	A	40.00	1040.00

This Period Totals

Taxable Pay	1579.00	Cash Equiv	.00	Pensions	151.00
Non-Taxable	.00			Voluntary	241.00
S.S.P.	.00	Tot Taxable	1396.00	P.A.Y.E.	358.75
Cl Hol Pay	.00	NI 'ERS	113.53	NI 'EES	113.53
S.M.P.	.00			True Net	714.72
Total Pay	1579.00				1579.00

Rounding		Breakdown		Coin Analysis		
True Net	714.72	Cash	257.90	Twenties	12	240.00
Less B/Fwd	.00	Cheque	4.10	Tens	1	10.00
		Glro	.00	Fives	0	.00
	714.72	Autopay	452.82	Ones	7	7.00
Add C/Fwd	.10	**Employees**		50p	1	.50
				20p	1	.20
Actual Net	714.82	Current	5	10p	2	.20
		Leavers	0	5p	0	.00
		Holiday	0	2p	0	.00
				1p	0	.00
To Date Totals						257.90

National Insurance

		Rate	'ERS	'EES
Taxable	5896.00	A	453.53	453.53
P.A.Y.E.	1198.75			
Pensions	376.00			
S.S.P.	100.00			
S.M.P.	.00			

Figure 10.6 Continued

Such a set of tables can be extracted before payslips and payments are issued. This will allow some last-minute checks before going ahead and making payments. It should be remembered, of course, that if a mistake has been made, we can go back and correct any data and then repeat the processes.

The next stage will involve the posting of the last Payroll run to the Nominal Ledger. Therefore it is imperative that checks are made now before going ahead with nominal postings if time is to be saved and accuracy achieved.

8 Perform the nominal analysis

Before performing this option it is always a good idea to spend time making certain that everything is correct. An effective way of doing this may be to examine payslips first, distribute them to employees and then make any required alterations.

The purpose of this part of the Payroll system is to post all relevant figures into the correct nominal accounts. The first thing to ensure is that the nominal accounts have been set up correctly. If they have not, then postings will be made to various suspense accounts, creating extra work for an operator at a later date.

From the Payroll parameters set up in the last chapter we had the following information with regard to the nominal codes:

Nominal Code		
	N.I.'ERS Cost	NI01
	N.I.'ERS + 'EES	NI02
	PAYE	PAYE
	Wages Control	W111
	Wages Suspense	W110

And from the payments and deductions part of these parameters, we will also need the following additional nominal accounts:

GROSS	W101	PENSION	W201
O/TIME	W112	INSURANCES	W202
O/TIME	W113	CAR LOAN	W203
O/TIME	W114	HEALTH INS	W204
BONUS	W115	CHARITY	W205
MORT/SUBS	W116	UNION SUB	W206
COMMISSION	W117	SAYE	W207
EXPENSES	W118		
SSP	W119		

Exercise

Using the Nominal Ledger system of the Pegasus package, go to nominal processing and set up these accounts to allow the Payroll details to be posted across.

In our example **all** PAYE for this Payroll is posted to the account PAYE, as is the case for the others stated above. Pegasus has what it calls a MASKING facility whereby, according to the analysis codes set up in each employee file, postings are made to differing accounts. This facility is explained in the manual. For now, the set-up given above will suit most applications. It may, however, be more normal to have different Payroll runs posting figures to different nominal accounts. As explained earlier, this can be achieved by using different company identifiers for each different set of Payroll data.

When using this option, you will be required to state which company identifier you are using to store your Payroll data. The idea of this is to allow the use of different company identifiers for different Payroll groups. After entering this identifier (a single alphabetic character), the analysis and posting will begin. Remember, salaried staff must be separated from weekly paid staff.

There are two stages. The first, illustrated in Figure 10.7, will work through each employee record, writing the data to the nominal accounts. This is carried out for each employee and, as a result, can produce a very long report. The summary report indicates what sums have been posted to their respective nominal accounts. In the event of the account not being available, a posting to the suspense account will be made.

03.03.90	Nominal Analysis of Payroll		Page 1
Nominal Code	Name	Dr	Cr
NI01	N.I. 'ERS COST	113.53	
NI02	N.I. 'ERS + 'EES		227.06
PAYE	PAY AS YOU EARN INCOME TAX		358.75
W101	FACTORY WAGES	909.00	
W111	WAGES CONTROL		714.72
W112	OVERTIME @ TIME-AND-A-HALF	57.00	
W113	OVERTIME @ DOUBLE TIME	10.00	
W115	BONUS PAYMENTS	325.00	
W116	MORTGAGE SUBSIDY PAYMENTS	155.00	
W117	SALES COMMISSION	55.00	
W118	EMPLOYEE EXPENSES	68.00	
W201	STAFF PENSION		151.00
W202	STAFF INSURANCES		10.00
W203	CAR LOAN		153.00
W204	STAFF HEALTH INSURANCE		10.00
W205	CHARITY CONTRIBUTION		20.00
W206	UNION SUBS		8.00
W207	S.A.Y.E.		40.00
	Entry No. 11	1692.53	1692.53

Figure 10.7

At a later stage, the operator will be required to make a number of nominal entries through the journal in order to:

(a) Transfer some of the figures to other accounts (especially those items posted to suspense accounts).

(b) Pass on some of the collected money to their respective bodies; such as passing on the PAYE collected to the Inland Revenue.

(c) Transfer money from the bank to employees in order to pay the wages and salaries.

Whatever amount of work is needed on the Nominal Ledger, getting to this stage once the parameter, employee records and permanent payments and deductions have been set up is very quick in comparison to that of a manual system.

An example of a nominal account after this has been done is shown in Figure 10.8.

WAGES CONTROL		Account W111				03 Mar 1990
Date	Entry	Type	Input By	Dr	Cr	Comment
03.03.90	11	Wages	WG		714.72	
		Account Total			714.72	

Figure 10.8

The nominal analysis has replaced the need for all the double entry normally required in a non-integrated or manual system. As can be seen, the documentation indicates that the automated posting is simply another journal entry.

Exercise

Execute the nominal analysis as suggested above, ensuring that all required accounts have been set up. Investigate the effect this has by producing details on some of the accounts and a trial balance. If required, move all suspense figures across to their correct accounts and use journal entries to pass on some of the collected money to the relevant organisations. Also, pay the wages to employees by transferring money from the bank to do so.

9 Produce any special reports required

From the Payroll menu, option 9, Special Reports, offers three special reports options:

1 Print P14's, and P60's.

2 Print P35's.

3 Payment/Deductions List.

Each is important to a Payroll system, although they are normally used at the end of a financial year rather than at the end of each Payroll run.

1 Print P14's, and P60's The form P14 is an end-of-year return and acts as a summary for each employee stating for the year:

- Amount of pay earned.
- Tax paid.
- National Insurance Contributions paid by employee.
- Earnings on which employee's contributions are payable.
- Any SSP and/or SMP paid.

Consequently, such a form is required at the end of the tax year and should be passed on to the Inland Revenue.

A P60 is exactly the same form, but is a copy that should be passed to the employee rather than the Inland Revenue.

2 Print P35's This is for an end-of-year summary called an Employer's Annual Statement, Declaration and Certificate. The details on this P35 must cover for each employee:

- The net amount of tax deducted or refunded.
- The total of both employer's and employee's National Insurance Contributions for the tax year.
- The amount of SSP paid.
- The amount of SMP paid.

3 Payment/Deductions List This option will produce printouts for each employee showing the amounts for any particular payment or deduction type.

In all three cases, the most likely time you will need to use the special reports in any detail is at the end of the financial year. For many firms it is worth investigating the possibility of sending the end-of-tax year returns as data on a disk rather than produce it on provided forms and stationery.

10 Make any last-minute alterations

Before the next stage is activated, the Payroll operator should make any last-minute changes or alterations. Queries on pay will frequently occur which will require further processing.

The case may arise where the operator has to recalculate and perform the stages again. This is quite permissible and should be encouraged rather than ignore any problems that crop up.

11 Perform the Payroll update

This final stage is used to clear down the files in preparation for the next Payroll run. Because of this, it is important that all details are complete and correct.

The option appears on the main Payroll menu as option 6 (payroll update). Before commencing with this stage, it is important that the data generated has been archived to either a floppy disk or another part of your hard disk. The system will guide you through this operation, which may require the changing of disks if you are using a system that uses only floppy disks.

SUMMARY

As a final step, it is essential that Payroll data is properly backed up, a topic covered in Chapter 13. In the event of any disaster during Payroll activity, a backup can always be restored and the processes repeated.

At the end of this operation, if archived data is on a floppy disk, it should be marked, dated and stored in a safe place in case it is needed at a later date.

In going through the Payroll run in this fashion, it is hoped that you have gained a sufficient insight into both Payroll in general and Pegasus in particular to be able to investigate some of the other facilities within the Pegasus Payroll.

Table 10.1 shows the effect of integrating the Payroll function with the Nominal Ledger function on the final trial balance. It should be noted that the grouping of nominal accounts is also grouped. The Nominal Ledger grouping is based on the first character of the nominal account name which was achieved by setting the nominal parameter option 2 to Y.

Even with the parameter setting correct, a period-end will be required in order to get the accounts set up in the correct order, namely account number order. In observing the trial balance, you should begin to appreciate the need to plan the coding strategy carefully with respect to the choice of nominal header account numbers. As you will see, in the example set out in this and earlier chapters, all accounts relating to Payroll accounts have a similar set of codes.

Table 10.1

Pegasus Users Enterprises		

03.03.90	Summary Trial Balance		Page 1
		Dr	Cr
C101	CREDITORS		9,000.00
C102	SHORT TERM BANK LOAN		10,000.00
Total Group C		.00	19,000.00
F101	CLOTHING – FACTORY STAFF	2,200.00	
F102	CLEANING – FACTORY	1,520.00	
F103	DEPRECIATION OF MACHINERY	2,000.00	
F104	DISTRIBUTION	1,200.00	
F105	ELECTRICITY – FACTORY	936.99	
F106	DEPRECIATION OF FIXTURES	12,000.00	
F107	BAD DEBTS	2,345.00	
F108	SUNDRY EXPENSES	580.00	
F109	ENTERTAINMENT ALLOWANCES	850.00	
Total Group F		23,631.99	.00
G101	CLOSING STOCK	21,000.00	
G102	BANK ACCOUNT	19,583.01	
G103	CASH IN HAND		258.11
G104	DEBTORS	117,655.00	
Total Group G		158,508.01	258.11
K101	SHARE CAPITAL		500,000
K102	PROFIT & LOSS		12,000.00
K103	DEBENTURES		200,000.00
Total Group K		.00	712,000.00
NI01	N.I. 'ERS COST	247.12	
NI02	N.I. 'ERS + 'EES		494.24
Total Group N		247.12	494.24
P101	PURCHASES – RAW MATERIALS	43,000.00	
P102	PURCHASES – COMPONENTS	34,500.00	
P103	PURCHASES – SERVICES	2,650.00	
PAYE	PAY AS YOU EARN INCOME TAX		147.00
Total Group P		80,150.00	147.00

Table 10.1 Continued

Pegasus Users Enterprises			
03.03.90	Summary Trial Balance		Page 2
		Dr	Cr
Q101	PROPERTY	253,000	
Q102	PLANT & MACHINERY	120,000.00	
Q103	FURNITURE	121,000.00	
Q104	FIXTURES & FITTINGS	154,000.00	
Q105	MOTOR VEHICLES	90,000.00	
Total Group Q		738,000.00	.00
R101	GOODS RETURNED – INWARDS	3,350.00	
R102	GOODS RETURNED – OUTWARDS		4,400.00
Total Group R		3,350.00	4,400.00
S101	SALES – HARDWARE		112,000.00
S102	SALES – SOFTWARE		115,981.89
S103	SALES – CONSULTANCY		78,000.00
Total Group S		.00	305,981.89
W101	FACTORY WAGES	20,554.34	
W102	ADMINISTRATION WAGES	6,048.50	
W103	SALARIED STAFF	12,032.00	
W104	DIRECTORS SALARIES	9.00	
W110	WAGES SUSPENSE	516.00	
W111	WAGES CONTROL		714.72
W112	OVERTIME @ TIME-AND-A-HALF	57.00	
W113	OVERTIME @ DOUBLE TIME	10.00	
W115	BONUS PAYMENTS	325.00	
W116	MORTGAGE SUBSIDY PAYMENTS	155.00	
W117	SALES COMMISSION	55.00	
W118	EMPLOYEE EXPENSES	68.00	
W201	STAFF PENSION		295.00
W202	STAFF INSURANCES		22.00
W203	CAR LOAN		263.00
W204	STAFF HEALTH INSURANCE		31.00
W205	CHARITY CONTRIBUTION		20.00
W206	UNION SUBS		28.0
W207	S.A.Y.E.		62.00
Total Group W		39,829.84	1,435.72
Grand Totals		1,043,716.96	1,043,716.96

11 Job Costing

INTRODUCTION

For many firms the use of the ledgers will prove to be an insufficient method of either controlling or monitoring costs. Instead, they may decide to analyse cost by job or department. For example, a building firm will take on a number of projects where it needs both to control costs and to assess the profitability of such projects. In addition to being able to monitor profits, such analyses of costs will always assist such companies in realistically assessing the costs of new projects and, as a consequence, being able to compete with other building firms for contracts.

Alternatively, a firm may break its operations down into cost centres or departments and will then wish to monitor costs of such departments, assess their performance and measure their profitability.

Some of the benefits of Job Costing can, therefore, be to assess the profitability of various sections within the organisation, to ensure losses on projects are not made or at least minimised, to improve the ability of a firm to tender for business without taking on loss-making projects and to help fix or alter selling prices, where appropriate, to ensure a profit.

The principle of Job Costing is that:

(a)   A job is identified.
(b)   Costs are attached to a job which will include labour, materials, expenses and overheads.
(c)   As transactions are generated in terms of acquisition of goods, service, materials and wages paid, the costs are then attributed to the various jobs.
(d)   Job cost reports are extracted indicating costs of the job, project or departmental activities.

In order for Job Costing to be effective, it requires details of its costs from some of the other functions within the Pegasus system. Consequently, Job Costing requires integrating with other functions, achieved by ensuring that parameters are correctly set across other functions. This area will be discussed later in this chapter.

The Job Costing system maintains and generates reports based on two files, a job record file and cost type record file. The Job Record File contains a record for each job currently undergone, shown in Figure 11.1.

Job No.	Job Description	Budget	Completion Date	Balance Forward or Open Item Cost Transaction	Completed Indicator
0401	Consultancy Tuck Suppl.	9000	22 10 90	0	

Figure 11.1

The **job number** is a unique field that identifies the job. In other words, each job must have a different number. The **job description** simply describes the job, section or department. The **budget** is an attempt at estimating the likely or projected cost of the job over its lifetime. In practice, it would be the aim of the firm to keep the cost of the whole job within this budget and, as the next field holds the **completion date**, to finish the project within the completion date.

Such jobs can be categorised as either **balanced** or **open** type records. Periodically, records will need to be re-organised. If the record is balanced, then only balances will be carried forward to the re-organised records, while for open accounts all individual transactions will be carried across and retained. The **completion indicator** simply indicates whether a job has been completed or not. If the job is complete the entry will be 'Y'. If the job is complete, then this record will be deleted after the re-organisation activity.

The second file that has to be maintained in this function is the job cost record file. This file holds a record for each cost type to be used with a job. Such records are illustrated in Figure 11.2.

Cost Code	Cost Description	Cost Rate	Payroll Payment Number	Overhead Allowance
C10	Consultant (on site)	15	1	14%

Figure 11.2

The costs indicated in the cost type records can be recorded against any job in one or more of the following ways:

(a) From employees' time sheets which requires integration with the Payroll function.

(b)   From analysed Purchase Ledger invoices which requires integration with both Stock Control and Purchase Ledger functions.

(c)   By journal entry into the cost ledger.

INTEGRATION WITH OTHER FUNCTIONS

Figure 11.3 illustrates the way Job Costing relies on information from other functions in order for its activities to operate.

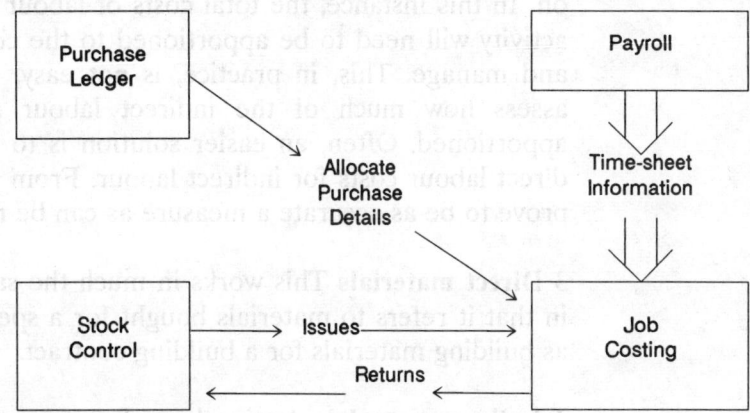

Figure 11.3

In order to integrate with the Purchase Ledger, the Purchase Ledger parameter file needs to be altered so that option 6 is set to 'Y'. With this set, any purchase made will be assigned a job number and cost code in order to assign the costs to the job.

Integrating with Stock Control will require you to alter the Stock Control parameters such that option 9 is set to 'Y'. As each stock record is created, a cost code will be required and associated with each item of stock. When stock items are both issued or returned, then a job has to be associated with that movement so the cost of a job can be altered to reflect the stock movement.

Integrating with Payroll requires no alteration to Payroll parameters. Using labour analysis within Job Costing, **time-sheet** information can be kept. This operates by associating any labour costs directly to a particular job. Such time-sheet details can be used to monitor job costs and can be used at Payroll periods to post details direct to the Payroll function, thereby reducing the work in running a Payroll.

Before starting, it is worth making clear some definitions for future reference.

1 **Direct labour** This refers to wages paid to staff who work within a department or on a specific job. For example, if the firm is a building

contractor, then staff will either be assigned to a specific contract (job) or recruited on a casual basis while the contract is in progress.

2 **Indirect labour** This refers to those labour costs that are not readily associated with a specific job or project, such as wages and salaries to managerial, supervisory and administration staff who work for the firm as a whole and not on any specific job or project. Using the example for direct labour, our building firm will need some kind of head office to co-ordinate the work of contracts, purchasing and so on. In this instance, the total costs of labour for this area of business activity will need to be apportioned to the contracts they co-ordinate and manage. This, in practice, is not easy, because it is difficult to assess how much of the indirect labour any contract should be apportioned. Often, an easier solution is to add a percentage to the direct labour costs for indirect labour. From past experience this may prove to be as accurate a measure as can be realistically achieved.

3 **Direct materials** This works in much the same way as direct labour in that it refers to materials bought for a specific job or project, such as building materials for a building contract.

4 **Indirect materials** Again, this refers to those materials that cannot be attributed to a particular job or project, such as administration costs and the costs associated with the business headquarters. As before, estimating such materials across contracts is not easy and adding a percentage to direct materials for indirect materials can prove to be a reliable and effective method.

5 **Direct expenses** As above but refers to expenses.

6 **Indirect expenses** As above but refers to expenses.

Before commencing with operating this function, it is useful to examine the structure of the job costing function and the activities within it, as shown in Figure 11.4.

From the structure, it should be clear how common activities have been grouped. All those activities that are concerned with maintaining the job records, cost type records and entering transactions data have been grouped as **job costing processing**. Those activities concerned with extracting reports have been grouped as **job cost reports**. The remaining activities fall into their own categories and tend to be less frequently used once the system has been set up and is being operated.

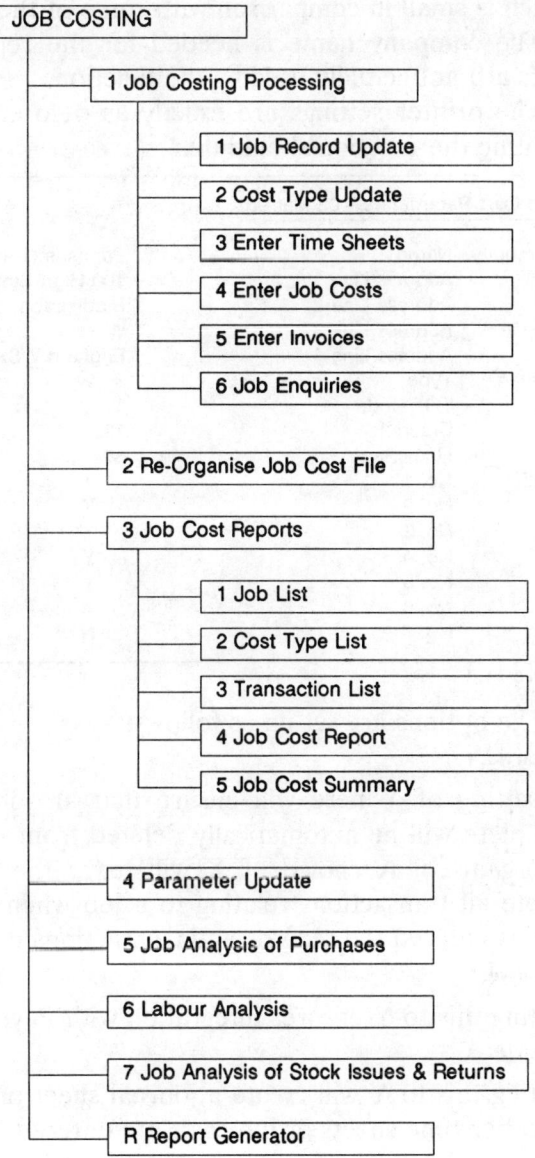

Figure 11.4

As with other functions before, especially Payroll, much of the work involves setting the system up. Such activities will need careful planning and thought.

GETTING STARTED

It should now be familiar ground that Pegasus functions require a parameter file to be set up before any work on a module can be started. The example in Figure 11.5 shows a complete parameter file, which is small in comparison with some of the others.

The company name is needed for the reports, while the address lines are not actually used by the function.

The printer settings are exactly as before, to indicate the type of printing the function should do.

Job Cost Parameters – 03 Mar 90		
Company	Name	Pegasus Users Enterprises
	Address Line 1	100 High Street
	Address Line 2	Biddlesdon
	Address Line 3	Wessex
	Address Line 4	England WSX 999
Printer	Type	0
	TOF Code	12
	Columns	132
	Lines/Page	66
Option	No. 1	Y
	No. 2	Y
	No. 3	Y
	No. 4	Y
	No. 5	Y
	No. 6	Y
	No. 7	N

Figure 11.5

The options are set up as follows:

Option No. 1   Y

A setting of Y here will ensure that all jobs that are recorded as complete will be automatically deleted from the job record file when re-organised. A choice of X will leave the record on file but will delete all transactions relating to a job when the file is re-organised. If N is entered the records and transactions data are left intact.

Option No. 2   Y

Setting this to Y ensures integration with Payroll.

Option No. 3   Y

Setting this to Y will create a journal sheet printed every time details of either time sheets or job costs are entered.

Option No. 4   Y

If set to Y a job description appears with transactions lists.

Option No. 5   Y

Setting this to Y ensures integration with the Purchase Ledger.

Option No. 6   Y

Setting this to Y ensures integration with Stock Control.

Option No. 7   N

This option is not used as yet and should be set at N.

Option No. 8

If you wish to use the password that you enter for access to the parameters in other areas of the job costing module, then enter 'Y' here. When items are selected from the menu of job costing, the user will be prompted for entry of the password before being allowed to proceed. The file reorganisation and integration routines use the password anyway.

Option No. 9

This allows you to print payment details on the labour analysis report.

As is usually the case, these parameters can be changed at any time in the future. If you change parameter settings, be careful not to allow the system to erase data files unless you particularly want to.

DEFINING JOBS AND COST TYPES

In this section there are six activities which fall into three main areas;

(a) File maintenance through job record and cost type updates.
(b) Transaction processing through entering time-sheets, job centres and invoices.
(c) Job enquiries.

Job Record Update is used to:

(a) Create new jobs. This is simply done by entering a new job number and then completing all other fields that make up the record.
(b) Amend an existing job. When an existing job number is entered, the system displays the existing record information.
(c) Delete a job. Entering the word DELETE in upper case in the job description field will cause the record to be deleted when the file is next re-organised.

Table 11.1 shows a list of jobs.

Table 11.1

Pegasus Users Enterprises		
03.03.90	Job List	Page 1
Job No.	Budget	Due Date
C0100 Jo Blake Bakeries	51,000	10.09.90
C1022 Davis Video Hire	3,400	10.06.90
C040 Tuck Shop Supplies	9,000	22.10.90

Cost Type Update works in exactly the same way as Job Record Update, except the fields are different.

Cost codes in the activity will play an important role. Each code is made up of 3 characters. The first character can be either a letter (A to Z) or a number (0 to 9) and is used to group common costs. For example, all raw materials may be prefixed with **M**. The following two characters can be used at will, except that codes ending in **00** are used to label group category. A description for M00 might, therefore, be raw materials.

The principle of cost type is an important one. Each cost type must fall into a category of either labour cost or general cost. Each cost type record will simply hold details of each type of cost and is used to categorise cost types which, during processing, will be used to generate a transactions list.

The description should be used to reflect the cost type accurately. For example, for a firm supplying computer systems to businesses, a cost type could be the supply of micro-computers. If this is the case then a description reflecting this should be used. This will help produce reports that can be easily read and understood later.

The Payroll payment number should be used in conjunction with the Payroll function. If you only have one type of Payroll payment method set up, which will be the case if you have kept to the examples in the previous two chapters, then the entry should be 1. If, on the other hand, another payment method has been set up and this cost type is against the second payment set up, then an entry of 2 is made. If you remember, we can set up differing Payroll categories to account for the different ways people are paid or we can set up a different Payroll for different jobs or departments. Up to 17 types can be set, it is important to know which number refers to which type. The purpose of this is to allow time sheets with these cost types to update the correct Payroll later. If the cost type is not a labour cost, then this should be left blank.

The rate indicates the cost per unit of cost type. For example, a firm offering consultancy services may decide to cost such a service at £20 per hour. If this is the case a figure of 20 will indicate this, as £20 per unit. It is then up to the operator to know this fact and, during transactions processing, to use the facility by entering (say) 3 units if a consultancy visit is to be costed at 3 hours. In using this for such an example, it is important to note that when integrated with the Payroll function this is NOT the Payroll rate for the employee, since this will already have been specified in the payments and deductions table in the employee details. Such a facility in this context, therefore, is used to assist us in determining the costs of the job.

A further illustration of the rate can be used with other costs. For example, if a job is to receive modules of Pegasus accounts then a rate can represent the cost we are to charge to a job for the supply of each Pegasus module. This can then be used to assist an operator in determining costs when entering transaction details.

The overhead field is used to record any indirect costs that should be added to the cost type. This entry can be a single value or a percentage. If it is a single value, then the figure will be added to the cost. If it is a percentage then a % sign should prefix the value entered. This simply adds the given percentage to the cost.

Table 11.2 shows a list of cost types.

Table 11.2

	Pegasus Users Enterprises		
03.03.90	Cost Type List		Page 1
Cost Code	Rate	Overhead	Payment No.
C00 Consultancy Activities			
C05 Advisory visits	20.00	30.00	1
C10 Maintenance visits	15.00	% 5.00	1
H00 Hardware Supplies			
H10 Microcomputer Systems		100.00	1
H20 Peripherals		% 9.00	1
H30 Accessories			
S00 Software Supplies			
S10 Packaged Software			
S20 Tailored Software			
T00 Transportation			
T10 Packaging & Postage			
T20 Delivery Service		% 10.00	

At this stage you should attempt the following exercise before going any further.

1   Set up the Purchase Ledger parameter file to integrate with Job Control by setting option 6 to 'Y'. When purchase invoices and credit notes are entered as a transaction, an operator will now be required to indicate which job number and cost type it should be costed to.

2   Set up the Stock Control parameter file to integrate with Job Control by setting option 9 to 'Y'. When stock issues or receipts are made within this function, an operator will now be required to indicate which job number and cost type it should be costed to.

3   Set up the Job Control parameters file as indicated in this chapter, making sure that you integrate with the other functions.

4   From the Job Costing Processing option use the job record update activity to create a number of jobs.

5   From the Job Costing Processing option use the cost type update activity to create a number of cost types.

6   From the Job Cost Reports option use job list activity to generate a list of the jobs created.

7   From the Job Cost Reports option use cost type list activity to generate a list of the cost type created.

TRANSACTIONS PROCESSING

Transactions can take two forms:

(a)   Time sheets which relate to labour costs.
(b)   Job costs which refer to other types.

Both activities are available from the job costing processing menu and have similar data entry screens.

Time-sheet entry

Time sheets will show the **Date** as the first field to be entered. The system date is shown as default, which can always be changed. The Employee number should now be entered. This number will need to be the same as in a Payroll employee file. Even with integration with the Payroll, no validation is made as to whether the employee exists. For many large systems, it is unlikely that you will have sufficient disk storage space to keep Payroll files **on-line**, that is, accessible by the Job Costing system (you should also consider that much of the Payroll data is personalised information and should be kept **off-line** if not really required). As a consequence of this, you will need to make your own validation check as to whether the employee number exists. The **Pay Frequency** will also have to match with the details kept in the Payroll and should be either W for Weekly, M for Monthly, 2 for fortnightly or **4** for 4 weekly. The entry can always be left blank if not required. The **Narrative** field is for documentation purposes only and can be used to record such information as time-sheet numbers or dates.

The remainder of the transaction entry will be to assign to jobs various time-sheet cost types. The result of this is to build up a transactions file of job costs. A **Job Number** has to be entered to indicate what job a labour cost is to be set against. The **Cost Type** indicates the cost to be charged. In both cases, they must exist within their respective files. If a **Rate** has been set within the relevant cost type, then this will appear in its column leaving the operator to enter the number of units used. The **Value** column is then calculated. Any of these columns can be manually altered. If the cost simply requires a value against it, then the units and rate column can be left blank. A **Payment Number** refers to the payment number set up in the job file and, if not showing, can be entered or altered. The Comments column is for reference purposes only and should be used to reflect the labour cost referred to.

Each line represents a transaction record that appends to the transactions file. You will be allowed up to 50 transactions records per entry. However, when finished, you should type **END** in the job number column.

Cost-sheet entry

Entering cost details against jobs is far more straightforward and works in exactly the same way. The input screen requires a **Date** in the same way as Time Sheets and a **Reference** that can be used freely by the firm. With the exception of the payment type, which does not appear, the entry of each transaction record in the entry is exactly the same as that for Time Sheets.

INVOICES AND ENQUIRIES

It is important to bear in mind that what has been explained so far is that having created both jobs and costs type, we have entered a series of transactions regarding costs associated with jobs. In order for a firm to make a profit, it will need to receive payments from such jobs. The activity of **enter invoices** available in the Job Costing processing menu will allow us to assign invoices against a job. The input screen requires the **Job Number** against which the invoice is made. A **Reference** is used for documentation purposes and may, for example, be used to store the invoice number. The **Value** is the amount received against the job and should include the VAT. The comment field again is for documentation purposes.

In the same menu is the **job enquiry** activity which will produce a summary of all transactions, including invoices, associated with a job number.

03.03.90			Transaction List (To-Date)		Page 1			
Job Number	Date	Type	Reference	Cost Code	Amount	Units		
C0100	03.03.90	Lab	M001 1M	C05	40.00	2.00	Jo Blake Bakeries	Preliminary
C1022	03.03.90	Lab	M001 1M	C05	20.00	1.00	Davis Video Hire	Feasibility Study
C040	03.03.90	Lab	M001 1M	C05	20.00	1.00	Tuck Shop Supplies	Investigative
C1022	03.03.90	Lab	M002 1M	C10	45.00	3.00	Davis Video Hire	Hard Disk format
C040	03.03.90	Lab	M002 1M	C10	30.00	2.00	Tuck Shop Supplies	Printer Jammed
C0100	03.03.90	Cst	Supplies	H10	2,500.00	0.00	Jo Blake Bakeries	3 x Microcomputers
C0100	03.03.90	Cst	Supplies	H10	12,000.00	0.00	Jo Blake Bakeries	File Server
C0100	03.03.90	Cst	Supplies	H20	10,000.00	0.00	Jo Blake Bakeries	Printers + Cabling
C0100	03.03.90	Cst	Supplies	S10	12,450.00	0.00	Jo Blake Bakeries	Software
C1022	03.03.90	Cst	Sales	H10	789.00	1.00	Davis Video Hire	Personal Computer
C1022	03.03.90	Cst	Sales	S20	400.00	0.00	Davis Video Hire	Pegasus Ledgers
C1022	03.03.90	Cst	Sales	H20	400.00	1.00	Davis Video Hire	Printer
C1022	03.03.90	Cst	Sales	T20	50.00	0.00	Davis Video Hire	
C1022	03.03.90	Cst	Sales	H30	330.00	0.00	Davis Video Hire	Paper + Disks
C040	03.03.90	Cst	Sales	H10	998.00	0.00	Tuck Shop Supplies	20 Mb Micro System
C0100	05.03.90	Cst	Disks	H30	100.00	0.00	Jo Blake Bakeries	80 * 3.5" Disks
C040	05.03.90	Cst	Disks	H30	50.00	0.00	Tuck Shop Supplies	40 * 3.5" Disks
C0100	03.03.90	Inv	INV100010		−20.00	0.00	Jo Blake Bakeries	Extra charge
C0100	24.02.90	Inv	Ch7611192		−20,000.00	0.00	Jo Blake Bakeries	First Instalment

Cost Type Totals		
Consultancy Activities	155.00	9.00
Hardware Supplies	27,167.00	2.00
Software Supplies	12,850.00	0.00
Transportation	50.00	0.00
Total Invoiced	−20,020.00	0.00

Figure 11.6

With all of these activities, there is now sufficient information to determine costs associated with jobs as well as determining whether a profit has been made.

The list of transactions in Figure 11.6 is an example of transactions records held in the job costing transactions file.

The transaction list shows cost entries as + amount while invoice figures are −. The reason for this is that invoices, which represent income, can be regarded as a negative cost. For any given job the aim should be to have total invoices associated with a job greater than the costs.

When a Job has been completed, the job record will need to be updated so that the completed indicator has a 'Y' in it. During the lifetime of any job, we will will want to regularly make enquiries on a job in order to see whether costs have been kept within budget.

Figure 11.7 is an example of such an enquiry.

C0100 Jo Blake Bakeries		Budget 51,000			By 10.09.90
			Amount	Overhead	Uplifted
Advisory visits Labour To M001 Preliminary		03.03.90	40.00	30.0000	70.00
Microcomputer Systems Costs Ref Supplies 3 x Microcomputers		03.03.90	2,500.00	100.0000	2,600.00
Microcomputer Systems Costs Ref Supplies File Server		03.03.90	12,000.00	100.0000	12,100.00
Peripherals Costs Ref Supplies Printers + Cabling		03.03.90	10,000.00	% 9.0000	10,900.00
Packaged Software Costs Ref Supplies Software		03.03.90	12,450.00		12,450.00
Accessories Costs Ref Disks 80 * 3.5" Disks		05.03.90	100.00		100.00
Invoice Sales Ref INV100010 Extra charge		03.03.90	−20.00		−20.00
Invoice Sales Ref Ch7611192 First Instalment		24.02.90	−20,000.00		−20,000.00
Total	Including Invoices		17,070.00		18,200.00
	Excluding Invoices		37,090.00		38,220.00

Figure 11.7

The enquiry in Figure 11.7 shows that the total cost of the job to-date has amounted to £37,090 against a budget of £51,000. Also it can be seen that income from the job has so far amounted to £20,020 from two invoices issued. The enquiry also shows the effect of the overhead. When the overhead is added to the actual cost amount, we get a column called uplifted. It is the uplifted value that all income should eventually cover.

As the job does not indicate it has finished, it can be assumed that more transactions will result from it.

Exercises

Before progressing any further, attempt the following exercises:

1. From the Job Costing Processing option use the Enter Time Sheets activity to create a number of time-sheet transactions. Be careful to match both employee number and pay frequency with the records held in the Payroll file.
2. From the Job Costing processing option use the Enter Job Costs activity to create a further number of cost transactions.
3. From the Job Costing Processing option use the Enter Invoices activity to create a number of invoice transactions.
4. From the Job Costing Processing option use the Job Enquiries activity to examine the effect the transactions have had on each of the jobs.
5. From the Job Cost Reports option use the Transaction List activity to generate a list of the transactions generated.
6. From the Job Cost Reports option use the Job Cost Report activity to examine the costs on each of the jobs.
7. From the Job Cost Reports option use the Job Cost Summary activity to examine a summary of job costs.

An example of a job cost report and job cost summary should show the benefits of being able to categorise costs into jobs. However, allocating costs in the way set out so far is only part of the story. The final section of the chapter will attempt to complete the job control function by examining the remaining sources of information.

ANALYSIS AND RE-ORGANISATION

By now you should have gained a fairly comprehensive knowledge of how the Job Costing function works. It is possible to operate the function fully without much further development in knowledge. However, the main problem at the moment is that no real use has been made of the fact that we can integrate this function with those of Purchase Ledger, Stock Control and Payroll.

Job analysis of purchase

Provided the Job Costing function is integrated with the Purchase Ledger, this activity will scan every purchase invoice and credit note in the Purchase Ledger to see if any items are related to any of the specific jobs. This offers an alternative way of entering job costs where job costs are identified when purchase invoice details are entered to the Purchase Ledger.

The case often arises when goods or services are directly related to a specific job. Identifying such purchases against particular jobs will need careful thought and organisation and may not always be practicable. If a purchase is not directly related to a specific job, then the job cost details in the Purchase Ledger can be left blank.

The extract in Figure 11.8 shows a hard-copy output of an analysis of purchase.

03.03.90	Job Cost Analysis of Purchases					
Cost Type	Date	Reference	P/Acc	Value		
C0100	Jo Blake Bakeries					
H30 Accessories	03.03.90	JOB C0100	0001	100.00	Williams & Sons Stationery	Printed Paper
H30 Accessories	03.03.90	inv303031	0003	18.00	Peaky Paper Supplies	Fanfold Paper
				118.00		
C040	Tuck Shop Supplies					
S10 Packaged Software	03.03.90	930023	0100	280.00	Account Software Inc	Packaged Software
				280.00		

Total Posted	398.00
Total Rejected	16,150.00
Total Purchases	16,548.00

Figure 11.8

Exercise

1. From the Purchase Ledger enter a number of purchase invoices indicating in the job costing columns both the job number against which the purchase has been made and the cost type to which it is to be attributed.
2. From the main job costing menu run the job analysis of purchase activity in order to update the Job Costing transactions file.
3. Now use the enquiry option within the Job Costing Processing menu in order to examine the effect on job costs.

It should be evident from this that a good deal of processing activity can be saved by identifying the jobs to which purchases have to be made at source.

Labour analysis

In purchase analysis, job cost details were extracted from purchase invoices and credit notes and generated transactions to Job Costing. In this instance some of the Payroll details are already held in Job Costing transactions in the form of time sheets. The purpose of this activity is to post these to Payroll and take away the need to enter the details again when operating the Payroll system.

The report in Figure 11.9 is a small demonstration of a printed report generated from the analysis, which should be run prior to the end-of-month Payroll run.

Pegasus Users Enterprises					
03.03.90	Labour Analysis (This Period)				Page 1
Cost Type	Date	Emp.	Units	Value	Uplifted
C0100 Jo Blake Bakeries					
C05 Advisory visits	03.03.90	M001	2.00	40.00	70.00
			2.00	40.00	70.00
C1022 Davis Video Hire					
C05 Advisory visits	03.03.90	M001	1.00	20.00	50.00
C10 Maintenance visits	03.03.90	M002	3.00	45.00	47.25
			4.00	65.00	97.25
C040 Tuck Shop Supplies					
C05 Advisory visits	03.03.90	M001	1.00	20.00	50.00
C10 Maintenance visits	03.03.90	M002	2.00	30.00	31.50
			3.00	50.00	81.50
	Grand Total		9.00	155.00	248.75
Company Pegasus User Enterprise			Monthly Payroll Updated		

Figure 11.9

It is also important to make sure that all time sheets are up to date and entered before the month or week end if this facility is to be taken advantage of.

Job analysis of stock issues/returns

This concerns itself with integrating Stock Control with Job Costing. In order for this activity to work you will need to ensure that:

(a)   Stock Control parameter option 9 is set to 'Y'.
(b)   Stock records will need a field of **cost code** to match a cost type code in Job Costing.

Given these conditions, when stock issues or returns are made within the Stock Control function, they are ready for automatic analysis within the job control function.

Exercises

As a final set of exercises perform the following activities:

1   Ensure that option 9 in Stock Control parameters is set to 'Y' and that a **cost code** that matches job cost types have been set for all relevant stock records. Altering cost codes in Stock Control will have to be done as a record-update activity in that module.

2   Now make a number of issues and returns within the Stock Control function ensuring that the job numbers required exist within the Job Control function.

3   From the main Job Costing menu run the Job Analysis of Stock Issues/Returns activity in order to update the Job Costing transactions file.

4   Now use the enquiry option within the Job Costing Processing menu in order to examine the effect on job costs.

5   From the Job Cost Reports option use the Transaction List activity to compile a list of the transactions generated.

12 Bill of Materials

DEFINING ASSEMBLIES

This chapter tackles an extension of the Stock Control system by examining the way some stock is actually used. In a manufacturing firm, a product may be manufactured using components held in stock. In other words, a group of components are used to create a single product, or even a single component for another product. The concept of Bill of Materials is to handle the way components are used to create **assemblies**, an assembly being a composition of components. (*See* Figure 12.1.)

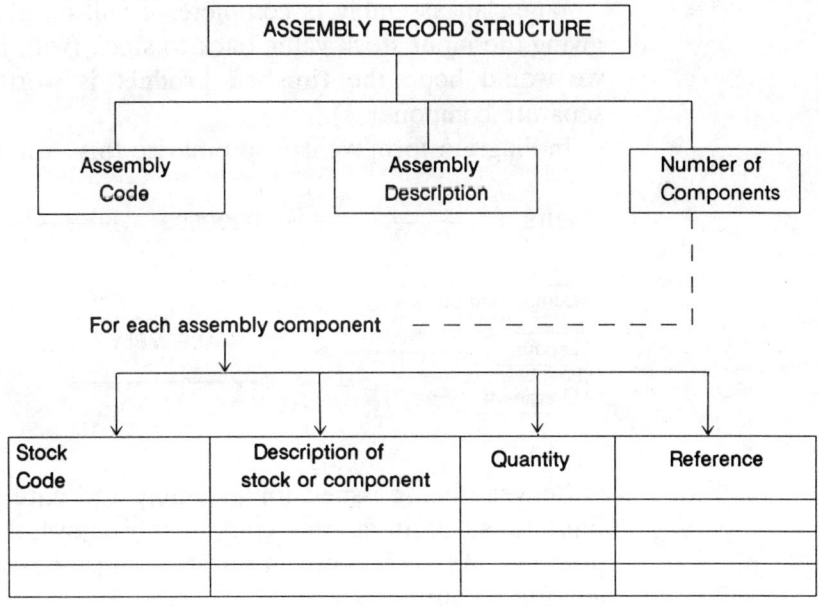

Figure 12.1

Note: From this structure, any single component within an assembly can be another assembly record, creating a hierarchical structure of assemblies and sub-assemblies.

One of the focal points of this function is the maintaining of records called **assembly records** which are held in an assembly file. Another name for these assembly records is an explosion record. In order to operate this function, there has to be a stock file maintained by the Stock Control part of the Pegasus system. In other words, this has to be integrated with Stock Control, as depicted by the diagram in Figure 12.1. An assembly (or explosion) record consists of the following details:

1   Assembly code to identify assemblies.
2   Assembly description to give it a name.
3   For each component (that must appear in the stock file)

   (a) Component code.
   (b) Number of components in assembly.

Work-in-progress

We now need to explain how the system handles stock movements with respect to this module.

When an item of stock is **issued** as a movement to appear in an assembly it is no longer an item in stock. As such, it will not appear in any stock valuation for accounting purposes.

When an assembly is complete, it will be placed in stock, thereby giving the input stock value back to stock (with a value added because we would hope the **finished product** is worth more now than as separate components).

In diagram form we can summarise this as in Figure 12.2.

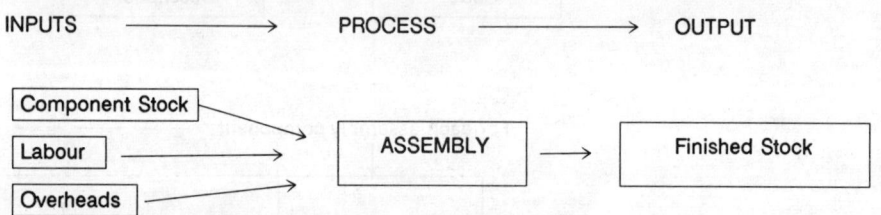

Figure 12.2

Between being issued for assembly and entered back in stock as a finished stock item, the component enjoys the status of **work-in-progress**. As such, work-in-progress must be valued at intervals for accounting purposes.

Allocating stock

An important feature of Bill of Materials is the information as to the availability of stock in order to make assemblies and to indicate what is required in the way of stock to meet future assemblies.

When deciding on an assembly for a finished stock item, the system must take out of stock and place into work-in-progress all those components that are required to make the finished products. Apart from being a major time-saving facility, it is also a useful way of assessing a firm's manufacturing potential at any given time.

Sub-assemblies

It cannot always be assumed that all assemblies are simply a collection of components with labour and overheads added in order to produce a finished stock item. An assembly may be made up of sub-assemblies which, in turn, can consist of further sub-assemblies. It is important to note that all assemblies and sub-assemblies will originate from components. Also, many components can be required by differing sub-assemblies and at different levels.

Figure 12.3 illustrates the main features of an assembly structure:

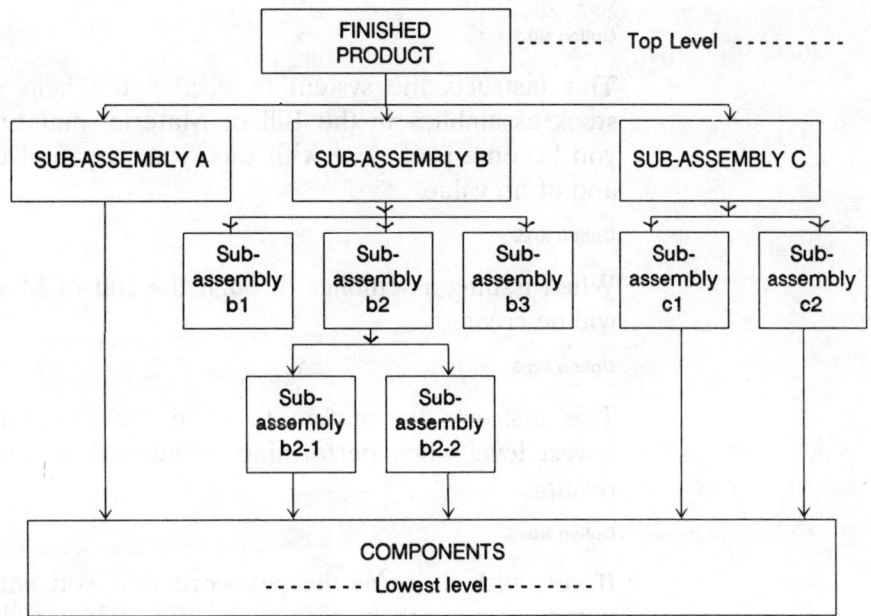

Figure 12.3

Whatever the structure of an assembly, the base of such a structure will be components, with records in the stock file as maintained by the Stock Control system.

GETTING STARTED

As usual, we need to set up the parameters required by the module, followed by setting up the records. From the Bill of Materials menu, there are five options:

1 **Bill of Materials Processing.**
2 **Re-organise Assembly File.**
3 **Bill of Materials Report.**
4 **Parameter Update.**
5 **Special Update.**

Option 4 will be required first.

The following is an example set of parameter settings with notes of explanation following:

Company Name   **Pegasus Users Enterprises**

This name is used to appear on Bill of Materials reports as headings.

Printer	**Type**	0
	TOF Code	12
	Columns	80
	Lines/Page	66

As before, printer details instruct the package about the kind of printer being used.

Option No.1   Y

This instructs the system to display the help menu when creating stock assemblies in the Bill of Material maintenance activity. After you become proficient with this, you may find the menu a nuisance and of no value.

Option No.2   Y

When issuing assemblies through the Bill of Materials, order records will be created.

Option No.3   Y

This instructs the system to issue the components through to the lowest level when performing an allocation, de-allocation, return or receipt.

Option No. 4

If you wish to enter the password that you enter for access to the parameters in other areas of the Bill of Materials module, then enter a 'Y' here. When items are selected from the menu of the Bill of Materials, the user will be prompted for entry of the password before being allowed to proceed.

MAINTAINING ASSEMBLIES

From option 1 of the Bill of Material Menu, Bill of Materials processing, you see another menu where option 1 deals with assemblies maintenance. The objective of this activity is to allow:

(a) Creation of new assembly structures.
(b) Deletion of old assembly structures.
(c) Amendments of existing assembly structures.

You are first required to enter an **assembly code** which must appear as a stock number in the stock file. This item forms the basis of an assembly which is made up of components.

As an example, I shall use an assembly of an adjustable computer desk to demonstrate the principle of Bill of Materials, as well showing the technical activities contained within the Bill of Materials function.

A crude look at how such a finished product is assembled is shown in Figure 12.4.

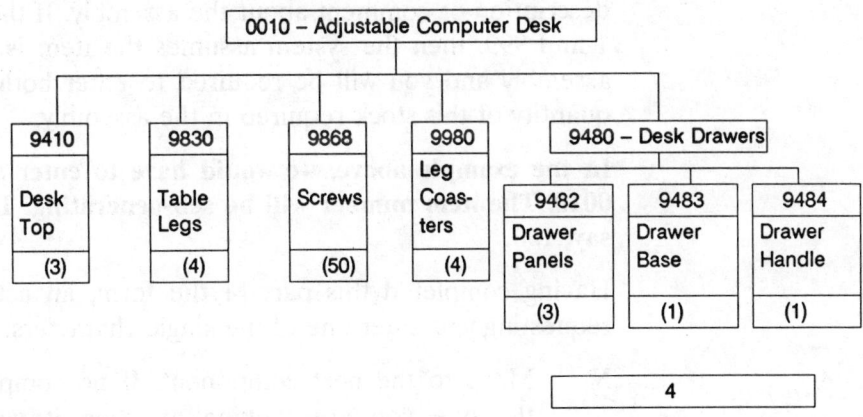

Figure 12.4

From Figure 12.4 it appears that the finished product is made up of five components, of which one, four Desk Drawers, is itself an assembly of three different sets of components. The figures in brackets indicate the number of components required in the finished product.

Table 12.1

	Pegasus User Enterprises			
05.03.90	Stocktake List			Page 1
Stock Reference		Location	Stock Qty	Unit Desc	Supplier's Part Number
9410	Desk Top	flr1	10		
9830	Computer table legs	flr1	55		
9868	Basic table screws	flr1	1200	box	
9980	Table leg coasters	flr1	40		
9480	Desk Drawers	flr1	22		
9482	Drawer Panels	flr1	100		
9483	Drawer Base		40		
9484	Drawer Handles	flr1	21		
9540	Computer Desk Drawers	flr1	89		

Before we can start, it is important that each assembly **and** individual component is in stock. The stocktake list in Table 12.1 confirms that all such items are in stock and that there are sufficient stocks available to assemble a few finished products. It is not good enough just to create stock record headers for this demonstration.

From the Bill of Materials Processing menu, the activity **Assembly** maintenance allows the setting up of an assembly structure.

The **item number** informs you which component is being displayed. If the assembly code is a new one, then 01 will be displayed here. This number is generated by the computer.

The **reference** will need to be a number between 0 and 999. If the number is ZERO then a box below will appear requesting a description or comment about the assembly. If the number is between 1 and 999, then the system assumes the item is a component of the assembly and you will be required to enter both stock code and the quantity of this stock required in the assembly.

In the example above, we would have to enter an assembly code of 0010. The item number will be self-generating. The reference can be, say, 100.

Having completed this part of the form, an action box will appear requesting you enter one of the single characters:

N Move to the next component. If no component exists beyond the one you are looking at, then it will prepare itself to receive details of a new component.

P Moves to previous component, if there is one.

S Move to a specific component. You will be asked to enter the item number of the component you wish to move to.

U Move up a level to the assembly for which this is a sub-assembly, if there is one.

D Move down a level to a sub-assembly. If one does not exist then you will have the chance to create one.

None of these will be of use when setting up a new assembly, because all of them assume a component exists.

CREATING A NEW ASSEMBLY

When creating assemblies and sub-assemblies, the codes below that will appear on the screen are the key to creating the structures outlined earlier in this chapter.

B To insert a component BEFORE the one in view.

A To insert a component AFTER the one in view.

C   Change the component on display.

E   Erase the component on display.

X   Erase the component on display and all other components after.

Table 12.2 shows the sequence of entries that are needed to create the assembly of the adjustable computer desk depicted in Figure 12.4.

Table 12.2

Assembly Code 0010   Adjustable Computer Desk

Item No	Reference	Component Code	Quantity	Action to follow
1	001	9410	3	A
2	002	9830	4	A
3	003	9868	50	A
4	004	9980	4	A
5	005	9480	4	D
1	501	9482	3	A
2	502	9483	1	A
3	503	9484	1	U

Press **Esc** key to finish entering the component

When entering the details of the assembly structure, you will need to keep a conceptual idea about how the assembly is structured. Once created, this same option can then be used to move around the assembly structure and make any necessary alterations. For example, the need will often arise when a component needs to be changed or new components added to an assembly or sub-assembly.

At the end of this activity, you should find yourself back at the **Bill of Materials Processing** menu. With this activity, therefore, you are able to define all assemblies and sub-assemblies and how they are broken down into components.

From here, you can select option 3, **Assembly Enquiries**. The record for component 0010 reveals the following information:

0010	Adjustable Computer Desk			
Component		Quantity	Cost	Value
9410	Desk Top	3	44.00	132.00
9830	Computer table legs	4	20.00	80.00
9868	Basic table screws	50	.80	40.00
9980	Table leg coasters	4	20.00	80.00
9480	Desk Drawers	4	30.00	120.00
Cost Price 462.00	Assembly Cost	452.00	Variance	10.00
	Selling Price	500.00	Profit	48.00

Figure 12.5

From the details in Figure 12.5 you can observe that the assembly has been broken down into the components that make up the assembly. Each component has a cost, with the value being the cost multiplied by the number of components. The summary reveals:

(a)   Cost price as £462, which was extracted from the stock file.
(b)   Assembly costs as £452, which is the total cost of ALL components that go into the assembly.
(c)   Variance of £10 is the difference between the above.
(d)   Selling price of £500, which was extracted from the stock file.
(e)   Selling price £500 – assembly price £452 = PROFIT of £48
      If the cost price as entered in the stock file were taken, then the profit would be £38 (£500 less £462).

However, you may have noticed that when we set up the assembly, component 9480 was a sub-assembly to 0010. The enquiry above has not revealed this fact. You will need to make a further enquiry to show a breakdown of this assembly which is shown in Figure 12.6.

9480 Desk Drawers				
Component		Quantity	Cost	Value
9482	Drawer Panels	3	3.90	11.70
9483	Drawer Base	1	5.00	5.00
9484	Drawer Handles	1	4.00	4.00
Cost Price 30.00	Assembly Cost 20.70		Variance	9.30
	Selling Price 30.00		Profit	9.30

Figure 12.6

At this point you should have gained a reasonable idea about what Bill of Materials is generally trying to achieve. Before examining the more general activities within the Bill of Materials function, it is worth examining how the function is structured, in Figure 12.7.

From the outline structure overleaf it should, therefore be clear that the function Bill of Materials is broken down into three distinct sections:

(a) Maintain assemblies.
(b) Re-organise files.
(c) Reports.

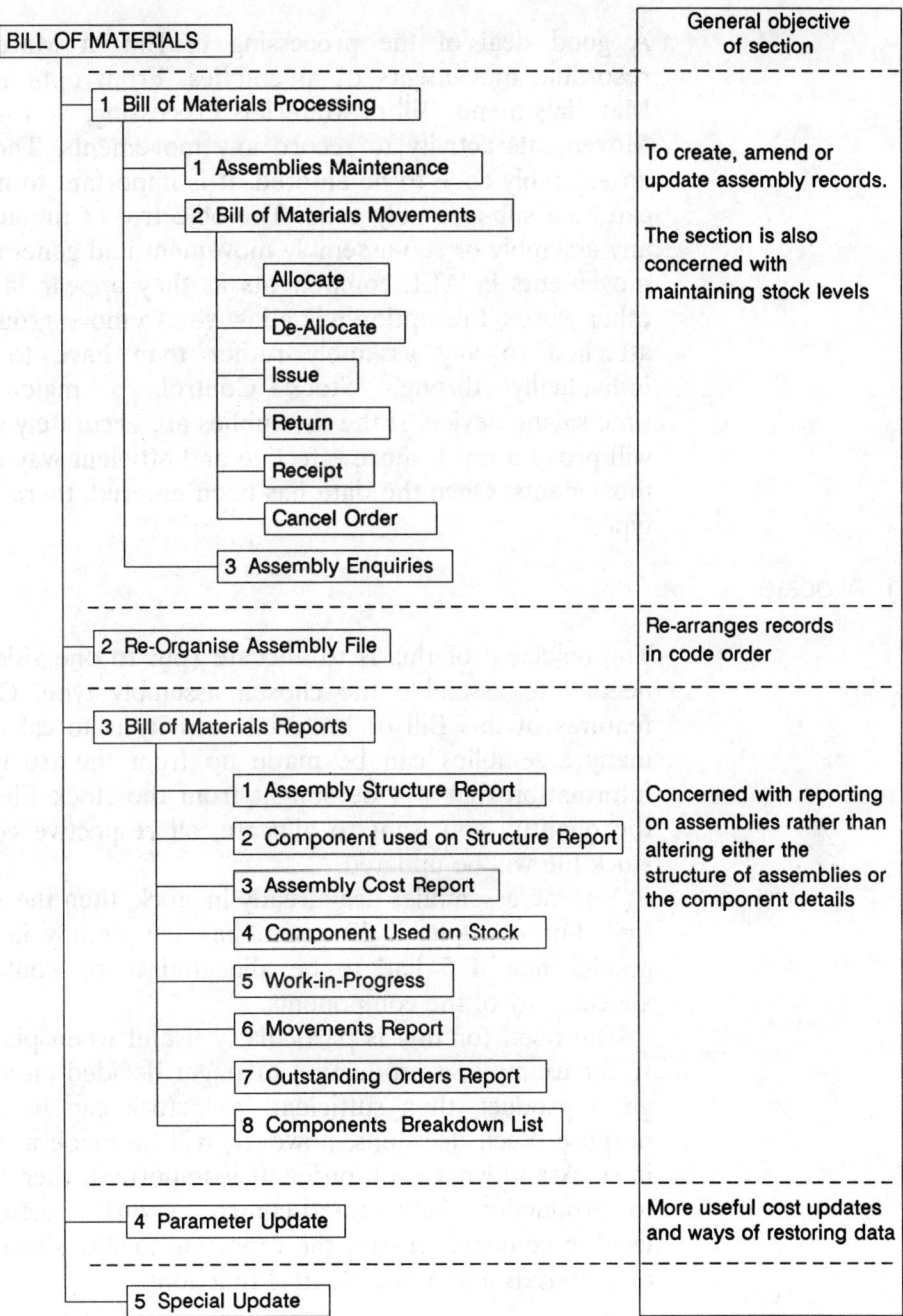

Figure 12.7

STOCK MOVEMENTS

A good deal of the processing of Bill of Materials will involve recording movements of assemblies. From option 1 of the Bill of Materials menu, Bill of Materials Processing, we use Bill of Materials Movements activity to record any movements. The activity requires an assembly code to be entered. It is important to note that this code can be a sub-assembly code. The objective of the activity is to record any assembly or sub-assembly movement and generate the subsequent movements in ALL components as they appear in the stock file. In other words, this option will allow you to move groups of components attached to any assembly rather than have to deal with them individually through Stock Control, a major and significant time-saving device. If the assemblies are accurately set up, this facility will prove a much more effective and efficient way of recording stock movements. Once the date has been entered, there are six movement types.

1 Allocate

The objective of this is to allocate (put to one side) all components needed to assemble the chosen assembly type. One of the useful features of this Bill of Materials activity is to calculate for you how many assemblies can be made up from the freely available stock, information that will be sought from the stock file. After indicating the quantity you want to allocate, all respective components in the stock file will be updated.

If some assemblies are already in stock, then these can be allocated first. For example, if 20 assemblies are already in stock as finished goods, then if 5 had to be allocated there would be no need to allocate any of the components.

The need for this is particularly useful when planning production. If, for example, a production manager decided on assembling 40 of a given product, then sufficient free stock can be allocated for this purpose. Such decisions, however, will be made according to what is in stock and what is on order. It is important, therefore, that in order for production planning and control to work effectively, this facility is used in conjunction with the reporting facilities available in both Bill of Materials and Stock Control functions.

2 De-Allocation

This simply reverses the process of stock allocation. In practice, this activity should be used sparingly. If, for example, a whole series of components have been allocated on the assumption that new assemblies were being made, then there is a good chance that a large number of purchase orders have been placed in order to preserve stock levels. If, subsequently, de-allocations are made, we could find ourselves with stock levels too high.

It is important, therefore, that careful production is made if rational stock-holding decisions are to minimise the cost of holding stocks.

3 Issues

The effect of issuing assemblies or sub-assemblies is to decrease the number in stock. Before making an issue, the system will again calculate the amount that can be issued based on the amount of components, sub-assemblies and assemblies that are in free stock.

When inserting a quantity, the system will ask whether the amount being issued has already been allocated. If in the past you made an allocation of stock for this issue, it is vital that you answer 'Y' to this question; if you do not, your stock levels will soon be too high.

If applicable, you will be requested to issue the stock against a job number. From the previous chapter, we examined the effect that integrating Stock Control with Job Costing had. This is simply an extension of this.

When the transaction is complete, all component stock affected will have their stock figures and histories updated. In many cases you will not want stock figures to be updated in this way. If this is the case, then enter the Stock Control function and update the stock record by inserting **** in the stock location field.

4 Returns

It is inevitable that some assemblies or sub-assemblies will be returned to stock, either because a user department or customer has changed its mind or there is something wrong with the order. In any case, such a return will have the effect of increasing stocks of such goods.

If option 2 in the Bill of Materials parameters is set to 'Y' then returns will be offset against past issues and, therefore, you will be requested to indicate against which orders returns are to be made. The system will extract up to 13 outstanding orders from the assembly for you to select from.

5 Receipts

This works in exactly the same way as that for returns.

6 Cancel Orders

When cancelling an order for assemblies or sub-assemblies, you will need to place the reference of the order in the reference box.

This now completes that section of the Bill of Materials that deals with maintaining assemblies. Before moving on to examine the reports, attempt the following exercises in order to build up a database and set of transactions to work with.

Exercise – Maintaining Assembly Records

1   Add two more assembly record types. In order to save time, Figure 12.8 gives two suggestions about products that can be made up.

Assembly	No.	Components and Description	No.	Sub-assembly Components and Description
0020	1	9021 (Hand piece)		
	3	9022 (Cables 3HR)		
	1	9023 (Scanner)	5	9023/1 comp111
			4	9023/2 comp89
			3	9023/3 comp911
0100	4	0100/1 (CHIP 100)		
	12	0100/2 (CHIP 200)		
	3	0100/3 (Case)	3	9023/2 comp89
			3	9023/3 comp911
	3	9022 (Cables 3HR)		

Figure 12.8

Before starting on this, you will need to update your stock file. Make sure you have plenty of the components in stock. To make sure, enter 100 of each component to start you off.

2   Use the purchase order system to ensure that over half the components have stock on order.

3   Use the Sales Order Processing function to ensure that both the assemblies are on order with customers.

4   Now use Bill of Materials movement to experiment with each of the movements types. Perform at least two of the following: Allocate, De-allocate, Issue Return, Receipt, Cancel order.

By the time you have completed these exercises, your knowledge of many other functions and the way in which it integrates with Bill of Materials will have been fully tested.

From now on we have the relatively straightforward job of extracting reports based on your work and interpreting their meaning.

BILL OF MATERIALS REPORTS

From the Bill of Materials main menu, option 3, the Reports function offers eight reports, all of which will serve as a useful source of information.

1 Assembly Structure Report

This report simply indicates the way an assembly is structured. Figure 12.9 shows the structure for our example of the Adjustable Computer Desk.

Assembly Structure			
0010	Adjustable Computer Desk		
		Ref	Quantity
9410	Desk Top	1	3
9830	Computer table legs	2	4
9868	Basic table screws	3	50
9980	Table leg coasters	4	4
9480	Desk Drawers	5	4
9482	Drawer Panels	501	3
9483	Drawer Base	502	1
9484	Drawer Handles	503	1

Figure 12.9

From this it can be seen the desk has five components of which the fifth, 9480, is a sub-assembly of three components.

2 Component Used on Structure Report

This report requires you to select a range of components for which you want to report on which assemblies they are used. Figure 12.10 shows details of the assemblies on which the selected components are used, along with the quantities used. Such a report quickly illustrates the extent to which components are used in production and can assist us in both purchasing and production planning decisions. For example, if a component is missing, we can at least see what assemblies cannot be completed.

Component Used On Report			
9023/2	comp89		
		Ref	Quantity
0100/3	Casing for bar reader	301	3
0100	Bar Code Reader	3	3
9023	Scanner	302	4
0020	Hand Scanner	3	1
0100/3	Casing for bar reader	302	3
0100	Bar Code Reader	3	3
9023	Scanner	303	3
0020	Hand Scanner	3	1

Figure 12.10

3 Assembly Cost Report

Figure 12.11 gives a listing of each assembly and sub-assembly, showing summaries of costs. You may notice in this report, that each variance (var) is zero. This was achieved by running **cost price update**, which is an activity available within the special update function from the Bill of Materials menu.

The assembly price is determined by adding up all the components costs that go into the assembly. The cost price is the price held in the stock file. The purpose of using cost price update is to alter the cost price in the stock file by making it the same as the assembly cost. The variance, therefore, will be the difference between the stock file cost price and the assembly price.

Assembly Costs Summary						
Assembly Code		Cost Price	Assembly Cost	Var	Selling Price	Profit
0010	Adjustable Computer Desk	414.80	414.80	.00	500.00	85.20
9480	Desk Drawers	20.70	20.70	.00	30.00	9.30
0020	Hand Scanner	221.00	221.00	.00	320.00	99.00
9023	Scanner	174.00	174.00	.00	200.00	26.00
0100	Bar Code Reader	482.00	482.0	.00	450.00	–32.00
0100/3	Casing for bar reader	84.00	84.00	.00	12.00	–72.00

Figure 12.11

The selling price is found in the stock file, with profit being calculated as selling price less assembly price.

Such reports can be extremely useful for:

(a) Determining selling price.
(b) Identifying where profits and losses are being made.
(c) Identifying any discrepancies between assembly costs and stock file costs.

4 Component Used on Cost Report

Figure 12.12 reveals similar information to the assembly costs report except that costs are based on components selected. From this report it becomes easy to see the cost of any component that goes into each assembly or sub-assembly.

Component Used On Costs Summary		Cost Price	Assembly Cost	Variance
9023/1	comp111			
9023	Scanner	174.00	174.00	.00
9023/2	comp89			
0100/3	Casing for bar reader	84.00	84.00	.00
9023	Scanner	174.00	174.00	.00
9023/3	comp911			
0100/3	Casing for bar reader	84.00	84.00	.00
9023	Scanner	174.00	174.00	.00

Figure 12.12

5 Work-in-Progress

Stock Ref		Quantity	Price	Value
9410	Desk Top	6	44.00	264.00
9830	Computer table legs	8	20.00	160.00
9868	Basic table screws	100	.80	80.00
9980	Table leg coasters	8	20.00	160.00
9482	Drawer Panels	24	3.90	93.60
9483	Drawer Base	8	5.00	40.00
9484	Drawer Handles	8	4.00	32.00
9021	Hand piece for scanner	2	17.00	34.00
9022	Cable 3HR	9	10.00	90.00
9023/1	comp111	10	16.00	160.00
9023/2	oomp89	17	10.00	170.00
9023/3	comp911	15	18.00	270.00
0100/1	chip 100	4	17.00	68.00
0100/2	chip 200	12	11.00	132.00
	Work-In-Progress Total			1,753.60

Figure 12.13

When stock is used for an assembly it will leave stock and go into work-in-progress until the assembly is finished and entered to stock. It is important that a business can value any work-in-progress, as this forms part of its current assets. (*See* Figure 12.13.)

6 Movements Report

This report, as its name implies, produces a report for a specified range of assemblies or sub-assemblies, on all movements made.

Bill of Materials Movements (To-date)			
0010 Adjustable Computer Desk	Type = Issue Date = 15.03.90		Ref = inv8991 Qty = 2
	Quantity Used	Total Alloc/Iss	Free Stock
9410 Desk Top	6	6	1
9830 Computer table legs	8	8	43
9868 Basic table screws	100	100	1050
9980 Table leg coasters	8	8	28
9482 Drawer Panels	24	24	64
9483 Drawer Base	8	8	28
9484 Drawer Handles	8	8	9
0010 Adjustable Computer Desk	Type = Allocation Date = 15.03.90		Ref = a1002 Qty = 1
	Quantity Used	Total Alloc/Iss	Free Stock
9410 Desk Top	3	3	1
9830 Computer table legs	4	4	43
9868 Basic table screws	50	50	1050
9980 Table leg coasters	4	4	28
9482 Drawer Panels	12	12	64
9483 Drawer Base	4	4	28
9484 Drawer Handles	4	4	9

Figure 12.14

In the example in Figure 12.14, it can be seen that two entries made with respect to this assembly resulted in a number of components being issued from stock. In addition to this, it can be seen what the position of free stock was after each movement.

Such a report reveals a history of assembly movement and can prove useful as a means of forecasting future possible movement. Such a report is also an indicator of the effect such movements have on the stock levels of components.

7 Outstanding Orders Report

Bill of Materials Outstanding Orders						
Assembly Code		Order Number	Order Date	Due Date	Order Qty	Balance
0010	Adjustable Computer Desk	inv8991	15.03.90	11.04.90	2	2 Overdue
0020	Hand Scanner	6734	15.03.90		2	2
0100	Bar Code Reader	90321-23	15.03.90		3	1

Figure 12.15

Such a report simply indicates all orders of assemblies that are still outstanding, and in some cases, are overdue. If an order has not completed by its due date, it will appear as overdue. (*See* Figure 12.15.)

8 Component Breakdown List

This report allows you to build up a 'shopping list' of components in order to assemble a collection of assemblies. In the example in Figure 12.16, we have chosen to assemble four adjustable computer desks, three hand scanners and two bar code readers.

Component Breakdown List
To Lowest Level

Component Breakdown List for the Following Assemblies:

0010	Adjustable Computer Desk	Qty = 4
0020	Hand Scanner	Qty = 3
0100	Bar Code Reader	Qty = 2

Component		In Stock	Quantity	Price	Value	
9410	Desk Top	4	12	44.00	528.00	*
9830	Computer table legs	47	16	20.00	320.00	
9868	Basic table screws	1100	200	.80	160.00	
9980	Table leg coasters	32	16	20.00	320.00	
9482	Drawer Panels	76	48	3.90	187.20	
9483	Drawer Base	32	16	5.00	80.00	
9484	Drawer Handles	13	16	4.00	64.00	*
9021	Hand piece for scanner	98	3	17.00	51.00	
9022	Cable 3HR	91	15	10.00	150.00	
9023/1	comp111	90	15	16.00	240.00	
9023/2	comp89	83	30	10.00	300.00	
9023/3	comp911	85	27	18.00	486.00	
0100/1	chip 100	96	8	17.00	136.00	
0100/2	chip 200	88	24	11.00	264.00	
				Total Value	3,286.20	

Figure 12.16

The resulting list indicates £3,286.20 worth of components.

The asterisks on the right-hand side of some of the components indicate there are insufficient quantities of this component to meet the assembly requirements.

Such a list can be extremely useful if we want to gather up a list of components for, say, a week's production schedule or gather a components list to meet an order, as it will tell us what additional stock is needed along with costs of components.

When using this option, you will be required to enter an assembly code plus a quantity required. When finished, entering **END** in the assembly column will generate the required report.

CONCLUSION

From the Bill of Materials main menu, you will observe there is a **special update** function which contains two activities.

1 Cost Price Update

As already indicated, this is used to ensure the cost of assembled stock held in the stock file has the same cost as the assembly cost. It should be noted, however, that this is not always desirable. For example, a firm may add in an extra assembly component such as labour which it does not want to appear in the cost of stock.

When there is a difference between assembly cost and stock file cost, this will be reflected in the variance generated in some of the reports.

2 File Reset

Periodically, this activity should be carried out to perform the following:

(a) Re-organise the assembly records into code order.

(b) Remove any unused assembly or component records which will return any work-in-progress to stock and release the stock records so that they may be removed from the file.

At this stage, practise with the reports and special updates.

By now you will have covered all the application functions available with the Pegasus Business Software. The next chapter will take you through some more advanced features available and give you the opportunity to see how the system can be customised to suit a business's added needs.

13 Retail Accounting

RETAIL ACCOUNTING

The facilities offered by the Pegasus modules so far examined may prove to be quite sufficient for a retailer's accounting needs. However, this additional module is specifically available for those retailers who serve their customers at a 'point of sale' (POS). Such a set-up simply means that when a customer enters a shop, or any other retail outlet, they will pay for their goods at some point of sale. It is at this point that many transactions with a customer are first carried out. The principle of POS is to capture this information at this initial stage and get it into the computer immediately. This will ensure that the initial data entry to the business is not repeated. In other words, retailers can easily establish the main 'data capture' point as being the point of sale, such as a cash register.

As with any module, you will need to start by setting up a parameters file. Beyond this, the Retail Accounting module offers the following functions: Parameter Update, POS Processing, Cash Reconciliation, Price Labels, Monitoring Stock Level, Printing Consolidated Statements.

1 Parameter Update

As with other modules, you will be presented with a series of options and requests to enter printer codes. Document designs are also required by the Retail Accounting module to produce invoices or receipts to customers. Clearly, if the POS is a cash register, then receipts will be an important output document to a customer.

2 POS Processing

The performance of these activities is largely dependent upon how the parameters are set. POS Processing makes extensive use of the function keys on your keyboard as well as the more conventional 'form filling' from the screen. A number of function keys (normally twelve) will appear on your keyboard either at the top or down the left-hand side. They can be recognised as labelled F1, F2, F3, etc.

Many application packages use these keys to allow you to perform a 'function' by hitting just one key rather than a series of them. The use of such function keys makes certain common operations easier, quicker and more accurate. Function keys allow you to:

- Create new sales accounts.
- Delete sales accounts.
- Amend account details.
- Perform *quick* sales.
- Store and recall partially held transactions.
- Perform till adjustments.
- Open the cash drawer.
- Perform an enquiry on a stock item.

Because such function keys are often used repeatedly at POS computer terminals, they will normally be labelled on the keys so that an operator can see more clearly what each function key can do.

Form filling via the screen allows:

- Making of sales.
- Production of receipts.
- Giving customer refunds.
- Posting receipts to accounts.

The use of either function keys and/or form filling is often entirely dependent upon the type of retail business being run. The module, therefore, has been intentionally designed to allow users the chance to tailor the product to their own business needs.

3 Cash Reconciliation

This activity will produce a report of all the transactions that go through the POS system which may include:

(a) An audit trail of all transactions.
(b) A breakdown of the payment types, such as cash, cheque and credit card.
(c) Daily summaries of: opening float, cash sales, refunds, account payments, adjustments, bankings and end-of-term balance.

This will allow an operator the opportunity of matching what actually appears in the till against what was entered.

4 Price Labels

This function can be very useful in that it simply prints product labels with their prices as stored in the stock or product file. Its effective use requires the business to keep stock files updated frequently.

5 Monitoring Stock Levels

This activity is used to monitor stock and inform an operator when stock levels fall below an acceptable level (i.e. the minimum stock levels). Such an activity is also available in the Stock Control function.

6 Printing Consolidated Statements

This allows the production of documents showing all the transactions for the same customer consolidated on to the one statement. It requires integration with the Sales Ledger and is a form of Statement of Account.

Conclusions

It is worth noting that sales can be made to customers who have accounts in the sales ledgers as well as cash. As for sales to account customers, the treatment of such transactions will require the updating of the Sales Ledger. Consequently, the use of this module will need integrating with the Sales Ledger function.

In much the same way, selling stock will mean that stock levels of items sold will begin to fall. Therefore, integration with the stock control system can result in very effective processing. If the Stock Control function is not used, the Retail Accounting function will require a product file in much the same way as Sales Invoicing.

With respect to VAT, most businesses must settle VAT net indebtedness (the difference between what they collect and pay) with Customs & Excise on what they invoice to customers and what they are invoiced for. This is an assumption that Pegasus makes. However, this module offers the option of settling VAT on what is actually collected and paid; a need for the very small business who can opt for such an arrangement with Customs & Excise.

In Chapter 15, case study 3: National Durable Supplies, we examine the implementation of Pegasus accounts in a retail outlet to perform the basic accounts and stock control in a store and linked to a wider area network. It should be apparent now that the availability of this module may be more appropriate than simply using the Sales Ledger and Stock Control functions.

14 Advanced Features of Pegasus

GENERATING REPORTS

Throughout this book, a good deal of the practical effort has been spent on the extraction of a whole series of reports. Although such reports are lengthy and extensive, the case often arises when certain information required is not in the format required in the reports available with the package. Report generation is, in effect, an extra way of extracting reports from the system. The difference lies in the fact that it is up to you what reports you want and the format you want them in. Using this facility is rather like programming the computer – you determine the rules and the output.

In addition to being able to print reports, we may also want to produce a report and incorporate it in a document of another kind that is to be generated by a word processor or a desk top publishing package. Later in this chapter, we will examine how this can be achieved.

In addition to generating reports, the need will often arise where information is needed for a spreadsheet package such as Lotus 1-2-3 or Multiplan.

Of the eight modules available in the Pegasus system, six have report-generator facilities: Sales Ledger, Purchase Ledger, Nominal Ledger, Payroll, Stock Control and Job Costing. Each report generator allows you to build up a report using the data fields within the module. You cannot combine fields between modules using the report generator.

As an example, we shall attempt to generate a report from the Sales Ledger module that will give us a list of all customers on the Sales Ledger that have a balance still outstanding. The first stage to this will be to enter the Sales Ledger function and select option R, report generator. This will reveal the following menu:

    1   Report Design.
    2   Data Selection.
    3   Sort Report.
    4   Print Report.

To start a new report you will need to select option 1, report design. The first stage will be to give the report a name of up to six characters of either letters or numbers, indicate that it is to be a new report and decide which disk it is to be stored on.

The first report screen will display a grid of ALL fields used in the Sales Ledger. From this grid, it is important to understand the nature of the field groupings. The first row of fields starting with a/c no. (master) down to balance, will be fields relating to a customer and, as such, will appear once for each customer account number. The next 2 rows relate to transactions records, where one record exists for each transaction. The fourth row is used to store customer account status, and will appear once for each customer, but will be periodically updated.

Before designing a report, you will need to be clear in your mind about the kind of report you want. In our example, we are simply interested in customer details and not transaction details. Figure 14.1 shows how the fields required in the report are selected:

```
PEGASUS                        CUSTNO Report Design                    30 May 90

A/C No. (Master)   :E:   A/C No (Trans)   : :   Type (I or C)    : :   Current Month   : :
A/C Name           :B:   Trans Date (1)   : :   Analysis Code    : :   1 Month Old     : :
Address Line 1     : :   Trans Date (2)   : :   VAT Code         : :   2 Months Old    : :
Address Line 2     : :   Age In Days      : :   Value            : :   3 Months Old    : :
Address Line 3     : :   Trans Type       : :   A/C No (Anal)    : :   4 Months Old    : :
Address Line 4     : :   Reference        : :   Anal Date (1)    : :   5 Months + Old  : :
Address Line 5     : :   Value            : :   Anal Date (2)    : :
Comment            : :   VAT              : :   Reference        : :
A/C Code           :A:   Paid Indicator   : :
A/C Type O/B       : :   Month Allocated  : :
Credit Limit       :D:   Day Created      : :
Turnover           : :   Bal Remaining    : :
Last Activity      : :
Balance            :C:
```

Figure 14.1

When selecting the fields, you must remember that details will appear in columns, such that choice A is the first column, choice B is the second column and so on. It does not matter what order the letters appear on the grid so long as they start with A and go through the alphabet in order.

If anything in the transaction fields were selected, then the size of the report would depend upon the number of transactions. In this instance, it is the number of customers on the Sales Ledger that will determine the size of the report.

To finish with this table and to move on to the next, use the down arrow key to run to the end of the table and into the next table. Having selected the table required, the next grid will require you to enter details of what fields are printed in the report and how they should appear.

The first feature is that in the left-hand row the selected fields appear in alphabetical order. You are required to enter, for each field, details for how that column on the report should appear. Figure 14.2 is an example of such a grid completed.

```
PEGASUS                    CUSTNO Report Design                        30 May 90

                      Tot   Line  Length   <-----------Selection Criteria----------->
A  :  A/C Code        : :   : :   :02:  :                                           :
B  :  A/C Name        : :   : :   :30:  :                                           :
C  :  Balance         :Y:   : :   :11:  : GT 0                                      :
D  :  Credit Limit    : :   : :   :11:  :                                           :
E  :  A/C No (Master) : :   : :   :04:  :                                           :
F  :                  : :   : :   : :  :                                            :
G  :                  : :   : :   : :  :                                            :
H  :                  : :   : :   : :  :                                            :
I  :                  : :   : :   : :  :                                            :
J  :                  : :   : :   : :  :                                            :
K  :                  : :   : :   : :  :                                            :
L  :                  : :   : :   : :  :                                            :
M  :                  : :   : :   : :  :                                            :
N  :                  : :   : :   : :  :                                            :
O  :                  : :   : :   : :  :                                            :

                   Seq  Item  Pos  Length              Item  Pos  Length Page
Sort Definition 1  :C:  :B:   :01: :30:  Total Break 1 : :   : :   : :    : :
Sort Definition 2  : :  : :   : :  : :   Total Break 2 : :   : :   : :    : :
```

Figure 14.2

The second column, **Tot**, requires you to enter a 'Y' if you want the column totalled. In this example, all the balances outstanding by customers will be totalled to give the total debt outstanding. The **Line** column requires a number in it as to how many blank lines to print after this column field has been printed. The **Length** column is filled in for you to indicate the number of characters the field is to occupy. In practice you will probably only want to increase this number rather than decrease it.

The **Selection Criteria** column is used to select which fields should be printed in the report. In the example here, **GT 0** indicates that only those fields where the balance due by a customer is greater than 0 will appear on the report. Another example is **NE 0** which means Not Equal to **0**. Other types can include such entries as:

LT 100	Less than 100.
GT O AND LT 1000	Greater than 0 and less than 1000 (between 0 and 1000).
EQ 10 OR EQ 100	Equal to 10 or Equal to 100.

If the field name is blank, then selection criteria should be a formula based on the values held in other fields. For example, if the column holding field C was the sum of fields A and B, the entry should be A + B.

Arithmetic operators for building up formula are:

+	addition
–	subtraction
*	multiplication
/	division
(	open bracket
)	close bracket

Brackets are used in exactly the same way as in defining any normal mathematical function. Also, numbers can be used to build a formula. For example:

$$((A + B) * D)/100$$

At the foot of the report design you are required to enter details about how you want the items listed in the report sorted. In our example, the report is to be sorted by a/c name, item B in the report. The first entry, **Seq**, determines the order in which items should appear; **A** for ascending order, **C** for ascending order irrespective of whether text is in upper or lower case and **D** for descending order. The **Item** entry determines the field by which sorting is to be done, in this case item **B: A/C Name**.

The next two entries determine what part of the field the sort should be based on. With **Pos** as 1 and **Length** as 30, the sort is based on the characters starting as position 1 and based on 30 characters from that position. If Pos was 3 and Length 2 the sort would be based on the characters starting as position 3 and based on just 2 characters from that position.

In the event that some fields are the same, typical if you have large groups of records with common fields, then you can set up a second definition.

The **Total Break** entries are used to indicate any breaks required in the report for such things as sub-totals, general groupings and page breaks. You can enter item, position and length in exactly the same way as for sort definitions to determine where the total breaks are to appear.

Having completed this, you will be required to enter details of the **Report Title and Heading**. The purpose of this screen is to allow you to enter details that you want to see on the report. The first entry requires a main report title. The enclosed boxes are used to place column headings at the top of each column. Underneath the enclosed box are letter codes indicating the nature of data items that go into each column. Apart from the length of each column, the information tells you what kind of data will appear: an asterisk, *, for text and 9s for numbers. The letter codes are explained in the lower part of the screen to help you determine what you should put at the head of each column.

Figure 14.3 is an example.

Report Title:	List of Customer Accounts			
A/C Code	Name of Customer Account	Account Balance	Credit Limit	A/C No.
A	B	C	D	E
**	*****************************	99999999999	99999999999	****

A A/c Code
B A/c Name
C Balance
D Credit Limit
E A/c No (Master)

Figure 14.3

Once this has been completed, you will be required to work through some relatively simple stages.

1   You are asked if you want to continue in **data selection**. If you answer 'Y' to this, the system will work through the Sales Ledger, extracting the fields in preparation for the report. Prior to starting, you will be asked on which drive you want the working data to be stored. Select an appropriate drive. If you answer 'N', then the activity will terminate, although you can always return to it later.

2   The system will now work through the files sorting and selecting fields for the report. Once complete, you will see how many records have been sorted and how many have been selected for your final report. You will then be asked if you want to continue. If you answer 'Y' the next stage will continue, which is to sort the selected records into the required order. Again, if you answer 'N', the activity will terminate, and you can return to it later.

3   Once sorting is finished, you can then print the report. If the report runs over one page you will see the same page heading as set up in your report title and column heading setting, with pages numbered.

Once the report has been completed, you are asked if you want the report data to be erased. If you answer 'Y', then, to run the report again, you will need to repeat stages 1 to 3 above from the report generator menu. You WILL NOT have to redesign your report.

The purpose of erasing report data is to reduce the number of files stored on your disk and, consequently, increase the space available. It is important to remember that disk space is not an infinite resource and can soon become cluttered up if not kept in check.

The report in Figure 14.4 shows the kind of output that can be achieved from the example we have gone through.

	Pegasus User Enterprises			
30.05.90	List of Customer Accounts			Page1
A/c Code	Name of Customer Account	Account Balance	Credit Limit	A/c No.
P1	A J Amber	1,313.72	900.00	0001
P3	A P Klingen	600.00	1,000.00	0101
B1	Blackman Software Ltd	10,444.53	5,000.00	0300
B5	Connells Enterprises Inc	1,120.00	6,500.00	0400
P3	K K Schwarz	110.00	1.500.00	0100
B1	Microchip Hardware Supplies	50.00	10,000.00	0303
P1	P M Bluesdale	1,020.00	1,500.00	0002
L1	Wessex County Council	11,715.00	0.00	0200
		26,373.25		

Figure 14.4

Exercise on Payroll

As another example, we shall experiment with the report generator using the Payroll files.

Perform the following stages:

1   Call up the Payroll module and select the report generator activity.
2   From here select report design and name your report **EMPLST**.
3   The fields that will make up the report should be identified as:

    A: Code
    B: Name
    C: Date of birth
    D: Sex
    E: Employee no.

Select these fields for your report and go on to determine the sort definitions.

4   The sorting should be by date of birth such that the youngest person appears at the front of the list. To do this, you will need to use the sort definition based on the year in descending order and use a second sort definition based on the month. The following parameters will achieve this:

	Seq	Item	Pos	Length
Sort definition 1	:D:	:C:	:07:	:02:
Sort definition 2		:C:	:04:	:02:

5   Carry on through the stages to print your report to produce something like Figure 14.5.

06.05.90		List of Employees		Page 1
Emp Code	Employee Name	Date of Birth	Sex	Emp No.
10	David Greenock	01.01.70	Male	M004
22	Kathy Pink	03.06.66	Female	K100
10	Jonathan Black	20.01.64	Male	M003
10	Joanne Red	25.11.60	Female	M002
10	Jack Blue	12.12.51	Male	M001

Figure 14.5

Remember to erase working data at the end of the exercise.

6   As a final exercise to this section, produce a report that will print labels for stock items. Such a label might consist of:

Line 1:   Stock reference
Line 2:   Stock description
Line 3:   Unit description
Line 4:   Factor

As a final point to this section, it is important to consider the different types of data when designing reports.

Master data Refers to data belonging to a database that will not change very often and is normally used to identify such attributes as stock reference, employee number or name, customer name and address.

Transaction data Data generated during transactions such as invoice number, stock movement details and payments this period.

Analysis data Data kept for analytical purposes only, such as category of sales or purchase type.

Calculated data Data that is calculated by the programs during execution such as customer debt outstanding, account balances or value of stock issued in a period.

When extracting data for a report you will need to bear these facts in mind. As a guide, Table 14.1 shows how the columns of data fields for selection are organised.

Table 14.1

Module Type	Type of data in columns (left to right)			
	Master data	Transaction data	Analysis data	Calculated
Sales Ledger	1	1	1	1
Purchase Ledger	1	1	1	1
Nominal Ledger	1	1	0	1
Stock Control	2	1	0	1
Payroll	3	1	0	0
Job Costing	1	1	0	0

Before carrying on through this chapter, have a go at producing reports with other modules. Here are some ideas:

1 Sales Ledger

(a)   A list of all customer debt outstanding for more than one month and in excess of £50.

(b)   A list of all sales made where VAT was collected.

2 Purchase Ledger

(a)   A list of all debt outstanding with suppliers for more than one month and in excess of £100.

(b)   A list of all purchases made where VAT was paid.

3 Nominal Ledger

(a)   A list of all journal entries, showing who made them, the value of the entry and in date order.

(b)   A list of accounts showing zero balance.

4 Stock Control

(a)   A list of all stock with VAT code 1 on them, in stock description order.

(b)   A list of all stock items that indicate they would incur a loss, and by how much, when moved. In other words, the report will show that selling price is lower than cost price.

5   Payroll

(a)   A list of all employees whose date of birth is before 1931. The list should be in age order such that the eldest is first.

(b)   A list of employees who have more than 10 days of Statutory Sick Pay (SSP) to their name.

6   Job Costing

(a)   A list of completed jobs, showing total costs and budgets.

(b)   A list of Purchases made against jobs, showing purchases in job order and sub-divided further into purchase reference order.

There is scope for plenty of imagination here, but you will need a reasonable amount of transactions data to do this successfully.

Linking reports with spreadsheets

A spreadsheet is the electronic equivalent of an accountant's ledger – a large piece of paper divided by vertical columns and horizontal rows into a grid of **cells**. The name derives from the **spread**ing of the organisation's accounts on a **sheet** of paper. The user can directly enter numbers, formulae or text into the cells. Each cell is referred to by its co-ordinates, like a map reference or point on a graph. For example, cell C12 is in column C row 12. Formulae can be entered to link cells. An example of linking cells is where a cell entry reads:

B1 * C1

which makes the value of the contents of this cell equal the value of cell B1 multiplied by the value of cell C1.

The spreadsheet effectively becomes a screen-based calculator capable of being printed or displayed as a graph.

Any figure can be changed at any time and the new results will be automatically shown, so-called **'what if'** analysis (for example what if sales were to increase by 10%). It is this facility of being able quickly to recalculate formulae that makes spreadsheets a powerful, useful and popular analytical tool.

Some spreadsheets are used in order to seek goals. For example, spreadsheets can be set up to depict the sales and costs of a business where a model is set up to determine what price will maximise profits.

Some examples of use are listed here.

● Financial plans and budgets can be represented as a table, with columns for time periods (e.g. months) and rows for different elements of the plan (e.g. costs and revenue).

- Tax, investment and loan calculations.
- Statistics such as averages, standard deviations, time series and regression analysis. Many statistical in-built functions are available in Lotus 1-2-3.
- Consolidation – merging branch or departmental accounts to form group (consolidated) accounts. This involves merging two or more spreadsheets together.
- Currency conversion – useful for an organisation with overseas interests such as a multi-national company.
- Timetabling and roster planning of staff within organisations or departments.

Pegasus has the facility of outputting any file to the disk in such a way that a spreadsheet, either Multiplan or Lotus 1-2-3, can read them in and manipulate the data in its usual spreadsheet way.

Output to Multiplan is achieved by using the report generator to output a report to a spool file rather than the printer or screen. When you are about to print a report-generated file, you are given the option of sending data to a Multiplan SYLK file; (SYmbolic LinK. The option is found by nudging through the options of how to output the report. Using Multiplan, you are then able to import the resulting file into a Multiplan spreadsheet. The file that is output, will have the same report name but with the extension **.MLP** after it. When Multiplan loads a file, it expects to find files with this extension after it.

To output to a Lotus 1-2-3 file, exactly the same method is used, except you choose the Lotus option instead. The file that is output will have the same report name but with the extension **.WKS** for worksheet file after it. When Lotus loads a file, it expects to find files with this extension after it.

In both the Multiplan and Lotus situation, you will need to refer to these packages to see how to process the data further.

In addition to the link with spreadsheets, there is also the facility of outputting reports to a **Comma Separated Variables** file. This output allows the report to be sent to a disk in such a way that many other packages such as dBase, Supercalc3-5 and Data Master can make use of the reports.

In order to practise any of these extra facilities available through the report generator, you will need a package such as Lotus and a knowledge of the package you are trying to link, an area beyond the scope of this book.

MORE ON FILES AND LINKING WITH WORD PROCESSING

In the first section the effort was geared to generating reports and sending them to various forms of output. This section will be concerned with sending ANY type of report for output in a way that can be used by a word processing or desktop publishing package, in other words, not just report generator output.

To begin with, a little familiarisation will be needed about the types of files available with the Pegasus system. Before going further, be sure you are aware of some of the basic operating system commands. An understanding of the operating system, although not essential to working with Pegasus, is very useful.

On inspection of directories, you will observe that all files that either make up or are created by the Pegasus system, have a file extension to them such as '.**dat**'. Files contain two elements:

(a)   A file name, which will be to the left of the decimal point. In MSDOS this is limited to maximum of 8 characters.

(b)   A file extension, which will be to the right of the decimal point. In MSDOS this is limited to maximum of 3 characters.

Such file extensions are designed to tell us and the computer something about the data stored in them. The following gives a list of the types of files and what they are used for.

1 Executable (.EXE) files

These represent the program files that make up the Pegasus system. For each Pegasus module, there will be a different set of these files. PEGLO-U.EXE, PEGMEN-U.EXE and PEGMOD-U.EXE are the main Pegasus programs that all modules need. The remaining files relate to specific modules. You can tell which module they begin with by the letter of the alphabet that starts the file name.

First letters	Module
SL	Sales Ledger
PL	Purchase Ledger
NL	Nominal Ledger
IN	Invoicing and Sales Order Processing
ST	Stock Control
WG	Payroll (WaGes)
JC	Job Costing
AS	Bill of Materials (ASsemblies)
RA	Retail Accounting
RP	Report Generator

BRUN10.EXE is needed to run the programs.

SUHELP.EXE is a program available that gives 4 pages of help indicating error codes that may appear during the operation of the Pegasus system. To run the program, type **BRUN10** from the operating system prompt.

2 Data (.DAT) files

These files are used to store the accounts of data generated by the programs. The file names indicate what data are stored in them. The first character is the company identifier. Hence, all files beginning with **B** will be company identifier **B**. The next 2 characters show which module the data belongs to, which matches the same 2 characters as for the executable files. The characters that follow the hyphen indicate the type of data held. For example:

(a) **XIN-PARM.DAT** stores **IN**voice parameters for company identifier **X**.
(b) **ASL-TRAN.DAT** store the Sales Ledger **TRAN**sactions data for company identifier **A**.

Some special files that can, on occasions, cause problems are the data files used to **lock** files. When certain files are being used by the Pegasus system, it is important to **lock** them from being used by others. For example, if an operator is performing an activity in the Sales Ledger that involves the updating of records, then other users will have to be locked out of similar activities while the updates are being carried out. The system, in this example, will change the name of a file called (say) ASL-FREE.DAT to ASL-LOCK.DAT. This, therefore, has the effect of keeping others out while certain activities are being performed. When such activities have been completed, the file will be changed back to ASL-FREE.DAT.

In the event of an operator attempting to perform an activity that they have been locked out of, the system will flash a message that the system is **active**. A problem could occur where the records are locked in error; this can occur when the system has been shut down wrongly in the middle of a process. If this does happen, then you will need to use your operating system to rename the file yourself.

This file-locking activity is required in a multi-user environment where more than one operator has access to the files.

As these data files represent the files where all Pegasus data is held, it should be apparent that it is these files that need to be **backed up** regularly to safeguard data against being lost or corrupted. With a clear definition as to what data files are used for what modules, you will now have the facility to be selective with your backing up.

Although much of this file handling requires a working knowledge of your computer's operating system, you will see later that Pegasus allows you to perform some of these activities from within Pegasus itself.

3 Spool (.SPL) files

These files are used to store files for either future printing or for importing into word processing or desktop publishing documents.

Throughout the modules you are given the choice of where to direct output: to the printer, screen or spool. If you select spool, the system writes the output to a file with the .SPL extension.

An example of a directory entry of such a file may be **NL120055.SPL**. The first two characters, NL, tell us that it is output from the Nominal Ledger. The six numbers are generated by the computer itself and is based on a calculation around the computer's own clock to ensure that every file generated is unique.

You can go on generating spool files and then print them all out at a later stage using one of the Pegasus utility activities. This has the benefit of deferring printing. Quite often, in a multi-user environment, it is not always convenient to print at all times of a day.

Spool files, as mentioned, can be used for importing into word processing or DTP documents. This ability is due to the fact that spool files are ASCII (or sometimes called DOS) files. In other words, the documents have no control codes or odd characters.

Once such documents have been imported into such packages, there will often be a need to process the imported text in order to make its layout compatible with the rest of the text in the document.

The main problem with using spool files in this way is that there is no way of telling what the file contains until you actually look into it, other than the module that created it. Also, the numbers generated when creating the spool file can be a little cumbersome to handle.

Nevertheless, the facility of having spool output in ASCII format is an extremely useful one.

4 Report (.CTL, SEL and KEY) files

These files are produced by the report generators as working files in order to print the required reports. As files, they serve no direct use to a user and should be cleared when the reports they represent are no longer needed.

5 Spreadsheet (.WKS and .MPL) files

These are Lotus 1-2-3 and Multiplan files respectively and are output by the report generators when requested.

6 Comma Separated Variable (.CSV) files

These files are requested output from the report generators that allows the report to be sent to a disk in a way many other packages can use.

PEGASUS UTILITIES

This final section gives you an overview of the last option on the Pegasus main menu, utilities. The menu displays nine activities.

1 Back-up/Restore Files

This activity does nothing other than instruct you to use your operating system to back-up or restore files.

Earlier it was mentioned how the Pegasus system stores its data in a collection of files that have a .DAT file extension to them. One effective way of backing up is to copy ALL files on the system with this extension to another disk or tape as a means of backing up. The Pegasus package itself does not require continual back-up because original copies of the software should be stored away from the very start.

Some users, however, prefer to back-up all of their files periodically. This is especially so if the system is hard-disk based and is a fairly large set-up with a large number of working files. Quite often, regular back-ups are made of complete disks on to a tape streamer or another hard disk.

2 Print Spool Files

This simply allows you to print one of the spooled files previously created. After naming the file required, you can align the paper on the printer by stating the paper is **not** aligned and entering the number of lines to align it. This process can be repeated until the printer paper is aligned.

After printing, you have the option of removing it from the disk. As mentioned before, it is unwise to allow unwanted files to be left on the disks. It causes cluttering up of directories and wastes disk space.

3 Spool File Map

This will list on all available disks the names of all spool files that can be printed. All such files have the .SPL file extension.

4 Data File Map

This will list on all available disks the names of data file groups which give an indication of what and where on the system modules are stored and files are kept.

5 Report File Map

This will list on all available disks the names of reports available for preparation and printing.

6 Multiplan File Map

This lists all the files that have been set up by the report generators for input to a Multiplan spreadsheet.

7 CSV File Map

This lists all the files that have been set up by the report generators for input to other packages through Comma Separated Variable files (CSV).

8 Lotus 1-2-3 File Map

This lists all the files that have been set up by the report generators for input to a Lotus 1-2-3 spreadsheet.

9 Reset Date and Company

This allows you to reset either the date or company, or both, without having to reload the program. The screen that appears when using this activity is the same as the opening screen when the Pegasus system is first loaded.

This facility is particularly useful when operating on more than one set of accounts or more than one Payroll grouping. Also, being able to alter the date allows an operator to pre-date or post-date transactions.

15 Implementing Computerised Accounts

This final chapter focuses on methods of implementing a computerised system. One of the problems is that the best strategy for one company may not necessarily be the best for another, although there are some basic and important rules to observe. Another problem is that the technology and related software is changing at such a rapid pace that an ideal solution now may not be the ideal solution in a few months time.

This chapter will present you with three **fictitious** case histories outlining the way in which companies went about computerising their accounting procedures (and other functions) and the varying degrees of success. At the end of each case study is a series of discussion questions which are designed to generate thought and/or discussion.

CASE STUDY 1: JAXAN LIGHT LTD

This case study is based around a firm that manufactures and markets domestic lighting equipment. The equipment manufactured can be quite extensive, but the mainstream of activity involves the manufacture of 30 different torches, 10 different ranges of light fitting, 10 types of table lamps and a range of specialist lights often made to customer order.

The company prides itself on meeting orders from retailers and overseas customers promptly. Some simple facts about the company may put the firm into some kind of perspective:

The facts

Number of employees:

Production shop-floor	15
Production administration	2
Marketing, sales and distribution	5
Dispatch	4
Accounts	3
Managerial	4
TOTAL STAFF	**27**

Turnover	£12 million
Expected number of orders	400 per month
Number of suppliers	100
Number of regular customers	650
Average stock value on premises	£2.5 million
Number of different items held in stock	5,000

Although the above depicts the state of the company at present, this represents a 50% growth in the volume of trade since five years ago when the company was formed.

Projected growth for the next five years is estimated at about 15% to 20% per annum. With such growth, it is anticipated that more capital equipment will be required and there is likely to be a need to employ more production shop-floor staff (probably two) and an extra person to cope with dispatch of goods. The company already has its production staff working on regular overtime, and equipment is working six days a week when production to meet orders needs to be high, hence the need for more staff and capital equipment.

The problems

All administrative procedures are, at present, done manually by clerical staff. Although the company sees no problem in coping with the extra capital equipment and staff, it anticipates a problem in information flows which cannot be overcome by simply employing more administration staff. In fact, information needs are not being properly satisfied by the current manual system. The company has identified the following information problems which will get worse with the projected growth:

1   Maintaining efficient stock levels becomes increasingly difficult. With the more essential stock items, such as differing types of flex (there are 50 in all), the company holds far more stock than is probably needed, because it cannot afford to run out. It is estimated that stock values are £500,000 higher than necessary, a figure that may well grow rapidly with expansion.

2   Keeping track of customer orders is becoming a strain, endangering the reputation the firm has for being able to meet customer orders punctually.

3   At any one time, there are up to 100 purchase orders with a range of suppliers, some of whom are overseas. Keeping checks on suppliers is becoming difficult because the information on orders still outstanding is coming to the production manager too late. On more than one occasion, the manufacture of key products had to be held up because of shortages of certain

components. The problem tends to be resolved by resorting to even higher stock levels of key components being held.

4. Information about customers owing money to the firm is not forthcoming at the right time. Quite often customer debt is left outstanding longer than it needs to be and customers exceed their credit limits because of lack of information coming quick enough. Of the average total of customer debt of £1.2 million, it is estimated that this figure could be reduced to an average of £800,000 without damaging company sales. Also, bad debts could fall by half to about £50,000 per annum.

Of the problems identified, it is important to stress that the company is far from disaster, but sees that if something is not done about these potential problems over the next two years, a serious problem could evolve.

The new system

The decision to computerise was taken as a result of a visit by a computer consultant, who advised that the company should acquire the following:

A computer network of four micro-computers. Each micro-computer had its own hard disk with a capacity of 40 megabytes and the file server, where the main files would go, holds up to 70 megabytes of information.

The full Pegasus Business Software system, with all modules being available for multi-user access. In other words, all four micro-computers could access and make use of all information held on the file server.

The strategy was to computerise the Stock Control function first, as this was identified as the main problem area. A decision could have been made to implement ALL modules simultaneously, but this was felt to be too ambitious. One thing at a time was regarded to be the best policy.

When the equipment was installed, one micro-computer was positioned in the production manager's office, one in stores and two with the production administration staff. The file server was also positioned in the production office where the two production administration staff were located. The consultant who organised the installation also arranged two days' on-site training for the production administration staff, the person in charge of stores and the production manager. The two-day training was focused towards setting up and running Stock Control and purchase order systems.

Getting prepared

The next stage was to place all stock information on to the stock control system. This process took the following form:

(a) The person in charge of stores had to ensure that ALL stock cards kept for each item of stock were up to date in terms of having one stock card for each item of stock, the description for each item was correct, cost prices were accurate and location where stock could be found was correct.

   During this exercise, some errors were found and corrected with improvements being made.

   The company always kept on stock record cards an estimated lead time for ordering stock quantities, re-order quantities, usual supplier and stock movement histories.

(b) The production team who were to be responsible for maintaining the Stock Control system had decided to scan carefully through the stock records, allocating new codes for their stock items. It was felt that this was long overdue and now was the best time to implement the system. Essentially, the stock codes that were already in existence would still be used, but each code would be prefixed with either A, B, C or Z to indicate the classification of stock. Basically, classification 'A' meant the stock was expensive and should be held only when needed in the short term. At the other end of the spectrum, 'Z' indicated very little cost involved in both buying and holding stock. The purpose of this was to get stock lists in the order they were required, a technique they learnt during training. Also, the stock code would have a 3-digit code following the classification code to indicate where in the warehouse the stock is to be located. Again, this produces a listing of stock that would prove useful for stores management, producing 'picking lists' and checking on stock quickly.

(c) When everything was complete and, as a result, the data was ready for input, the decision was made to create all the stock records on computer during the weekend. The weekend chosen was soon after making sure the manual stock records were ready, as there was always the fear that if this process is delayed for any time, the figures would soon be out of date. A Saturday was chosen, with four operators working through the day on the four micro-computers, to get the information on to the computer. Two of the staff needed a little training, but by the end of the day, all records were entered on the computer.

At this point, the only thing missing on the stock records was the actual stock level. This was intentionally left until last, because the problem of a time delay getting any information on to the computer would render all stock levels as useless. Before progressing further, a printout of the stock details entered was extracted and a few alterations were made, as well as 3 records being added that had been omitted.

Another visit from their consultant led to the advice that all such records should be backed up before proceeding further. The micro-computer in the production manager's office was designated as the system where Stock Control files would be backed to. A simple procedure was designed to allow this. It was also agreed that such a backing-up procedure would be carried out, as of habit, at the end of each day. (A simple batch file called STCBK.BAT was written on the micro-computer to do all the necessary work.) The production manager has recommended to the board that at a future date, the file server should be equipped with a tape streamer that would be capable of backing up everything on the file server at the end of each day within 10 minutes.

Getting started

The next stage was to enter all stock quantities and implement the system. It was decided to do this on the following Friday and Saturday. During these two days, stock levels were taken and used to adjust the stock quantities to reflect actual stocks in the warehouse.

The responsibility for keeping stock levels up to date was that of the person in charge of the stock. As from the Monday, every issue or receipt of stock was entered as a stock movement. This implementation went extremely smoothly, without too much disruption to the normal business. The company went on using the system almost unhindered for a month. It became apparent to the production manager that the ability to sit at a terminal and enquire about stock quantities at any time was an invaluable tool to his job, especially when planning production. Also, it was found that the low stock reports were extremely useful when planning what orders to place with suppliers.

Only one problem occurred when, as an error, the stock files were corrupted on the file server. This happened at 10.45 one morning. The production manager telephoned the consultant and soon put things right by restoring the stock details from the previous day (which had been backed up on to his machine) and re-entering the morning's movement figures. The whole process wasted just two hours, soon to be recovered during the day's work.

At the end of the month, another stocktake exercise was made to see how closely it matched the computer system. The differences were minor, and were easily corrected and new procedures for the collection and input of data were quickly drawn up.

Further developments

During the month, the production administration staff were sent on a computer appreciation course for two days. As a result of this, they requested the facility of a word processing package for their machines to replace the need for a typewriter. The production manager, commending them for their insight and enthusiasm, promptly purchased two single-user versions of Wordstar Professional Version 5 for their machines. Within one week, both staff were using their packages in preference to their typewriters. In addition to this, they learnt the technique of outputting reports to a file and then using the word processing package to incorporate the Stock Control output into reports and letters to a professional standard.

One of the obvious problems with the computerised stock system was the fact that low stocks could not automatically generate an order for new stocks because it did not take into consideration what was already on order. It was felt, therefore, that the next stage was to implement the Purchase Order System (POS).

The first step was to decide on the pre-printed stationery to be used. The existing stationery for generating order forms was used and a local stationers was commissioned to produce the forms as continuous stationery.

When the stationery arrived, the parameters for the POS were set up and, after a lot of trial and error, the printing of orders matched the stationery. One of the production administration staff quickly placed all outstanding orders on to the system and found that printing orders to suppliers using this system was relatively quick and easy and a substantial improvement on typing orders and having to file away copies of the order to a file.

Other benefits

Almost immediately, the implementation of the POS enhanced the Stock Control system and made it easier to see any outstanding orders that had not been received after the dates expected. Also, the ordering of more stock when stock levels reached their re-order levels was much more effective. Within a few weeks of the system running, and responsible staff becoming more capable and confident with the system, stocks held on the premises could be reduced, as the need to hold stocks was controlled.

One of the other benefits to be derived from the computerisation of both stock recording and purchase ordering was the fact that staff had more time on their hands to study the supply of stock from suppliers and 'shop around' the market place for better purchases.

In all it was estimated that the value of stock in hand fell by £200,000 (saving an estimated £13,000 a year in holding costs) and about £10,000 would be saved in a year through better prices by switching suppliers.

System evaluation

The company board, at an evaluation meeting, had come to the conclusion that the computerisation project was a resounding success and should be extended into accounts. The accounts manager, therefore, was given the job of investigating the feasibility of computerising sales, invoicing and sales order processing functions of the business. This interest was largely a result of the production manager complaining that the effectiveness of Stock Control was hindered due to the fact that it was not clear from the computer what stocks were earmarked for sale. If it was clear what stocks were allocated for sale, it would be easier to decide what needed re-ordering more accurately and, more important, more rational decisions could be made regarding production planning; too much time was still being wasted switching production schedules at the last minute in order to meet pressing orders. Meanwhile, the production manager was given the go-ahead to implement Bill of Materials as a way of enhancing the Stock Control system.

Computerising the sales function

The accounts manager began by using the same consultant to help decide a strategy on computerising sales. The first stage involved acquiring three extra micro-computers and upgrading the existing file server to allow these additional micro-computers to be linked to them. Additional printers were also acquired. One micro-computer was installed in the accounts manager's office, one in the main accounts office and one with the sales clerk.

As soon as the system was upgraded and the additional hardware installed, four members of staff, one of whom was the accounts manager, were trained on using the computer and the relevant Pegasus modules (Sales Ledger and Invoicing) by a trainer who came to the firm and trained the staff on-site. The training lasted two days.

From here, the four staff formed a small committee, chaired by the accounts manager, to decide on a plan of action. The plan took the following form:

1   Design and order special continuous stationery for both the invoices and sales acknowledgement forms.

2   Set up the parameter files for the Sales Ledger, Sales Order Processing (SOP) and Invoicing systems.

3   Collect details of ALL customers and enter this information to the Sales Ledger, placing an adjustment into each account to indicate how much is owed by each customer.

4   Enter every invoice, credit note, debit note and accounts adjustment details to the Sales Ledger until ready to implement the Invoicing system.

These first four stages were implemented smoothly, although staff did not appreciate the benefits of entering such details other than being able to print customer statements of account. This system was left to run one month before extending it. Meanwhile, the following preparations were being made:

Each stock record was being prepared with an analysis code. The method chosen was designed to allow future sales analysis to indicate categories of lights to be grouped. For example, all table lamps were prefixed with T.

Each stock item had attached to it a VAT code.

This was all done in conjunction with operating the Sales Ledger by itself for one month. In the second month, the next stage could go ahead.

As each customer was about to be invoiced or sent a credit note, the operator would use the Invoicing function to achieve this. This went ahead with remarkable fruition. It meant that the stock file was now being updated with an issue almost immediately the transaction had occurred. In addition to this, the whole process of invoicing had been speeded up. The operators soon got into the habit of processing such transactions as a batch processing run at 11.00 am each weekday.

The information being supplied to both the accounts and marketing personnel proved invaluable. In fact, for the first time, the marketing department could now analyse sales performance almost as soon as it happened.

In addition to this, keeping a check on customer credit limits more effectively meant fewer customers were being allowed to go over their credit limits without proper authorisation.

Within one month of this, Sales Order Processing was also implemented. This proved easy because most of the preparation had been done. As a starting point, all outstanding orders were placed on file and then all orders received from customers were processed through the computerised SOP system. Operators soon realised the benefits and found themselves with more time to concentrate on customer relations and promoting their products.

In addition to many of the accounting functions being met, those responsible for maintaining stock levels not only knew what was in stock at any time, but also what was on order and what stock had been allocated to sales.

Completing accounts

After six months of computerisation, a number of minor errors had been ironed out and the company was running the system with a good deal of success.

The next stage in the development of the system was to extend the role of computerised accounts to include both the Nominal Ledger and Purchase Ledger.

Starting with the Nominal Ledger, the company soon had this function set up and integrated with the rest of the operation. All journal entries were at first carried out by the accounts manager. The first set of automatic postings from the Sales Ledger to the Nominal Ledger caused a few problems, but these were soon sorted out.

During this development, Bill of Materials had also become well established within the computerised system.

Further development

After eighteen months the company had seen its information systems develop a long way. One of the main future developments will be to extend the size of the system to allow more users to access the information on the system. The marketing personnel's information requirements are such that they need a good deal of information on sales. A micro-computer was installed in their office to facilitate this requirement.

Over time, as the system developed, the company had organised itself quite effectively in order to get data on to the computer as quick as possible with as little fuss as possible.

The major problem caused as a result of computerisation is that the company now finds it much more difficult to recruit staff of the right calibre, even when it has increased its staff salaries to reflect the additional skills required to perform the tasks.

At present, the company now has computer expertise among its managers who have a number of developments they wish to get under way, Payroll almost certainly being the next project. It is anticipated that the information processing over the next few years will go on changing.

The latest evaluation report showed that the company was meeting its information needs well and would be able to cope with future expansion easily.

Case study discussion exercises

1. Trace the history of the computer development, indicating time scales involved. When doing this, try and show the development as a diagram depicting the sequence of events with time scales.
2. What role did staff training take in the development exercise and to what extent did it help?
3. Could the company have started with computerising the accounts function first followed by Stock Control in much the same way as covered in this book?
4. What developments can you see for the future in this company?
5. Outline

    (a) The benefits of the new system.
    (b) The costs of the new system.

CASE STUDY 2: PAPERLOT STATIONERY SUPPLIES

This case study is based around a stationery firm that supplies stationery through one retail outlet and distributes supplies to a large number of companies and individuals. The firm has three categories of clientele:

1. Customers through its retail outlet.
2. Corporate organisations who are supplied in bulk and receive sizable discounts.
3. Small firms and individuals who order goods based on a widely distributed catalogue – mail order.

Although this firm has a large customer base, its supplier base is relatively small, three large UK based firms and about 15 overseas companies who supply to the firm via agents; this avoids Paperlot having to handle importing procedures.

The facts

The following facts will help give some perspective about the company.

Number of employees:

Retail staff	2
Driving and dispatch	2

Storekeeper	1
Administrative	2
Managerial	1
TOTAL STAFF	8

Turnover	£2.4 million
Expected number of orders	250 per month
Number of suppliers	18
Number of regular customers – corporate	26
mail order	800
Average stock value on premises	£150,000
Number of different items held in stock	2,000

Background

The business has developed over 4 years of trading and was founded by its manager Jack Staples. The business has grown rapidly with the mail order side of the business being the latest part of their activity which was launched one year ago.

Staples envisages that the retailing and corporate sides of the business will grow less than 5% per annum over the next 3 years. On the other hand, if it can get its marketing and distribution right, the mail order side could double over the next 2 years.

In order to develop the mail order side of the business, Staples believes that the sales side of the business will need to be computerised in order to cope with the growth in administrative activity.

Getting started

Staples took the following actions:

1 He organised national newspaper and magazine advertisements for his catalogues. The advertisements are designed to coincide in all publications in one month's time.

2 He ordered from his printers a new batch of catalogues.

3 He bought a micro-computer with a 20 Megabyte hard disk, colour screen and a printer. The micro-computer was one of the latest and looks extremely stylish; he is always fussy about appearance.

4 He purchased copies of the three Ledgers and Sales Invoicing modules through a Pegasus dealer. He learnt about this package from an accountant friend at his golf club who used Pegasus for other business accounts.

After taking delivery of the computer hardware and software, Staples spent many hours struggling with the manuals to get the system set up and installed. Eventually, with a little help from a friend and a few phone calls to the dealers who sold him the computer system and Pegasus software, he got the Pegasus system installed.

Two weeks after having the system, he decided to appoint one of his administration staff to operate the Pegasus system. Judy was sent on a 3-day course to learn about the Pegasus package. Because the course did not start exactly when he needed, four weeks had passed before Judy started the course. This coincided with the mail order advertisements. On top of the normal business load, Judy was on a 3-day Pegasus course and requests for 3,000 catalogues had suddenly accumulated. All staff were now working overtime in order to get the catalogues delivered, with some orders from existing customers being held up for a day or two.

When Judy returned from her course she was now required to set up the Pegasus system with a view to implementing the Sales Ledger immediately to incorporate the new customer accounts on the mail order side of the business. Judy spent many hours setting the Sales Ledger up and entering all the customer details for existing mail order customers. The time spent doing this meant further neglect of normal processing activities in the firm; again orders were being delayed because invoices were not being set up correctly.

Crisis management

After another two weeks, new customer orders were coming in at about 90 a day, and the administration could not cope. Staples, in a near state of panic, contacted the local job agency and recruited two temporary staff to help handle request for catalogues, production of invoices and some basic accounts work for the shop. In addition to this, he employed the services of a consultant from a neighbouring firm who was experienced at setting up computerised accounts for such firms.

With the help of two temporary staff, who needed a good deal of supervision, and a consultant, a plan of action was drawn up.

The two staff in the shop concentrated on managing the shop and doing something about getting the backlog of work sorted out. Many stocks were low in the shop by now and disgruntled customers complaining of some stocks not being available. In addition to this, some accounts work had been neglected.

The two temporary staff and the other administrator concentrated on getting the mail order and corporate customer orders backlog sorted. This largely involved getting orders processed and invoices made up so that goods could be dispatched.

The storekeeper and drivers concentrated on coping with the extra dispatches. A much larger proportion of dispatches had to be sent by post in order to cope with the extra work.

During all this activity, Judy Punch was able to get the Sales Ledger set up properly and enter all invoices through the Sales Ledger. By the end of the second month, the processing was up to date and customers received their first computerised set of statements of account.

Getting settled

It was difficult to assess whether any real damage had been caused by the introduction of a computer and the transition period that occurred, but Staples felt certain that ground had been lost with some of its mail order customers and orders were lost with two large corporate customers. In addition to that, Staples spent a good deal of money paying overtime, employing temporary staff and paying consultancy fees. It was also certain that his advertising campaign to expand the mail order side of the business had not had the impetus it was designed to have.

However, in spite of everything, growth in business activity was expected, albeit not as large as originally planned. With the help of the consultant he hired, the decision was made to start the Nominal Ledger as soon as staff training was adequate. One of the shop staff was trained on the Pegasus system, along with Staples himself.

Meanwhile, one of the temporary staff left the firm and the other took on a full-time job; Staples felt the growth in the mail order side of the business now justified the extra member of staff.

Once the training was over, the decision was made to set up and run the Nominal Ledger. On this occasion, the transition went smoothly. It only took a few days to set up the accounts and enter the opening balances. Staples learnt from previous experience and from the training course that adequate pre-planning and preparation was an important factor when converting manual files to computerised ones.

It soon became evident that the system, with only one micro-computer, was not sufficient for the business information requirements. He was advised to install a network of three micro-computers. Consequently, he needed two extra micro-computers and a file server. The new system was set up with two computers placed in the main office and one with the storekeeper for future development. Staples regretted not being able to anticipate this early on because the adaptation to a network cost more than would normally be necessary and it meant having to retrain staff for the different skills required of them. It also caused a little staff resentment.

Very soon after this, both shop workers had got used to the computerised system and found that it was saving them time. Also, Staples had learnt how to extract the information he wanted from the ledgers and was soon planning effectively for changes in sales and keeping closer tags on customer debt.

Expanding the system

After two months, the system had settled well and Staples was ready to utilise the Purchase Ledger, Sales Order Processing, Invoicing and Purchase Order. He sent his storekeeper on a Pegasus course to learn how to set up and maintain the product files needed for the operation of the additional modules.

As soon as the storekeeper felt ready, he began to prepare the stock records by ensuring that all stock cards were complete and accurate. It was decided that stores would be kept separate from the shop. When goods were moved from stores to shop, it would be treated as a stock issue from stores in much the same way as issuing stock to customers through mail order to the corporate customers. The storekeeper converted all records to the computer in about one month and soon learnt to keep the records updated, especially with prices.

A major problem occurred because Judy Punch left the firm for another job, as she felt, with so much computing expertise behind her, that she could command a much higher salary than Staples was willing to offer. Staples had to recruit another employee to bring him to full staff strength. Finding another member of staff with the necessary expertise proved difficult. Eventually he found someone, after increasing the salary offered by 20%. This new person still needed training in Pegasus and needed some time to be able to get to grips with the way Paperlot went about its business.

The transition period between Judy leaving and the new person being taken on and able to work fully went on for about two months. During this period, some potential trade was lost, along with some credibility with many customers. Unfortunately the usual backlog of work had built up. Staff morale had also taken a little knock.

It took nearly three months for the expanded system to finally settle and for all the data processing to be up to date. Much of the management information was only just becoming of real use to Staples.

After one year of activity, Paperlot had expanded its business on all activities, especially the mail order aspect. Staples, on reflection, felt that computerisation was a success but realised that it could have gone much better with more careful planning, better handling of the staffing situation and better use of informed advice.

Case study discussion exercises

1 Trace the history of the computer development, indicating time scales involved. When doing this, try and show the development as a diagram showing the sequence of events with the time scales.
2 In your opinion, did Staples start off correctly? Explain the reasoning behind your answer.
3 To what extent did the lack of staff training and involvement influence some of the problems that occurred?
4 At what stage did Staples really get involved with the package? Did it help matters?
5 What can be done to improve staff morale, performance and the likelihood that they will stay with the firm longer?
6 What developments can you see for the future in this firm?
7 Outline

    (a) The benefits of the new system.
    (b) The costs of the new system.

CASE STUDY 3 : NATIONAL DURABLE SUPPLIES

This case study is based on a large firm that retails durable goods through a national chain of stores. The company has organised itself with a central headquarters in the north of England, five regional centres with depots for distributing to retail outlets in each of its regions. The organisation chart in Figure 15.1 indicates how the company is set up.

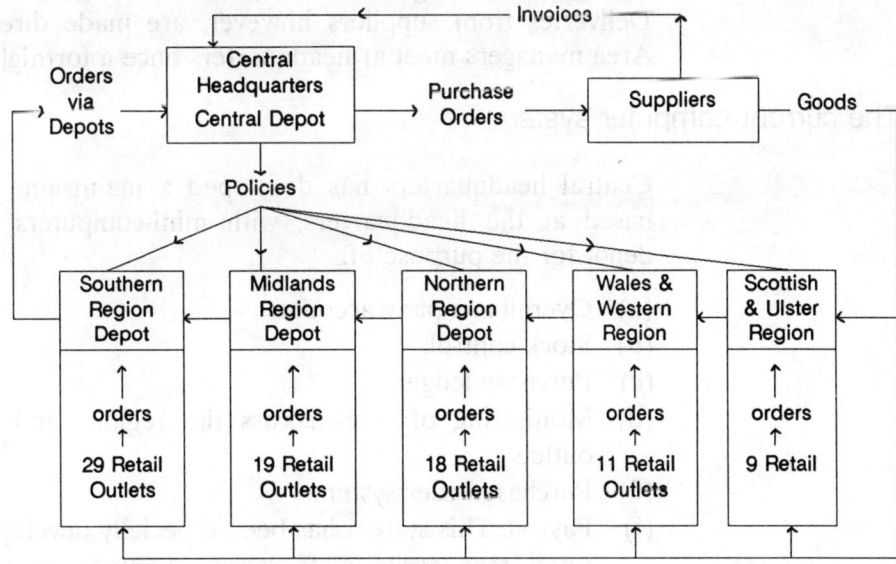

GOODS ARRIVE AT OUTLETS VIA REGIONAL DEPOTS

Figure 15.1

The role of central office is to:

(a) Make ALL purchasing decisions and order supplies centrally to ensure maximum discounts from suppliers.
(b) Determine sales policy as to exactly what each retail outlet is to sell and at what price. This ensures the company develops a clear national corporate image and can market its retail outlets in a more effective way.

Each retail outlet is headed by a local manager with a deputy manager and up to four full-time assistants and part-time staff. The number of staff at each outlet will vary from store to store depending on the time of year and the size of store.

Local retail managers decide on shop layout, although general guidelines are issued from headquarters, ordering stocks from their regional depot, hiring and firing part-time and full-time assistants and attending weekly regional meetings. Retail managers and their deputies receive basic salaries plus bonuses linked to their retail outlets' sales performance. Also, retail management can find their bonuses suffering if they recruit too many staff to justify the sales volume.

Each region has an area manager and assistant manager who have the task of coordinating the activities within their region, organising and overseeing staff training and development and managing the distribution of stock. Also, regional centres manage the depots and are responsible for keeping stocks replenished. It is important to note that ALL ordering for stock is made through central headquarters. Deliveries from suppliers however, are made direct to the depots. Area managers meet at headquarters once a fortnight.

The current computer system

Central headquarters has developed a mainframe computer system based at the headquarters, with mini-computers at each regional depot for the purpose of:

(a) Overall company accounts.
(b) Stock control.
(c) Purchase ledger.
(d) Monitoring of sales across the regions and within the retail outlets.
(e) Purchase order system.
(f) Payroll. This system has been especially developed to ensure that retail managerial staff receive bonuses to match their sales performance.

(g) Monitoring receipts of goods from suppliers to regional depots.

(h) Management information systems.

The system has taken ten years to develop to its current stage and will go on being developed by the company for the foreseeable future. Each regional centre mini-computer has a direct link with the mainframe at headquarters via modems. The modems enable data transmission between headquarters and each region in much the same way as any other data communication link. The mainframe has a set of modems, one for each region, so that all regional centres can interact with headquarters simultaneously. The company, therefore, has set up for itself a 'wider area network' (WAN).

The software on the system has been tailored by the company's own programming staff. The company employs a senior systems analyst and two junior analysts whose function is to oversee the entire computer system, its operations and development. There are six computer programmers who work under the supervision and instruction of the senior systems analyst. In addition to this, the company has four maintenance staff who are responsible for ensuring that the computer systems function.

At retail level, there is virtually nothing in the way of computer systems other than electronic tills that keep a simple set of accounts. The retail deputy managers have the responsibility for submitting sales reports each day on specially designed sheets which are posted to their regional depot.

The problems to overcome

A major problem with the system is the fact that information about stock levels and sales at retail level can take up to one week to be entered to the computer system. This is because the retail shops have to fill sales sheets by hand, post them and then have the information on the sheets keyed into the computer at the region. Exactly the same problem occurs when retail managers order stock; order forms are again completed by hand and sent to the regional depots. In addition to the fact that information available was taking too long to form part of the management information system, it was felt to be too time-consuming on staff at both the regional and retail levels.

A feasibility study was commissioned to investigate the possibility of installing computing facilities at retail level with the following brief terms of reference:

1   To reduce the time lag between sales at retail level and the information being available on the headquarters mainframe.

2   To allow retail management to place orders with their regional offices by computer link rather than filling in stock requisition sheets.

3   Still maintain each retail outlet as an entity. That is, to ensure that a complete stock, sales and personnel profile can be kept on each retail outlet. One of the major functions of the management information system at headquarters is to monitor and compare retail performance, analyse national, regional and local trends and many other statistical analyses that require individual retail performance figures.

4   Ensure that any new system can be piloted first, then phased in over time.

5   To provide information for retail managers to assist them in both managing stock and being more effective as sales centres.

With this outline, a feasibility study team was set up which was chaired by the company's systems analyst and made up of the junior analysts, two programmers, three regional area managers and six retail managers.

The feasibility study was carried out with regular meetings every month, with each member of the team being given a different task to perform. At the end of six months the team agreed and recommended a strategy to the board of directors which was accepted by the board, with implementation to be carried out immediately.

The strategy

1   A sample of five retail outlets was to be selected to run a pilot scheme where each shop would be equipped with a micro-computer, a modem, printer and communications software.

2   Each micro-computer would have a copy of Pegasus Sales Ledger, Purchase Ledger, Nominal Ledger, Invoicing and Sales Order Processing and Stock Control.

3   Both manager and deputy managers of all retail outlets would go on a week's intensive course in Pegasus, to be held at one of the regional depots.

4   Managers would then go back to their retail outlets to implement the systems within a specified time.

5   While training was being carried out, two of the programmers would set up the Pegasus system with all the required parameters and report generation details in such a way that the reports would reflect what had to be sent to the regional offices. Such reports would be printed to a spool file and then

transmitted from the retail outlet's micro-computer to the regional office down a telephone line via modem.

6 Managers would be required to meet each month for six months to report on the success and failures of the new system, drawing from their experiences and contributing ideas about how implementation should take effect in future.

7 After this six-month pilot scheme, the team would submit a report of their experiences along with recommendations about how the scheme should be implemented universally.

The pilot scheme

The first step was taken by purchasing five micro-computers equipped with hard disks, five printers and five sets of data communication kits. Each machine was fitted with the communication boards that would allow each machine to connect to the telephone system. These communication boards are effectively a modem built into the computer rather than having a separate box. The systems staff then installed an operating system on to each disk and tested the computers fully. The Pegasus software was then installed with all the parameters set in a way that ensured it was correctly configured for the retail outlets. The analysts also set up a wide range of reports that would be needed by the regional centres.

The programmers, meanwhile, had to write a suite of programs to enable reports being sent down from each retail outlet to be used to update the mini-computer files as well as being used to transmit details to headquarters.

Five micro-computer systems were quickly set up and distributed to the five retail outlets that made up the pilot scheme. There was a delay, however, because the software that was being developed for the mini-computer system took longer than expected to write and test. Once the system was fully tested the five managers and their deputies could then go on a training course.

The one-week training course went off without too much trouble, although three of the managers complained that too much was being taught in too little time and that they feared they could not remember everything expected of them.

The managers then went back to their respective stores with clear instructions and deadlines about how to implement their systems. The instructions, in brief, went as follows:

1 Build up the stock files to reflect current stock situations. Time allowed was one week, after which regular updating would have to be made.

2   In week 3 implement the Purchase Order System by first placing current outstanding orders on to file and then processing new orders from a low stock list.

3   From week 4 ALL new purchase orders would be printed to a spool file and then, with aid of company written software, be transmitted to the mini-computer at regional office.

4   Once the system had settled, each retail outlet should then implement the Nominal Ledger and send a detailed trial balance each day to the regional office in the way that orders were sent.

5   In week 5 the Sales Ledger would be implemented, which meant placing all credit sales and cash sales on to the computer. Existing debtors did not need placing on the system, only new ones. Once done, these too would be sent to the regional depot.

6   Because credit control was handled at regional level, retail outlets would receive details about those customers who had made payments towards their accounts on a daily basis. This meant having to collect data from the regional office, print it and then use the information to update the Sales Ledger.

7   Sales analysis reports would also be sent to the regional centre on a daily basis as soon as they were available.

In order to ensure that feedback from managers was effective, it was decided that the retail management would meet after the first two weeks to report on their progress.

Feedback

After two weeks the managers met with the systems staff to discuss and share experiences. Out of the five managers, four reported that it took longer than one week to get the stock files to a position where they could start regular updating. One of the problems found was that managers were not doing a thorough manual stocktake before building up the files. It was established that the best way to do this was to generate special stock cards with all required fields on the cards and filled in during stocktaking, and record the dates when stock information on an item was compiled. With the larger shops it was felt that conversion should be done in four stages by splitting up the stock into four categories and setting them up one at a time. Also, stricter checks needed to be kept on sales and getting the figures into the computer in a more systematic way; in other words, establishing a simple routine of updating stock. All retail shops, however, had the stock files converted. The managers decided to meet again in four weeks' time.

At the next meeting all managers reported success at setting up and implementing the purchase orders system. One of the retail outlets attempted to print orders to a spool file and send them down a line to the regional office. The attempt failed because the system at the regional centre had not been set up properly to receive the information. When eventually the orders were sent, the software at the regional centre had not been correctly written to translate the information into orders, so there were some bugs in the software. At the meeting, the chief systems analyst reported that the problems had been sorted and managers could implement the sending of orders by modem to their regional offices rather than sending them by post or carrier.

During the next two months, managers had succeeded in achieving the remaining implementations, in approximately the predicted time span. The only problem managers really found was that of handling the data communications hardware and software. However, after the two months they all felt they had just about mastered the skills needed to operate the system.

The scheme ran for another three months before the next meeting. At this meeting plans were drawn up for implementing a system in every retail outlet in all regions. The members of the meeting agreed to form a steering committee to draw up a plan for phasing the new systems into the retail outlets. From their own experiences they were soon able to identify some of the pitfalls to look out for and were better able to define training needs. In addition to this, all the hardware and software problems had been solved.

Corporate strategy

The plan involved starting off three outlets per month in the Southern region, two per month in the Midland, Northern and Wales & Western regions and one per month in the Scottish & Ulster Region.

Implementation would take much the same form as that for the pilot schemes, with managers and their assistants first going on to a one-week intensive training course before actually implementing the systems in their shops. Each manager would also have a well-documented 'action plan' which formed a corporate strategy to work from during the process of transition.

The implementation went ahead, in most cases, extremely well. A good deal of trouble-shooting was needed, especially towards handling equipment. Another problem occurred because a few shops experienced a change in management during the transition period, although the situation never occurred where both manager and deputy left together. During the project, regional meetings between retail management and the visiting of each other's shops became far more common, because managers felt they needed to share and draw upon experiences. This extra liaison activity between managers had an unexpected beneficial side-effect because managers often learnt from each other about new sales skills, marketing techniques and shop layouts.

Case study discussion exercises

1. Trace the history of the computer development, indicating time scales involved. When doing this, try and show the development as a diagram showing the sequence of events with the time scales.

2. How long would it take to complete computerisation in all retail outlets?

3. Could the company have either saved time or money developing its own software rather than purchasing a package like Pegasus to do the job instead?

4. Discuss the role of staff training during the project and how staff training might play a role in the future development of this company.

5. How does this company benefit from having such a large number of retail outlets computerising compared with a small business that may only have one or two retail outlets?

6. From your knowledge of Pegasus, identify those parts of the package that were not used and examine whether there might be a role in the company for some of the other functions available in Pegasus.

7. What developments can you see for the future in this firm?

8. Outline

   (a) The benefits of the new system.
   (b) The costs of the new system.

Appendix 1 Glossary of Terms

Abort. Stopping the excution of a program while it is still running. If you are in the middle of, say, updating a record, you may need to abort to avoid a serious error. Usually done by hitting the **ESC** key.

Access. The activity of referring to data stored in a file. For example, disk access is needed if a Sales Ledger activity is going to keep customer records updated.

Algorithm. A series of instructions set up in logical order designed to perform an activity such as sorting stock records into stock number order. The algorithm will be capable of being converted into a computer program.

Amend. The activity of changing a record in a file. For example, altering a customer address details in the Sales Ledger is a form of file amendment.

Analyst. A person who has the job of analysing various activities, such as a systems analyst, database analyst, cost analyst. Systems analysts are often concerned with analysing computer-based information systems or manual systems with a view to computerising them.

Application. A specific use to which a computer is put to such as Payroll, Sales, Job Costing. Such applications are often performed on a computer by a software package, or part of an integrated software package.

Audit trail. Such a term can take many forms but is largely a way of recording a sequence of transactions in a way that any transaction can be traced back. Such audit trails can take the form of printed transactions lists, called transactions files. Such audit trails are required to allow auditors to check accounts, or personnel to track errors or restore lost transactions data to a computer-based database.

Background printing. A process where the computer prints a document and still allows an operator to go on using the computer or computer terminal to process data.

Backing storage. Often referred to as secondary storage, it allows data to be stored on media such as disks for long-term purposes called off-line data storage.

Back-up. A process of copying all data from one source to another for safe keeping

Bar code. Often found on retail products, is a set of pre-printed vertical bars that holds on it information about the product, such as where it was made, who made it, weight or size of product. Such bar codes are useful as computers are able to read them quickly using a bar code reader. Such details can, for example, help computers determine a price for the product by accessing a related record in a database.

Batch processing. The process of grouping transactions together and then processing them all in one go. For example, a firm may choose to enter all invoice details sent to it by suppliers at pre-defined times in the week, rather than entering them up as and when they arrive.

Bootstrap. A small program built into the computer that instructs the system about how to set itself up when switched on. Part of the bootstrap is often held on disk, which is also needed when a machine is switched on.

Buffer. A part of memory used as a temporary store to hold data from an input device. For example, most printers have a buffer memory for storing data prior to printing it. Also keyboards often hold at least one line of data before it is sent to the computer's processor.

Bug. An error in a program.

Bus. A communication channel which data travels along. Such communication channels consist of a control bus, data bus, address bus and a peripheral bus.

Byte. A measure of computer memory, normally containing 8 single bits. Each byte often represents a single character. 1024 of these bytes are referred to as a Kilobyte.

Cache memory. A form of buffer memory that works at high speed and is capable of keeping up with the computer's CPU. It acts as a buffer between the CPU and the slower main memory. Because the CPU is not delayed by memory access, processing speed is faster. The operating system will load segments of programs into cache memory from disks.

Card reader. An input device that reads data from cards. The data on such cards can be in magnetic form or simply holes punched into the cards.

Carriage return. A single control character sent to the computer, activated by pressing the RETURN key on the keyboard. Such carriage returns are often used to release data from the keyboard buffer to the computer's processor.

Central Processing Unit (CPU). Often referred to as simply the processor, it is the main unit of any computer system. The processor accepts its data from input devices, processes such data and sends it to output devices such as screens and printers, or sends it to backing store for saving.

Character. A single element in coded form for the processor, such as a letter or a single number digit. Such characters are normally 8 bits, or one byte, long.

Clock. A processor contains an electronic pulse generator that is used to transmit such synchronised pulses to different parts of the computer for the interpretation and execution of instructions. Such synchronisation will be set at a speed that determines the computer's CLOCK SPEED. Such clock speeds are measured in Megahertz (MHz). The faster the clock speed, the faster the internal processing speed of the computer. For most business applications, it is the access time to disks that is more important to processing speed than the clock speed.

COM. (Computer Output on Microfilm). A form of computer output that offers an effective form of long-term data storage that is both compact and durable. Such output is especially useful as a means of archiving data.

Command. An instruction to the computer to perform a given task; *see* Appendix 2.

Computer Aided Design (CAD). The use of a computer with graphics software to design using electronic drawing. Main applications areas are in the field of engineering drawing, product design, fashion design and technical drawing.

Computer bureau. A commercial enterprise offering computing services to organisations. Many firms still use computer bureaux to manage their Payrolls. Some computer bureau firms can offer on-line services by installing a terminal into the firm and thereby offering computing time on a time-sharing basis.

Control unit. That part of the computer's CPU or micro-processor that controls the movements of data within it.

Corruption. A term used to refer to the loss, or corruption, of data. Data corruption is of a particular problem when it occurs on a disk. Such corruption can often render data on a disk useless, hence the importance of regular backing up of data.

CPU. *See* Central Processing Unit.

Cursor. A small image such as a block or dash on the screen to indicate where data will be entered from the keyboard.

Daisy wheel printer. A type of impact printer that prints characters by striking the character images through carbonated ribbon. The characters appear on the end of spokes on a small wheel. The characters on paper are of a high quality but the print style is limited to the characters on the wheel. Several different wheels are available, giving some choice of style. Particularly good for letter or report writing.

Data. An element that will need processing to form the basis of information. It can be an electronic pulse, a magnetic particle, a hole in a piece of paper, a particle of light or any other physical form that can be represented in one of two states. It is the pattern of these data that will be processed by the computer.

Data capture. The way in which data is captured, collected or input for processing. Methods of data capture can vary from entering data by bar-code readers, scanners, optical character recognition, and source documents requiring keying in. The methods of direct input to the computer are increasing, as data capture is often the most time-consuming and error-prone part of general data-processing operations.

Data dictionary. A way of classifying data definitions, data names, characteristics and inter-relationships within a database. The dictionary is needed to overcome the problem of identifying data names which tend to differ in various parts of an organisation which uses a corporate database. Programmers will, as a result, be restricted to using the data definitions, names, characteristics and inter-relationships defined in the dictionary. The data dictionary can be extended as required, but the concept ensures the effectiveness of a corporate database within an organisation.

Database. The collection, in a structured form, of all data that represents the basis of information for an organisation's business applications. In practice, the Pegasus database will be the collection of all data files depicted by the '.DAT' file extension.

Database Management System (DBMS). Software that manages computerised databases such as updating, creating and interrogating. Such software also manages the efficiency of data storage, data security and integrity.

Datel. The Post Office data transmission facility available to commerce and industry. It allows the transmission between points of data on either private or public telephone lines. Datel offers a wide and varied service to meet the needs of differing data communication systems.

Dedicated computer. A computer system set up to perform one specific task or set of tasks. For example, a cash dispenser, or electronic cash till.

Default. When offering a choice to users through software, a default value is assumed if no choice is made.

Delete. The process of removing data from a system, such as a customer record or transaction.

Diagnostic routine. A program used to detect errors in either existing software or hardware. Many diagnostic routines will operate in a way that does not interfere with normal operations and is not apparent to a user.

DIP (Dual Inline Package). An integrated circuit socket or switch having two rows of connector pins. Most printers have DIP switches which allow settings to be altered to make the connections to the printer compatible with both a computer's hardware and software.

Disk drive. A peripheral device for storing data generated by the computer's processor and for retrieving data by the processor. Disk drives can be either floppy disks or hard disks.

DOS (Disk Operating System). Part of the software that is contained on disk, is loaded into computer memory and is used to operate the computer system.

Down time. The amount of time a computer is not functioning.

Download. The process of loading a program into computer memory.

Driver. A part of the operating system software that is used to control certain peripheral devices.

Duplex. A communications concept that allows simultaneous data transmission down a line in both directions.

EFTPOS (Electronic Funds Transfer at Point Of Sale). This allows funds to be transferred from a customer account to a trader's account as a transaction takes place, thereby avoiding cash transfer.

Electronic mail. A process of transmitting messages and mail between computers electronically. Such mail can be stored for future reference.

EPOS (Electronic Point of Sale). An example is the check-out system in supermarkets that can scan bar codes and price the products.

Exception reporting. A process of reporting any circumstances that are unusual or not normally permitted, such as large customer orders, or low stock levels on items of stock.

Expert system. Software orientated, it enables a computer to diagnose problems, given the symptoms. Such expert systems often contain information about past events and calculate likely causes of problems through statistical analysis.

Fibre optics. A cabling medium for transmitting data. As an alternative to coaxial cable, it transmits data via light pulses and allows a much greater and reliable capacity than coaxial cable.

Field. An element of a record that is a collection of characters such as that which makes up a customer name or stock number.

File. A collection records that are related in some way. A stock file, for example, may be a collection of stock records.

File protection. A method of protecting files from corruption or accidental erasure. A common way of protecting a file is to 'write protect' it, which means files can be read but not written to.

Firmware. Software that is set on Read Only Memory and can be easily replaced in the computer. It offers a reliable source of software and is particularly useful when an application is used often.

Floppy disk. A backing-store medium used to store data. Such disks require a disk drive in order for the computer to both read from them and write to them.

Flowchart. A diagrammatic form showing how functions and sequences of events are related within a system or sub-system. Examples are program flowcharts depicting the way a program runs or systems flowcharts showing the way a system works.

Form feed. A process where a printer FEEDS a sheet of paper through the printer. This is often used to align continuous paper on a printer to the top of the next sheet.

Format. The way data is structured on disk, paper or screens. With respect to disks, it is important that new disks are formatted in a way that is compatible with the computer system before they can be used. This usually means the size of data storage on the disk, e.g. 360K, 720K or 1.4M.

Fourth generation languages (4GL). A programming language that has a high level structure that allows programming to be done by English style statements. Such 4GLs have normally been tailored for certain applications, such as a database.

Front-end processors. A method where some processing for a large computer system is done by terminals or micro-computers such as, screen layouts, communications transmission, editing, data validation and verification.

Function. A general term used to identify a specific group of related tasks, such as the accounting function, Stock Control function or Payroll function.

General purpose computer. A computer that can be adapted to a wide range of applications by loading the appropriate software.

Generation of files. Often referred to as the grandfather-father-son principle, creates a generation of backed-up files. With the cost of storage being relatively cheap, it is often prudent to keep many generations of backed-up files.

Hacking. A term used for the act of trying to gain unauthorised access to computerised information, such as using modem equipment to gain access to private information held on computer databases.

Half duplex. A process of data transmission where data can be sent in both directions down a communication line, but NOT simultaneously.

Handshaking. A process where both computer and peripheral tell each other that data transmission is ready to commence. A printer requires this because it is normally unable to print data as fast as it can receive it, so the principle of handshaking ensures that data is sent down as and when the printer is ready, thereby preventing loss of data.

Hard copy. Printed output from a computer.

Hardware. The physical components of any computer system.

High-level language. A programming language that is constructed of statements containing English style words. Such high-level languages vary in type and sophistication. Examples are COBOL, BASIC, Pascal, C, Fortran, Modula-2.

Housekeeping. A term to describe the practice of reducing unwanted information on disks and tapes. Good housekeeping will prevent disks from becoming cluttered, speed up processing and lessen the chance of filling up a disk unnecessarily.

IBM. A trade name for International Business Machines.

ICL. A trade name for International Computers Limited.

Icon. A pictorial or graphic representation of programs, document files and options available for executing or processing. Icons are often used as an alternative to text menus and directories.

Image processing. A process of transmitting, in digitised form, pictures and images.

Impact printers. A category of printer that creates images on paper by physically hitting the paper, such as dot matrix or daisy wheel printers.

Interface. A general term used to describe the processing of data between two systems or sub-systems. For example, a disk interface refers to the process of transferring data from processor to disk and back. Such interfaces are collections of both hardware and software.

Job. In a computing context, this refers to either routines or applications being run on a computer system at any one time.

Job costing. The process of attributing costs against a specific job. In accounting terms, this could be a specific contract or the manufacture of a particular product.

Key field. A field within a record that identifies the record itself and is used to access the record.

Keyboard. One of the most used forms of input devices, laid out like a typewriter keyboard.

Kilobyte (K). Used to measure data quantity and represents 1024 bytes of data.

Kimball tag. Either pre-punched or magnetised card containing information about an item. Often seen in retail outlets, they are used as a storage medium that can hold details about a product. An appropriate computer input device can then read them.

Laser printer. A type of non-impact printer giving high quality printed output. It uses similar techniques to photocopiers.

Line printer. Low-quality, very high-speed printers that print complete lines at a time.

Local Area Network (LAN). A system that connects a number of micro-computers together so that they can share common resources such as a database or printer. While resources can be shared, each computer on a network is still able to act independently.

Logging in. A method of getting access to a computer's information. Designed for security, the process of logging in requires an operator to enter identification and, normally, an associated password.

Logging out. Signing off a system, an activity that should be carried out whenever an operator has finished work on a computer.

Magnetic disks. A storage medium for data which fits into a disk drive. There are many types of disk suitable for different types of application and computer systems.

Magnetic Ink Character Recognition (MICR). Typically used by the banks, magnetic ink characters are read by the computer as a way of inputting data to the computer. Magnetic characters typically appear on the bottom of cheques and are used to assist banks in processing a large volume of cheques.

Magnetic tape. A form of backing store medium that is mounted on to tape drives that can store data serially. Magnetic tapes offer an effective and cheap form of back-up storage for systems with a large amount of data. They are also used for storing programs that are subsequently loaded into computer memory.

Mainframe computer. An exceptionally large computer often capable of supporting many hundreds of computer terminals, micro-computers, storage units, printers and other peripherals. Quite often mainframe computers are used as a large central processor supporting remote systems by data communication links across long distances.

Management Information System (MIS). Often used in conjunction with other data-processing activities, it is used to extract a whole series of reports. With most MIS packages, users are able to identify their own information needs and extract reports to meet these.

Matrix printer. An impact printer that creates an image on paper through a dot pattern on a matrix. Such matrix printers are effective for printing, at low cost, graphics as well as near-letter-quality text. Such printers are often quite adequate for most smaller businesses using computers for accounts, word processing and management information.

Merge. Combining two related files, normally with the same structure if they are data files, together to create one larger file.

Micro-processor. The more common description for the processing unit of a micro-computer.

Mini-computer. Similar to a mainframe computer but on a smaller scale. The distinction between a mainframe and mini-computer is not an obvious one, but mini-computers are often multi-user/tasking machines that can support many peripherals (about 100) on both a local or distributed processing basis.

Modem (Modulator/Demodulator). A device for both sending and receiving signals down a telephone line, thereby allowing data communication between computer devices. Such modems will be needed at both ends of a line to allow data communications to work.

Module. A function within a program package that can often be used in isolation to other modules. For example, in the Pegasus system there is a Sales Ledger module, Purchase Ledger module, Nominal Ledger module and so on.

MSDOS. A trade name for MicroSoft Disk Operating System.

Multiplexor. A communications device that receives data from a number of computer devices and then sends such data down a single telephone line. There will be a slowing down in data communications transmission from each device as more of them transmit data, but such devices can reduce the costs of data communications quite considerably.

Numeric control. The process by which a computer automatically controls machines. Such computerisation will be most common within a factory.

Off-line. A general term referring to data or part of computer system being inaccessible. In other words, data on a disk which is not in the computer disk drive is said to be off-line.

Off-line data processing. A process of working on data away from the main computer system or on, say, a micro-computer before interacting with the main system. With the cost and power of micro-computer, it often makes sense to prepare data, such as invoices, off-line and then batch process the work to a mainframe or mini-computer later. Off-line processing can also involve many manual operations such as preparation and validation of data before computerised (on-line) processing.

Operating system. Software that is used to operate the computer and its peripherals.

Operator. A term used to describe a person who operates a computer. This is different to the person who programs a computer, a computer programmer.

Optical character reader. A computer input device that recognises characters, usually in typed form. Such devices can be a considerable labour-saving device when text that has already been typed needs to be entered to the computer.

Parallel running. A process of running two systems together; typically a computer system and a manual one together. This may be a necessary prerequisite to automating a manual process with computers. Such parallel processing will help to detect any errors or bugs in the new system. Eventually, such parallel running will end in most cases.

Parameter. A value that is required to control a situation. In nearly all the Pegasus modules, parameters have to be set in order to control the way the module is to function.

Password. A way of ensuring that only authorised personnel have access to parts of a system. Passwords are only effective if they are kept secret from everyone excluding authorised persons. Passwords are also set up in way that ensures different people have access to different parts of the system.

Payroll. The function of paying employees, for which computers can be particularly useful.

Peripheral device. Input, output and storage devices of a computer that constitute part of a system's hardware.

POS. Point-Of-Sale.

Prestel. A public database service offered by British Telecom.

Protocol. Communications protocol is a standard of data communications that tries to ensure compatibility in the way data is communicated across lines.

RAM (Random Access Memory). A part of the internal memory in a computer that starts off blank and is used to load in:

(a) The rest of the operating system which is read from a disk. The process of building up the operating system in this way is called BOOTING UP.

(b) Applications software which is normally LOADED in from the hard disk.

(c) Business data generated. Such data will be directly related to the business and is normally WRITTEN to your hard disk where it has a more permanent home.

Such RAM is volatile, in that it is lost when the machine is switched off.

Random file. A file organisation principle that allows the computer to directly access any record without having to read all records preceding it sequentially. Naturally, such files are normally stored on disk medium.

Read/write heads. A device contained within a disk drive or tape drive that either reads data into the computer or writes data on to a storage medium from the computer.

Real-time processing. A concept of ensuring that files and databases are updated by transactions as the transactions occur. To achieve real-time processing, procedures for operating a computer system are just as important as having the hardware and software capabilities to do it.

Remote job entry (RJE). This is the process of entering data to a computer where the entry is geographically separate from the central processing unit. RJE is typified by a remote terminal being linked by modem to mainframe or mini-computer.

Report generator. A part of a software package that allows users to design their own reports based on their information needs. It allows much greater freedom in the way a user can extract available data from the system.

ROM (Read Only Memory). A part of the memory in a computer used to store programs in a permanent way. Part of a computer's operating system (e.g. BIOS) is stored on them. Some systems will also have applications software built into ROM.

Run. The actual execution of a program.

Scheduling. A process of determining the order in which jobs are performed or executed. Such activities can be done automatically or by the operator, with priorities being set on certain jobs.

Scrolling. The process whereby text is moved up the screen when you want to view data past the bottom of the screen. The alternative to scrolling is to clear a screen in such a way that one complete screen at a time is viewed, sequentially.

Sequential access. A file-reading method where data is read in a defined sequence. With magnetic tape, the order of sequential access is the order in which it was saved. Programs are also read sequentially on whatever medium they are stored. Some files support an index which allows files to be read in different sequences.

Sequential file. A file where data is stored physically in the order in which it is generated.

Silicon chip. A small piece of silicon-based material used to hold computer circuits to form a micro-processor. New technology has allowed many thousands of transistors and diodes to be stored on one single chip.

Simplex transmission. A method of data communication where transmission of data can be made in ONE DIRECTION ONLY.

Soft copy. A term used for screen output.

Software. All computer programs, from operating system to applications software.

Sort. A data-processing term used when rearranging files into a different order.

Source code. The program as written by a computer programmer before it is compiled to form object code. High-level languages, for example, are first written in source code and the computer uses a compiler to convert this source into something it can run from.

Spool. Often referred to as a file awaiting printing. When outputting data, you are often given the option of spool output, which means output is to file for future processing or printing.

Stand-alone system. A computer that is capable of working in isolation to any other system. Most micro-computers are stand-alone systems.

Status. A signal indicating whether a system is active or not.

Storage capacity. A way of measuring the amount of data that can be stored. Storage capacity is normally measured in Kilobytes (K).

Suite. A set of inter-related programs. A term often used instead of package.

Systems analysis. The job of analysing systems, both manual and computerised, with a view to implementing new systems or modifying existing ones. The job of a systems analyst will often require communications and business management skills as much as computing ones.

Telecommunication. Refers to the general concept of sending data from one device to another down a telephone line.

Teleprocessing. The use of telecommunications in order to achieve on-line data processing. In other words, to interact with a database from a remote distance using transmission lines and a terminal.

Telex. As part of British Telecom's datel service, it is used for transmitting text only from one terminal to another, producing printed output at the receiving end.

Test data. Data generated and specifically used for testing systems and software. Often, copies of live data form a useful set of test data. However, test data may have to be specially created when being used to test a new system of software.

Time sharing. A technique where a processor shares its time among more than one user. Some operating systems have time-sharing built in.

Transaction data. Any data generated from the result of a transaction such as a sale, purchase or stock movement. Such transaction data will often be stored as a record per transaction in a set of transaction files and will be used to update master files.

Turnkey system. Simply means switching on and starting. Such systems are normally supplied by outside agencies or consultancy services, specifically for the business.

Unix. An operating system associated with mini-computers or large multi-user micro-computers. The operating system is a standard that is used on many different models of machines and is not associated with one particular manufacturer.

User friendly. A term often associated with the way software is designed to guide a user through processes when using a computer application package.

Utility program. A program that can be used to manage files or perform activities outside the normal scope of running a program such as file back-up, retrieving lost files and deleting unwanted files.

Validate. A process of checking whether data conforms to expected input, such as a valid date or ensuring alphabetical characters are not entered when the computer expects a number.

Verification. A way of confirming with an operator that data input is complete and correct or a certain action is what is required (the 'ARE YOU SURE' message).

Virtual storage. This is a technique whereby the computer uses backing store, usually disk, as part of the processing area in addition to that of internal memory. This has the effect of allowing use of very large programs that are normally beyond the memory capabilities of the machine they are running on. An example is the way in which only a small part of the Pegasus Business Software is loaded into memory at any one time.

Vision display unit (VDU). The screen that displays text and graphic output as soft copy.

Winchester drive. A storage device that holds a hard disk. The hard disk is non-removable, but offers high storage density and capacity and is generally very reliable.

Window. A method of sectioning the VDU in such a way that an operator can see different parts of a document or run, and see different applications at the same time.

Word processing. An application that involves processing words and spending time perfecting format, spelling and so on before producing hard copy. Word processors are replacing typewriters at a growing rate.

Xenix. An operating system associated with large multi-user micro-computers. The operating system is a standard that is used on many different models of machines and is not associated with one particular manufacturer.

Appendix 2 Error Codes and Messages

The following is a simple guide to the kind of errors that can occur when running the Pegasus system, along with suggestions about what to do to overcome them. In some cases, the problem cannot be solved simply and extra help will be needed.

1   **System Active.** Some special files that can, on occasions, cause problems are the data files used to **lock** files. When certain files are being used by the Pegasus system, it is important to **lock** them from being used by other users. For example, if an operator is performing an activity in the Nominal Ledger that involves the updating of records, then other users will have to be locked out of similar activities while the updates are being carried out. The system, in this example, will change the name of a file called (say) XNL-FREE.DAT to XNL-LOCK.DAT. This, therefore, has the effect of keeping others out while certain activities are being carried out. When such activities have been completed, the file will normally be changed back to XNL-FREE.DAT. If someone shuts down a terminal in the middle of doing this, the system can lock. To get out of the problem, return to the operating system and change the file names to the correct form.

2   **Illegal function Call in 2120.** The system is attempting to read a date from the system. This error indicates the date cannot be read in. You should use the operating system to reset the date.

3   **Disk Error 52 Bad File Number.** The system is attempting to open a file. The best way of overcoming this problem is to copy the back-up files and use them. File corruption can be the result of a whole host of reasons. If it happens too often, you may have to get your system checked. If the data files are on floppy disk, then dispose of the disk and use a new one.

4   **Disk Error 53 File Not Found.** The file the program is seeking is not on the disk. You will need to restore the missing file.

5   **Disk Error 54 Bad File Mode.** Usually caused by having more than one **D** line on an invoice. To correct it reformat the invoice with one D line.

6 **Disk Error 55 File Already Open**. The same as with System Active. If renaming files does not work, you will have to revert to a back-up.

7 **Disk Error 57 Operating System**. This error is an operating system generated error. You will need to check your system. Starting the machine again may solve the problem.

8 **Disk Error 58 File exists**. Free and Lock files are on the same ledger. To correct this simply delete the lock files.

9 **Disk Error 61 Disk Full**. Either all available room on the disk has been taken up or there is no room in the directory for more file entries. You can correct this by removing unwanted files, but the only long-term solution may be to use a system with more disk space.

10 **Disk Error 62 Input Past End**. Normally a result of failing to save an upgraded parameters file. You might be able to correct this by return to the parameters and saving them again WITHOUT erasing the old data files.

11 **Disk Error 63 Bad Record Number**. The system is unable to access a part of the file, you may have to revert to a back-up to correct it.

12 **Disk Error 67 Too Many Files**. There is not enough room in the directory for any more file entries. A way around this is to store the data files in a sub-directory. You should be aware of the fact that the number and nature of file entries will vary from one system to another.

13 **Disk Error 70 Disk Write Protected**. The system is unable to write to the data disk. You will have to remove the write protection sticker or notch from the disk.

14 **Disk Error 71 Drive Not Ready**. Either the disk is not in the drive or the drive has been left open.

15 **Disk Error 72 Media Error**. The disk is corrupt. If you are using a floppy disk, replace it with a new one. If it is a hard disk, it will need to be checked.

16 **Disk Error 99 DOS Not Available On System**. You will need to load a DOS disk.

Other problems may occur which cannot be easily diagnosed. When software is purchased, it is normal practice for buyers to be given a 'hot line' telephone number that they can use for a limited time in the event of problems. Such a facility will normally see you through most of the problems that will typically happen in the first months of using a new package and system.

If a problem looks severe, it is always wise to seek professional help.

Appendix 3 Pegasus Senior

This book has concentrated on the Pegasus single-user version. A good knowledge of this will allow a user to easily adapt to the other versions offered by Pegasus.

PEGASUS SENIOR

Pegasus Senior is an enhanced version of the Pegasus single-user, with better screens, more user help, better techniques of finding records and easier methods of paying and receiving money. One of the more important features of the 'senior' version is the availability of foreign currency accounting. This is particularly important for firms buying from and selling to overseas markets. Pegasus Senior also makes effective use of the function keys in order to help speed up and simplify many of the commonly used activities.

The 'senior' version is also available for the following:

(a) **IBM OS/2** This operating system allows you to work on more than one module at the same time. This is possible because the OS/2 operating system has *multi-tasking* capabilities. You can, for example, look at the stock file on the screen while processing invoices; or you can process sales orders while a lengthy report is being printed.

(b) **Senior Xenix/Unix** Xenix and Unix are now fairly well-used and standard operating systems used on multi-user systems. They tend to be employed to operate larger computer systems used by bigger companies. Because of the nature of the operating system, it means that different users are able to access different parts of the package simultaneously on different terminals attached to the main computer.

(c) **Senior Network** As the name implies, this is the senior version available for a computer network. Thanks to a number of micro-computers attached to a file server, where the software is installed, different users are able to access different parts of the package simultaneously.

SALES HISTORY

This is an 'add-on' module that can be used to enhance your Sales Ledger function. It offers, in addition to the normal Sales Ledger function activities, the following extra activities:

(a) Much more detailed information and breakdown on sales invoices and credit notes.

(b) Summary analysis of sales for the previous 24 periods (two years if a period is a month).

(c) Enhanced reporting facilities that allow an operator a greater say in what is reported and how.

(d) Enhanced accounts enquiry facilities that allow an operator a greater say in what is reported and how. (For example, you might want to study the buying patterns of principal clients.)

(e) Up to 26 sales biographies (profiles). Again, this is particularly useful if you want to analyse sales of a particular key customer or sales to a particular country.

FIXED ASSETS

This offers the facility of maintaining details of company assets in a more comprehensive way than can be achieved by the Nominal Ledger alone. Many facilities offered by this module are important to a business when controlling and monitoring its fixed assets. They include:

- Nine differing methods of measuring depreciation.
- Leasing and hire purchase.
- Valuing transfers, additions, write-offs and insurance.
- History of assets.

Index

Computerisation in Business
David Royall and Michael Hughes

This book answers the vexed question, 'What can computers do for my business?'

Business people sometimes fail to appreciate that they need not become computer experts in order to derive significant benefits from the introduction and use of computer systems in their business. But even for those who have progressed beyond this stage, the increasing range of IBM and IBM compatible hardware and software now available, although offering wide choice and good prices, makes the final purchase decision a tough one.

This book provides a very welcome guide for the uninitiated: from making the decision that computerisation is worth investigating; through deciding what to buy; to getting the system installed and working and to managing it thereafter.

Computerisation in Business is likely to appeal to business owners wishing to explore the 'how to do it' and benefits of computerisation, especially those operating in the retail and other service industry sectors. Business managers and students will also find much constructive information and advice here.

Paperback, 192 pages, ISBN 0 273 03247 X

Computerisation in Business is a title in the NatWest Small Business Bookshelf. For details about other titles in the series, contact the publishers.

Training Guide: Pegasus
David Royall

The Training Guide to Pegasus has been designed to provide a practical introduction to the Pegasus software package.

The Guide:

- contains carefully structured instructions, tasks and exercises to teach the user the various commands and reinforce his/her learning
- can be used under supervision of the lecturer/teacher or as a self-instruction guide
- is jargon-free, therefore easy to understand
- covers all the main functions – e.g. loading, creating, quitting, locating, altering, storing, etc.

Other titles in the series are:

Training Guide: Lotus 1-2-3
Alan Jones
ISBN 0 273 03037 X

Training Guide: Ventura
Alan Jones
ISBN 0 273 03175 9

Training Guide: DataEase
Tony Tambyrajah
ISBN 0 273 03264 X

Training Guide: MS-DOS
Clifford Mould
ISBN 0 273 03172 4

Training Guide: SmartWare
Dexter Booth
ISBN 0 273 03206 2

The Training Guides are available from all good bookshops and direct from the publishers: Southport Book Distributors, 12-14 Slaidburn Crescent, Fylde Road, Southport PR9 9YF United Kingdom

Pitman

BRITAIN'S BEST SELLING BUSINESS ACCOUNTING SYSTEM

Senior

PEGASUS
SENIOR·RANGE

Pegasus Business Software today enjoys an envied reputation as the number one
supplier of Accounting Business Software in the UK. Pegasus software is now
used by over 70,000 organisations countrywide. Our reputation for giving
users the best solution available is second to none.

PEGASUS·BUSINESS·SOFTWARE

Pegasus Software Ltd.
35-41 Montagu Street, Kettering, Northants. NN16 8XG
Tel: 0536-410044
Fax: 0536-81796
Tlx: 341297 PEGASUS G

The Pegasus Business Software

EDUCATION RANGE

**Single-User
Senior Standalone
Senior Network
Senior Xenix/Unix/Aix**

The educational systems are full working versions of
The Pegasus Business Software range and differ only in the file capacity.
They can be bought in modular form or as a completely integrated system for
whichever version of Pegasus accounting.

Also available

PEGASUS COURSEWARE

A combination of course notes and manuals from the Pegasus Training
department which forms an exclusive training compendium for students.

PEGASUS COMPUTER BASED TRAINING

A unique method of interactive study from Pegasus Training for students
requiring an introduction to Pegasus Senior.

Education
establishment _____

Department _____

Contact _____

Position _____

Address _____

_____

*For further information please indicate which
elements of the educational range you are
interested in*

Single-User	☐	Senior Standalone	☐
Senior Network	☐	Senior iX range	☐
Courseware	☐	Computer Based Training	☐

Pegasus Software Limited
35-41 Montagu Street, Kettering, Northants NN16 8XG
Telephone: (0536) 410044